RECKLESS
SEX, LIES
AND JFK

Detective Mike Rothmiller LAPD OCID
and Douglas Thompson

First published in the UK in 2024 by Gemini Adult Books Ltd, part of the Gemini Books Group

Based in Woodbridge and London

Marine House, Tide Mill Way,
Woodbridge, Suffolk IP12 1AP

www.geminibooks.com

Text © 2024 Mike Rothmiller and Douglas Thompson

Paperback ISBN 9781802471830
eBook ISBN 9781802472318

A CIP catalogue record for this book is available
from the British Library.

Every reasonable effort has been made to trace
copyright-holders of material reproduced in this book,
but if any have been inadvertently overlooked the
publishers would be glad to hear from them.

Printed in the UK
10 9 8 7 6 5 4 3 2 1

New York Times-bestselling author MIKE ROTHMILLER has enjoyed a distinguished career in law enforcement working across US federal and state agencies and with American and international intelligence services. He served for ten years with the Los Angeles Police Department (LAPD), including five years as a deep undercover detective with the Organized Crime Intelligence Division (OCID). He was a member of the United States Department of Justice Organized Crime Strike Force and provided secret Grand Jury testimony regarding the assassination of Senator Robert Kennedy. He conceived and directed global intelligence operations targeting multi-national crime groups, terrorism, and political corruption, from Caracas to Washington and London to Moscow. In his long career Mike Rothmiller has encountered all manner of mendacity and atrocity, but he remains most shaken by his investigation into the death of Marilyn Monroe. He regards the book *Bombshell* as the rich and important culmination of a lifetime of inquiries which will achieve legal redress, posthumously in some cases, and correct the fabricated history about the death of Marilyn Monroe and those who used her. Alongside his dedication to public service, Mike Rothmiller established a media career producing television documentaries and working as a correspondent and presenter for America's PBS, ESPN and other television markets. He is a regular commentator on law enforcement and worldwide intelligence matters across America and throughout the world. He is the author of twenty-three non-fiction books.

Sunday Times-bestselling author DOUGLAS THOMPSON is the author of many non-fiction books, covering an eclectic mix of subjects from major Hollywood biographies to revelatory bestsellers about remarkable people and events. Four of his books are at present being developed for global television and another, *Devil's Coin*, as a Hollywood film. With Christine Keeler, he wrote her revealing memoir *The Truth at Last*. That instant bestseller was revised as *Secrets and Lies: The Trials of Christine Keeler* and the audio version recorded by actress Sophie Cookson, who played Christine to critical acclaim in the successful BBC television series. Douglas Thompson's works, published in a dozen languages, include the television-based anthology *Hollywood People* and a worldwide-selling biography of Clint Eastwood. He collaborated with Michael Flatley on the bestseller *Lord of the Dance*. A director of one of the UK's leading literary festivals, he divides his time between a medieval Suffolk village and California, where he lived as a Fleet Street correspondent and columnist for more than twenty years.

www.dougiethompson.com
@dougiethompson

For Tom Polhaus, with salutations to the US
Freedom of Information Act, 4 July 1967.

CONTENTS

CONTENTS

'The problem with putting two and two together is that sometimes you get four, and sometimes you get twenty-two.'
Dashiell Hammett, *The Thin Man*, 1934

PREFACE

Hubris

'... *for we possess nothing certainly except the past.*'
Evelyn Waugh, *Brideshead Revisited*, 1945

Havana, Cuba, 1957

The devil is in the wiretap. The voices are rough, crude, like their vocabulary, too alive to be in the past tense and coherent in translating the action involving three dexterous Cuban girls, a two-way mirror, and a future American President.

Who, what and where leave little to the imagination.

The venue is the corner fourth-floor suite of the Comodoro Hotel and Casino, Havana, with extravagant views out to the warm Atlantic Ocean and, from adjoining room 418, of dedicated professional sexual endeavour. On speaker is the cursing of Santo Trafficante Jr, an omnipotent great survivor and boss of the American Mafia, complaining to his lawyer that he hadn't the clairvoyance to film Senator John Fitzgerald Kennedy being enthusiastically compromised.

It's December, and peak tourist season, and JFK and his philandering pal, Senator George Smathers, are completing one of their regular 'fact-finding' tours of Cuba (Kennedy didn't gamble but each evening of the five-day visit is enraptured by the exotic chorus girls of the Tropicana nightclub floor show) and will be home with their families for Christmas.

There is irritation in Trafficante's tone as he reports the orchestrated happenings and the loss of the rich blackmail opportunity:

'If only I'd got that son-of-a-bitch on camera…'

Apparently, there was retribution for a cohort's inept attempt to take still photographs of the Mob-arranged honeytrap: the latest Minox camera, the size of a cheap cigarette lighter, mounted on a delicate, four-legged stand to keep it steady, failed by lack of available light, through the prism of the voyeurs' mirror. Yet, none immediately for the two young and eagerly ambitious politicians who witlessly engaged in their fun, believing themselves simply irresistible.

All his life, JFK expected to be serviced. For most, sex is an optional side-order of the day, for him it was compulsory, a manifestation of his majesty, his power, a display of entitlement and God-like behaviour, the detritus of which was for others to clean up. Smathers laughs with his friend that 'women will be the death of us' and for Jack Kennedy that was prescient.

PART ONE

Sugar Daddy

'The Galton household had hot and cold running money piped in from an inexhaustible reservoir. But money was never free. Like any other commodity, it has to be paid for.'

Ross Macdonald, *The Galton Case*, 1959

PROLOGUE

Act of Congress

'Mr [Joseph] *Kennedy always called up the girls Jack was taking out.'*
JFK girlfriend Mary Pitcairn on Kennedy's father, 1977

The Kennedy Compound, Palm Beach, Florida, 1957

The Kennedys were a dysfunctional family led by a patriarch who believed his money and influence could in his time, among other things, appease Hitler and buy the White House. For him one out of two, was clearly a result. Telling his children they could walk on water was foolhardy for, of course, there's every chance of drowning. For Joe Kennedy that cognitive dissonance was king-of-the-hill arrogance, the innocent, and regularly the complicit, collateral damage.

The Kennedy men had humid hearts. Power was an aphrodisiac. Risk was a turn-on, women simply a release, the world an entity to control, they'd get into bed with anyone and the metaphorical couplings were often the most troubling. Out of the many, there's one luminous Joe Kennedy story which illustrates so much. It hides, designated as a footnote amid the millions of pages of academic study and literature about the Kennedy dynasty.

As majority leader of the US Senate in 1957, Lyndon Johnson, while recovering from a heart attack, is invited to speak in Palm

Beach and, as a courtesy, is asked by family matriarch Rose Kennedy to lunch at their oceanfront estate. Johnson, with his wife Ladybird and his aide, Bobby Baker, sit down for lunch with his hostess and JFK and family friend, young Senator George Smathers and mentally notes the absence of Rose's husband Joe Kennedy. At that moment, reports Bobby Baker, 'Old Man Joe comes in with a seventeen- or eighteen-year-old girl. Doesn't say boo. Walks right in and goes upstairs and engages in what, clearly and noisily, is sexual intercourse.'

After some distracting ceramic clatter, the lunch proceeds as if nothing is happening (the girl was Joe Kennedy's golf caddy from the South of France, flown in 'to help with my swing'). Ladybird slips LBJ a glass of dissolved aspirin with his lunch, a little something for his shaky Texan heart. He would need stronger medicine in his next half dozen years with the Kennedys.

Chapter One

An Extraordinary Joe

'There ain't nothin' more powerful than the odour of mendacity, it smells like death.'

Big Daddy, *Cat on a Hot Tin Roof*, Tennessee Williams, 1955

For a time there, JFK ran the world like a player with loaded dice. He'd learned the value of an edge from the father he was forever in awe of. Better odds, yet still a game of chance.

The Kennedy men, father and sons, risked their lives in parallel with that other nefarious American dynasty, the Mob. With them they shared interests and lovers. They both operated within tight parameters. They expected everyone to follow them and their rules. What brought rancour and provoked tragedy was only one side kept to these rules.

The Mafia do not forget or forgive if they are betrayed in any way. The great sins, lack of respect, lies and theft, bring the ultimate sanction. No one is above being made an example of. Punishment is their life insurance, medieval in application to induce such shivering fear to dissuade others from making similar errors of judgment.

The Bureau of Investigation opened a file on Joseph Kennedy Senior in 1935, the year 'Federal' was added to their title. They were a little late, and Kennedy's quid pro quo relationship with the Director J. Edgar Hoover had everything to do with it. Kennedy was a multi-millionaire before the end of the First World War and in troubled times you don't do that without cutting corners. He was a Boston boy, born on 6 September 1888, when being of Irish heritage hurt your chances of prospering in business and politics. Young Joe turned that idea topsy-turvy and, through intelligence and street smarts, went from Harvard to banking and, at age twenty-five, was the boss of the city's only Irish-owned financial institution, the Columbia Trust Bank. A year later in 1914, as the war began in Europe, he married Rose Fitzgerald, the daughter of the city's ebullient mayor, John Francis 'Honey Fitz' Fitzgerald, a man who gave him scholarship lessons in how to win in city politics. It involved much corruption. Joe Kennedy was an excellent student.

He avoided wartime military service by taking a reserved occupation at a shipbuilding plant and, when peace allowed, he immediately returned to the financial world with a brokerage firm. In what he'd get jailed for today, insider trading, selling stock using information before it went public, he made an absolute fortune which for decades bankrolled his political ambitions. In what displays the once sacrosanct and elevated view of the Kennedy family, it was not until many years after the fact – and the Kennedy patriarch's death in 1969 – that revelations of his close associations with the American Mafia circulated, and then quite cautiously. In 2024, files showed his contacts with the Mob, and some of organised crime's more colourful and lethal characters, began during Prohibition (1920–1933), when alcohol was outlawed, and afterwards when he was officially in the liquor business. In *The Roarin' Twenties* world of speakeasies and flappers he was a number one man, supplying booze to bars and clubs throughout America – he had the monopoly on importing good whisky. He employed his own tough guys to front up hoodlums. He told his unfortunate bootlegging staff not to be intimidated by 'men with guns', which was a little reckless when one of his Prohibition partners was the engaging Abner 'Longy' Zwillman a founder of Murder Incorporated, a.k.a. Murder, Inc.

Kennedy's 'cover' was that through euphemistic *financial influence* – bribes – he received permits from the US government to import 'medicinal liquor' into Sag Harbor on eastern Long Island, New York. At his tenth Harvard reunion Cape Cod party in 1922, he over-served his guests with Haig and Haig Pinch whisky brought directly from a boat anchored at Plymouth Harbor, telling his former classmates, 'It came ashore the way the Pilgrims did' – courtesy of Frank Costello, one of America's most powerful Mafia bosses ever and a lifetime fan of Joe Kennedy. Much of what Joe Kennedy got up to went on, with his blessing, in some way or other under the cover of the night.

Longy Zwillman, a killer, was one of his more amiable partners and a powerful and influential New Jersey underworld figure, a supporter along with some of the founding fathers of the American Mafia of the young Frank Sinatra and talked of as in the league of gangster infamy as Al Capone. He was one of the first major organised hoodlums to launder his profits from gambling and prostitution in Hollywood where, for a lively time, Joe Kennedy would be a powerful presence. Kennedy and the Mob had parallel ambitions: to amass fortunes and power and, in time, to legitimise it.

The future was in being an honest crook.

Up, of course, to a point.

Prohibition provided the launch platform for them both.

Zwillman had helped one governor of New Jersey get elected and offered $300,000 to aid another; all he wanted in return was to choose the Attorney General, the state's top lawman. He'd compromised Hilton dynasty patriarch Conrad Hilton by linking him with mobster Arnold Kirkeby and washing cash through the Kirkeby-Hilton hotel chain and felt he was being generous: he could have asked to choose the legislature.

Of course, that was the Holy Grail, the lawbreaker as lawmaker. Zwillman was Joe Kennedy's kind of guy. As so too, as it would emerge so many decades later, were Zwillman's associates.

The American Mafia evolved as rapidly as the Kennedy family fortunes. Joe Kennedy became a welcome guest of some of the most unwelcome people in America. They included the dapper-dressed Frankie Yale, who had been born Francesco Ioele in Reggio Calabria, the home in Italy of the brutal, earthly 'Ndrangheta Mafia. He was now Americanising their methods in Brooklyn. Everything he touched was intended to appear as a legitimate business but was always a front for rackets, protection, gambling joints and the supply of booze and girls. Yale's pioneering organised crime outfit, from which feuding empires would emerge, was known as the 'Five Points Gang'. He put his profits into the Harvard Bar, Coney Island, and it was there that a waiter called Al Capone had his face badly scarred. He'd upset the sister of a very drunk mobster who in a lopsided attempt to cut Capone's throat slashed his face instead. It didn't make Capone a freak show – many of his bruised, bashed, shot and knife- and razor-cut fraternity had features like something the neighbourhood dog had been playing with. By the time Joe Kennedy set up a New York headquarters, 'Scarface' Capone had moved on in the underworld to Chicago. Still around Frankie Yale were his in-house killers, like cold delivery man Albert Anastasia and Willie 'Two-Knife' Altieri who, you get the idea, didn't use a gun but got his job done.

If you weren't part of their business, you had no problems with them. Yale himself was so useful a killer that Capone invited him west to Chicago for some political murders he didn't want botched. But the mobsters' friendship was upset by their constant companion, greed. They had no comfort zone.

Although there is little dispute (and none of it evidentiary) that Joe Kennedy smuggled high-end Scotch to America from Europe, there is confusion in archive reports on the senior Kennedy's involvement with the import of booze from Canada; some file documents appear to mistake a drinks industry businessman, Daniel Joseph Kennedy, who went by his middle name, with the Boston-born one. The other Kennedy sold *Kennedy's Jazz Cocktails*, which were produced in Canada and smuggled across the border by Joseph Kennedy Limited of Vancouver, British Columbia, (founder: D. Joseph Kennedy) along with bootleg whisky and gin.

This anomaly, according to law enforcement sources, may have saved Joe Kennedy much grief, if not his life. Frankie Yale imported Canadian liquor and supplied it to Capone, charging for the bootlegged whisky and the protection of it on the run to Chicago. Any successful hijacks of the convoys were just bad luck: you couldn't legislate against it. But there were too many booze heists. It stunk of an inside job. Capone suspected something was wrong – was Kennedy the supplier involved? – and sent in a spy to find the culprit. He reported back that Yale himself was stealing the liquor and reselling it. Often to Capone. A high-proof double-dip. A fatal one too, in time.

First, to get the dirty water off his chest, Capone dealt with a double-crossing underling and just after Fourth of July in 1927 the not-too-clever Jimmy D'Amato was shot down as he crossed a street in Brooklyn. Getting on for a year later, on 1 July 1928, Yale got a call at his Sunrise Club that his wife was unwell. He drove off in a panic, piloting his new armour-plated Lincoln coupe toward home. He was intercepted by a Buick carrying four assassins. They machine-gunned the coffee-coloured car, but the customised armour stopped the bullets. Not so the glass. The car dealer had cheated Yale and scrimped on the 'bulletproof windows', which were shattered by the gunfire blasts. Yale's car careened into a brownstone building. One of the killers leaped out with a .45 and finalised the contract by sending a chamber of bullets into the rival gangster's head.

The boys gave the Brooklyn Beau Brummell – at his death he was wearing a gift from Capone, a belt buckle engraved with his initials in seventy-five diamond chips – a wonderful funeral, the best. It was a gangland event. Thousands watched the procession, as a couple of dozen cars carried the floral tributes and around one hundred Cadillacs purred along with the mobster mourners. Dozens and dozens of roses were scattered into the air by the sleek crowd gathered around the grave, before the opulent, twenty-five-thousand-dollar silver casket was buried. The only moment of discord, one Joe Kennedy could fully comprehend, was when three women began arguing over which one was Frankie Yale's real wife. As it transpired, it was easier to work out who'd kill him than who was married to him.

Or who would fill the New York power vacuum he left.

For the next three years there was a machine-gun debate in which at least sixty mobsters with ambition died. The discussion was straightforward, the *Sicilian Way* against the *American Way*. The new, young guard was led by Charles Luciano, the Palermo-born Salvatore Lucania, who emerged as a charismatic, clever, wily and lethal leader of a multi-ethnic criminal conglomerate. He'd had an impressive adviser. As a nine-year-old he'd started a protection gang working in and around the Lower East Side. He offered little Jewish boys the choice of paying up or being beaten up. Most handed over nickels and dimes.

Maier Suchowljansky, who'd not long arrived with his family from Grodno in Poland, where he'd been born in 1902, wasn't taking any such nonsense. His reply to paying ten cents a week was a rapid *fuck off*. Luciano, attacked for his brutal nature, said he had to. His opponent fought back just as hard for he didn't know any different. The fighting finished, it was the beginning of a dark friendship between 'Lucky' Luciano and the boy who he came to know as Meyer Lansky. Lansky also became friendly with another young tearaway, the Brooklyn-born Benjamin Siegel, the son of Russian Jewish immigrants, who began his gangster career, like so many, by trading protection for dollars. They formed the Bug and Meyer Mob, dealing in muscle and murder and mayhem for the Prohibition-busting gangs of bootleggers operating throughout New York and New Jersey.

Benjamin – 'Bugsy', but never to his face – Siegel was a psycho-pistelero, a cowboy of a monster who wanted to be in at the kill if not pulling the trigger himself. Yet, as did Luciano, he listened to the counsel of Meyer Lansky, who – although as much a killer as his associates – had a corporate brain inside his head. Lansky, they said, could see round corners. He could also cut them. He and Luciano and Siegel worked with the addicted gambler and genius Arnold Rothstein. He was known as having a great criminal mind, cold and calculating. He envisaged a nationwide crime organisation. It was an idea he talked about with his students, who also included the decade-older Francesco Castiglia, who as Frank Costello was the greatest corrupter of politicians and policemen and judges, those known as the *foreign dignitaries*. Costello worked as a bootlegger alongside Joseph Kennedy and said the Kennedy patriarch and Rothstein were the only men he ever admired. He was clearly fonder, or at least felt less threatened by, Kennedy, who was amassing huge amounts of cash through stock manipulation, and clever enough to see the financial dark clouds gathering and to escape the 1929 Wall Street Crash which would destroy so much and so many. Costello also looked to the future. Rothstein, teetotal, non-smoker, saw his life and future as a spreadsheet. 'The Brain' appeared in Scott Fitzgerald's *The Great Gatsby* in 1925 as Meyer Wolfsheim, who wore human teeth as cufflinks.

Wolfsheim/Rothstein supposedly fixed baseball's 1919 World Series but the fact is that Rothstein probably only profited greatly from it. He only followed *hot horses*, those that always, always won. Never a play a game that isn't fixed. He was an able tutor and his class was eager, hungry for knowledge and opportunity. He taught them about forming organised groups, affiliations for no other reason than business, of 'looking after' politicians at local and national level, that the dollar was non-denominational and its nationality was profit. Money and the making of it was, he said, an international business. 'Have gun, will travel' was a crucial job description. So too was utter allegiance to profit. Never get in the way of making a dollar. His students, inhibited by him, believed they would prosper without him.

When Rothstein, at forty-six, was shot in Room 369 at the Park Central Hotel in November 1928, a single bullet went through his custom-tailored Harry Beck silk shirt, blasting a hole where the initials 'A. R.' had been handstitched. It was a nasty gut-shooting and Rothstein died the next day. The murder was never truly investigated by the New York authorities and dismissed as a falling out over gambling debts.

Rothstein, the great fixer, was fixed.

His students were never brought into inquiries about their mentor's passing. In gangland politics it was a landmark moment, like the Stock Market crash in October the following year for the straight world. Rothstein's acolytes had learned well. What happened outside their world was of no importance. They had their own agenda. When that battle for gangland dominance ended with a couple of assassinations in New York in 1931 it was already abundantly clear the boss was 'Lucky' Luciano, which for him and Lansky was neat diplomacy. Luciano kept the Italian factions content while his quieter – and privately equal – partner brought in the Jewish mobs who, unknown to the Italians, outnumbered them. That year saw the establishment of the New American Mafia, the National Crime Syndicate: gambling, prostitution, graft, corruption, numbers, loan-sharking, hijacking, criminal receiving, counterfeiting, pornography, smuggling, white slave and narcotics trafficking and all other nefarious and profitable activities on the wrong side of the street, were about to prosper.

The savagery, the unconscionable number of deaths fostered by Luciano and Lansky to establish point position, sped a high Richter rumble across gangland America. The old had been shaken out by men who had grown up faster than anyone could remember, a bunch as young as they were single-minded and ruthless. The New Deal gangsters expanded their enforcement arm, Murder, Incorporated. It recruited rubout men from the Meyer Bug Gang and comprised a bunch of made men including Siegel himself, Louis Lepke Buchalter and Albert Anastasia, the 'Lord High Executioner'. Still, no task for Murder, Inc., was taken forward without the personal approval of Meyer Lansky. He signed off on every deal, as it were. Other triggermen included Martin Goldstein and colourful, if nervy, Abraham 'Kid Twist' Reles who killed from a sweet shop known as Midnight Rose's. The hitmen got a salary and two to five thousand dollars a successful kill. The higher price was for the difficulty, not the target.

The Mob would kill anyone. Especially anyone standing in the way of them earning even one dollar. It remains puzzling why such a clued-in operator as Joseph Kennedy, who operated hands-on with such venal business partners, was disdainful over the years of this fact of Mafia commerce. He was a most arrogant man. He believed he should be allowed to simply be allowed to get on with his business. In one 1926 transaction he defied the need to pay his Mafia tithe to Lansky and his associates.

A year later Kennedy imported Irish whiskey – estimates of value peak at a couple of hundred thousand dollars – which he had brought ashore on Carson's Beach south of Boston. Many, many families in Hyannis Port and along eastern Long Island survived the early hurt of the approaching depression, and the proper bite of it, with good pay for unloading crates of Kennedy's bootleg booze. The value per bottle all but doubled if the booze was sold in New York so it was taken by Kennedy's trucks to the city.

Lansky's men hijacked the booze and in the gunfight one dozen drivers and guards died. The casualties were all Kennedy men. The mass deaths were covered-up by a staged 'drowning incident'. Kennedy didn't want Press attention, it was all 'an accident'. The Irishman fumed that not only had he lost a fortune but the families of his drivers were annoyingly chasing him for compensation. Kennedy could not sooth his anger with revenge. Lansky had the upper hand.

Myron Sugerman, eighty-six in 2023, who styles himself as 'The Last Jewish Gangster' worked with Gambino and Genovese in his decades as one of New York's outlaw entrepreneurs. His father Barney Sugerman operated alongside Lansky and his consigliere 'Doc' Stacher, and Myron himself visited them during their 1970s' exile in Israel. He told Douglas Thompson in 2017 that Joe Kennedy for ever wanted revenge – 'a deadly revenge' – against Lansky and the Mob and swore to 'get them'. He suggested that antipathy toward the gangsters bubbled away and was passed down to his sons JFK and Bobby Kennedy, although the business-first and pragmatic Joe carried on working and flirting with the Mob to enhance his fortune – and to ask favours. And sleep with their women.

Myron Sugerman offers unique insight into the times of which he or his father were primary witnesses. One gangster – identified only as a Cosa Nostra lifer by the FBI – said Myron was 'the last living testament to the National Syndicate, his experience with and exposure to the "fathers" of organised crime are invaluable resources that will soon be lost to history.' Myron himself put it another way over a boisterous lunch: 'I know a lot of stuff.' He said Joe Kennedy was actively involved in gangland pursuits – 'anything to make lots and lots of money'. He said that with the muscle of Murder, Inc. ('They killed enough guys to fill up their own cemetery') and wealth, every official, be it a judge or a politician, could be recruited by intimidation or bribe. Previously highly classified executive branch reports endorse him. As do faded State Department files, historical police records like those of the Los Angeles Police Organized Crime Intelligence Division (OCID) and declassified but still somewhat retracted reports from the FBI – J. Edgar Hoover reluctantly opened an official file when his friendly contact Joe Kennedy was flirting with the US government. There are statements and a great deal of circumstantial evidence about the links between the early Mafia men and Joe Kennedy. Many files are still restricted 'Eyes Only' (often because of bureaucracy rather than sensitivity) and although we have had access to hundreds of CIA files there are estimated to be more than one million of that agency's documents still too delicate in subject matter for release. Still, pressure on governments worldwide for more transparency about the past, and repeated Freedom of Information Act (FOIA) requests, provide details and revelations, pieces to one of America's most fascinating political jigsaws.

With hindsight, what appears astonishing is the concerted effort to ignore Joe Kennedy's life with the gangsters, and Establishment support for the constant denial by the Kennedy family of his bootlegging. The Canadian government were investigating him in 1926 as part of an inquiry into their alcohol exported to America during Prohibition. But it's only now, decades later, that *written record* of the Royal Commission on Customs and Excise have been disclosed. The Canadians weren't so much interested in catching bad guys but getting paid the tax on the booze by American importers, who included, along with Kennedy, in that order book Al Capone and Jake Guzik.

Jake 'Greasy Thumb' Guzik was the important Mob pay-off man who spearheaded the corruption of politicians and the police: his hands really got dirty and sticky counting so much cash. The commerce with the Canadians was worth a fortune, production of Hiram Walker Canadian increased by almost five hundred per cent to accommodate Kennedy and Capone's thirsty customers. Because it's such an emotive connection – Al Capone is shorthand for a violent, turbulent American era, celebrated for flappers and fun, condemned for the brutality of the St Valentine's Day Massacre – Joe Kennedy side-stepped around any direct 'embarrassing' personal links. Yet, hidden in the archives – time stops corroboration by primary witnesses – is the story that Kennedy negotiated a deal with Capone to smuggle his liquor into America across Lake Michigan, a safe route protected by the gangster. Anecdotal testimony by John Kohlert, on a tape made weeks before his death aged ninety-three, in 1994. Kohlert was a professional piano tuner who Capone favoured and employed to care for the instruments at his Chicago speakeasies and at his home. One evening Capone invited Kohlert to stay for a spaghetti dinner: they were 'having a special guest'. Kohlert sat listening and watching as Capone and Kennedy made a side deal involving the gangster's Canadian supply and Kennedy's Seagram's higher proof brand.

(In London during the Second World War, Kohlert was arrested on an immigration charge: he'd escaped the Nazis and contacted Kennedy, the US ambassador to the UK, with the message 'I hope you remember me from that spaghetti dinner in Cicero.' The next day, Kennedy arranged Kohlert's release.)

As ever, in the world of secrets and lies, it is in the early years that pivotal deals and alliances are determined and never more so than with the Kennedy dynasty and the sins of the father. Also, there is never a one hundred per cent assurance of discretion on the part of others, no matter how unlikely disclosure may seem. Take Joe Kennedy's great admirer, Frank Costello, a most discreet man, even the executions he ordered were carried out without a fuss.

As such, he kept his business and his business associates a private matter, especially under the government spotlight of the Special Senate Committee on the Investigation of Syndicated Crime led by Senator Estes Kefauver from Tennessee. That was in 1951 and the inquiry was into the Mafia, which the FBI's J. Edgar Hoover was still insisting did not exist. But there was Frank Costello on the stand, one of the Mafia's greatest godfathers. He was one of an astonishing bunch of characters who appeared before the ambitious politician.

From Davy Crockett's state, Kefauver had an Abe Lincoln look and a folksy-frontiersman way about him as he peered through his big, horn-rimmed spectacles at Costello and a parade of gamblers, thugs, hoodlums, crooked cops and sheriffs, caricature criminals, sweating and tapping their fingers nervously under the bright lights, every word recorded, every movement seized by the television cameras. These were guys who talked in broken English. Others, who couldn't count to five, were looking at their hands before taking the Fifth Amendment, including Greasy Thumb Guzik, who didn't want to 'criminate' himself.

When the Kefauver Committee got to New York, the proceedings were broadcast to dozens of stations across the country. The city was obsessed with it: Broadway theatre and cinema audiences dwindled, as, for eight days, the Mob put on their show – a carnival of criminality, scandalous and wonderful all at the same time. It was theatre – tragedy and comedy, dark Jacobean and Shakespearean slapstick – featuring the likes of the 'Lemon Drop Kid' and gunsels such as 'Golf Bag' Hunt, who were far more sinister than the comedy of their names. But the leading man was Frank Costello, the New York boss who, with his deputy Joe Adonis, ran casinos, slot machines and crap games.

For Joe Kennedy and his sons, it was a difficult time. Congressman JFK was preparing to run for the Senate. Only Joe Kennedy knew the extent of his dealings with Costello. He had nothing to fear. The mobster refused (in his hoarse voice – the result of a botched childhood tonsil operation) to testify, as the microphones would prohibit him from privately consulting with his lawyer sitting next to him. Kefauver compromised: the TV cameras would not show his face but focus only on his hands.

On live television, the cameras followed his meaty hands as he fingered the spectacles resting on the witness table, or moved to dab a handkerchief to his off-screen face as he dodged question after question. Mr Sinister in action. When asked to name one thing he'd done for his country, Costello growled: 'Paid my tax!' He also paid for his silence, being indicted for contempt of the Senate and for a decade he was in and out of state and federal prisons. He never said a word about anything – or anyone. Until, aged eighty-two, he wanted to 'put the record straight'. He let it be known to journalist Peter Maas that he would talk, and after months of elaborate courtship, he did. For ten days. The gangster known as the 'Prime Minister of the Underworld', who regularly advised Carlo Gambino, the American Mafia's most respected crime lord and the template for Brando's 'Godfather', suddenly died on 18 February 1973. His heart gave out. It was front page New York news on 27 February, the secret story that was almost written. Peter Maas, who himself died in 2001, told *The New York Times* that in his 'interview' time his most difficult job was getting this seminal Mafia man to talk about the Mafia. 'He considered himself a man of stature. His attitudes, even his manner, said that he felt he had maintained a life on a level far above the conventional rackets,' said Maas. Costello was intent on discussing corruption in high politics: 'He was much more interested in talking about himself in relation to Joe Kennedy, [Louisiana Governor] Huey Long and [New York Mayor] Fiorello La Guardia.'

In June 1972, Maas received the nod that Costello might talk. In December, the mobster who led the Family created by Charlie 'Lucky' Luciano went to the writer's apartment on East 57th Street for a meeting. For three hours Costello drank coffee, smoked cigarettes and listened. 'I told him that he was a legitimate figure in American history, and I meant it. There isn't a level of society that his career didn't touch.' They met once a week through to the end of January 1973.

Maas, the author of *The Valachi Papers*, the story of the Mafia soldier who turned informant, and *Serpico*, which became a movie with Al Pacino as former detective Frank Serpico investigating police corruption, said Costello told him that he and Joe Kennedy were partners in importing illegal liquor. Costello, he said, revealed that Kennedy had made the initial contact with him.

Law enforcement files show Costello, born Francesco Catiglia in Calabria, Italy, took over a smuggling Syndicate in the 1920s with Joseph Reinfeld, an associate of Longy Zwillman, and one of the canniest and most successful of Prohibition profiteers. Reinfeld bought booze in Europe and guarded its delivery to warehouses in St Pierre, off Newfoundland, in vessels owned by the Mob. The contraband was shipped to Rum Row, off Nantucket and eastern Long Island, or smuggled directly into New York Harbor. Costello bribed Federal and city officials and cops to look the other way as the consignments were safely landed.

Costello's evidence and assertion that he made Joe Kennedy wealthy during Prohibition – something continually denied by some of his heirs – is emphasised by official confirmation that Costello and Reinfeld, on behalf of the fledgling mobster Syndicate, controlled the largest ship-smuggling venture on the East Coast during Prohibition. Most are bemused by the family denials of a bootlegging Joe Kennedy and loyal supporters of the Kennedy myths may be dismayed by newly discovered documents, first discreetly registered in 2013, which show Kennedy bought during Prohibition, through his Columbia Trust Bank, eight hundred barrels of whiskey – that's forty-two gallons of liquor a barrel; a great many pints of whiskey to sell throughout the gangland controlled clubs of New York. The gangsters said they made Kennedy fabulously rich – the Reinfeld Syndicate imported almost half of the alcohol drunk in America during the thirteen long years of Prohibition. This is further corroborated by New York Mafia chieftain, Joe 'Bananas' Bonanno, who became a Family boss toward the end of Prohibition. In his autobiography (*A Man of Honor*, 1983), he includes photographs of dapper businessmen in the 1920s: himself and Joe Kennedy. The mobster's son, Bill, said in an archive interview that his father knew Kennedy during Prohibition and that Kennedy landed liquor at Sag Harbor on Long Island. (Bill Bonanno revealed his father met with Joe Kennedy in Arizona in the 1950s when he visited to recruit support for JFK's Presidential run.) Interestingly, the Mafia men only spoke after Kennedy and his sons JFK and Bobby Kennedy had died: was it fear of contradiction or reprisal?

Peter Maas had no doubts about Kennedy's bootlegging after his suddenly truncated conversations with Frank Costello. Indeed, he said Costello and Joe Kennedy worked as partners in the booze business until 1946, thirteen years after Prohibition ended. Maas said of Costello, 'He certainly didn't hold in awe some of the Mafia leaders of the past who are revered by everybody else in the organisation, yet he spoke with great regard about Meyer Lansky.' Another man with whom Joe Kennedy marked his card. As was gangster Owen 'Owney' Madden, a.k.a. 'The Killer', born in

Leeds, England, in 1891. He was one of the first to confirm that Joe Kennedy was a bootlegger.

Madden survived as a primary witness to the bullet-ridden madness of Prohibition and its violent aftermath, 'retired' to Hot Springs, Arkansas, which became an outlaw retreat and – to his own surprise – died of natural causes in 1965. He left his stories behind. He revealed Kennedy's high-price liquor was served in that most famous of naughty time 1920s' nightclubs, the Cotton Club, which Madden ran in Manhattan. Kennedy closely watched Madden's methods and how it brought him wealth and influence.

Like Kennedy's ancestor Patrick Kennedy – father of the dynasty – who had fled the Irish famine, arriving in the intimidating world of east Boston in 1848, Madden arrived in America with nothing but his wits about him. When his mother was widowed, she emigrated to New York to become a maid, leaving her three children in an orphanage. By 1896, she'd saved enough money to pay for them to join her. Owen Madden grew up on the streets of New York quickly, learning how to look after himself with whatever was at hand – knives and bats and knuckledusters, but in particular a weighted blackjack which he wore in a belt holster. His Hell's Kitchen friend and personal driver George Ranft would become the Hollywood star George Raft. Madden celebrated his twenty-first birthday as leader of the Gopher Gang, which controlled through terror most of Manhattan from 4th to 42nd Street and 7th to 11th Avenue. Much violence, murders and a prison term later, he returned to business as a hospitality entrepreneur, one who in time would control a couple of dozen of the city's nightclubs and restaurants by bribes and intimidation and having friends in high places.

In 1923 he opened the Cotton Club, at 142nd and Lennox and operated during Prohibition and Jim Crow racial segregation ('Jim Crow' being the pejorative term for African-Americans); as Madden served Kennedy booze, the absurdity of the white-only customers (paying an expensive two-dollar minimum cover fee) was evident; his customers were entertained by legendary black entertainers, including Louis Armstrong, Billie Holliday, Lena Horne and Count Basie. The Cotton Club was briefly closed, for selling booze, in 1925. After interventions by 'an influential businessman' and contributions by Madden to the New York City Police Fund there was not another problem with the cops. Indeed, the Cotton Club 'drinks menu' was extended.

A clever, numerate man, Madden admired Joe Kennedy's business strength and determination and his way with corruptible politicians – he paid them. Madden used his profits to buy shares and influence in the Stork Club in Manhattan, which would become one of the world's most influential and famous nightclubs. Reflecting the business fashion of the times, the Stork Club was funded by 'irregularities', the profits of bootlegging by original owner, the fastidious Sherman Billingsley and established at West 58th Street in 1929. Billingsley, proudly from Oklahoma, was 'acquainted' with Joseph Kennedy, who liked the Stork Club atmosphere: fresh flowers everywhere, discreet bar and mirrored dining rooms and the availability of showgirls.

The club policy was to have 'beautiful women everywhere' and that included the wall-to-wall oil painting portraits in the club room. Entry to the Club Room was via a factotum who was known to Joe Kennedy and his friends as 'Saint Peter'. One of those friends was the media voice that mattered, the ruthless Walter Winchell.

Winchell who broadcast his radio programme from Table 50, the roost where for decades he ruined lives, or, on kinder days, careers, reputations and marriages. Barking into a microphone or his centrepiece table telephone, neatly circled by notepads and pencils, he spread venom at two hundred words a minute (they timed him on a stopwatch) across America. He also wrote his column for the *New York Journal-American* from there. In one, the audacity of Joe Kennedy was kept to a snappy and anonymous item: 'A top New Dealer's mistress is a Mob widow'.

Joe Kennedy's lover, showgirl Evelyn Crowell Fay, had indeed become a widow, and most dramatically, on New Year's Eve 1932, when her racketeer husband Larry Fay was blasted away in a fury of bullets at the Casa Blanca Club in Manhattan, which he co-owned. A fussy and flashy dresser, who imported many outfits from Bond Street, London, for the first time in months he'd not worn his bulletproof vest because it spoiled the cut of his dinner jacket. An enterprising 'businessman' gambler, he was renowned for his Prohibition parties out on Long Island, fanfare affairs which made him mistakenly a suspect as inspiration for Fitzgerald's Jay Gatsby. Fay *was* the inspiration for James Cagney's gangster Eddie Bartlett in the landmark film *The Roaring Twenties*, 1939, and was the 'guest star' gangster in his own name in an episode of the 1960s' television series *The Untouchables*.

The lavishly magnetic Mrs Fay turned the momentarily besotted Joe Kennedy blind to her late husband's compromising enterprises. Indeed, it is suggested, Kennedy first met Mrs Fay when her husband was still very much alive and handling consignments of Scotch whisky, champagne and rum which was landed on the Canadian side of the border before being trucked to the city on Kennedy's behalf. When Kennedy and Mrs Fay became intimate is not on any Department of State timeline but they were often seen socially with Owney Madden, who in this small gangland world was a partner in the El Fay nightclub on West 54th Street with Larry Fay. It was in this world, in which Joe Kennedy was contently comfortable, that the Mob's political fixers helped get city officials – and, in time, American Presidents – elected. It was also in this world that the dollar ruled and nothing was ever quite what it seemed. Madden and Fay, until he went out of fashion, ran a protection racket on their own clubs, marking off the cash paid against the shares of profits paid out to their 'silent investors'. Joe Kennedy thought he was a step ahead of the gangsters, sleeping with their wives and girlfriends. He never was.

Federal files, meetings, minutes, memoranda reluctantly declassified by request and coaxed by time telling the truth, American and other intelligence reports and more memos and minutes as well as memoirs through the Eisenhower, Kennedy, Lyndon Johnson and Richard Nixon Presidential libraries and interviews over many years indicate why Joe Kennedy believed he was omnipotent. He had a protective shield. He had no fears running illegal booze or openly chasing every woman he met because his business had the protection of the Mafia – they got their cut – and his personal life was off limits to newspapers. Walter Winchell's 'blind' item was an anomaly but even Winchell, in 1935 the nation's most powerful media presence, shied from naming Kennedy.

After the publication of what was casual New York after-hours gossip, Kennedy befriended Winchell and instantly they found shared self-interests. A beautiful friendship began, with Kennedy feeding Winchell 'news' which would harm his opponents and amuse or enrage but most certainly entertain his new best friend's listeners and readers. Another friend, J. Edgar Hoover, deployed similar tactics. The FBI would 'cancel' critical newspapers and offer exclusives to friendly ones. One of Hoover's deputies, William Sullivan, is quoted by Beverly Gage in *G-Man: J. Edgar Hoover and the Making of the American Century* (Simon & Schuster, 2023) bragging, 'They were our Press prostitutes. Our strength was in the small dailies and weeklies; and with hundreds of these papers behind him, Hoover didn't give a damn about papers like *The New York Times*. A negative story which appears in a newspaper published in a congressman's home District hurts him more than any article in *The Washington Post*.'

In turn, as Gage points out, when it came to getting funding from Congress, Hoover got more money than he asked for. It was all politics: 'You scratch my back and I won't put a knife in yours.' The ironically pliable Winchell comprised part of Joe Kennedy's ongoing manipulation of the media, of a public always desperate for comic book superheroes to believe in. As his plans developed and his international machinations intensified, eminent newsmen enjoyed expensive gifts from Kennedy who as an extra also supplied one Pulitzer prizewinner, *New York Times* political editor Arthur Krock, with women. He was about to learn, and earn millions, from the world of those who did make-believe for a living.

Joe Kennedy watched masters of the dark arts in action and keenly adopted their wicked ways. He was also a very early disciple of someone whose activities would inextricably influence world politics and directly bring tragedy to the Kennedy family, the man who truly wrote the book on telling the public, the voters, what to think. And others how to act. Guided by him, and with the collusion of his family, with the manufacture of myth and legend, lies euphemistically explained after scrutiny as omissions and distortions, he got his son elected to the role of the American President.

Chapter Two

Sweet Deals

'It rechristened its territories "Banana Republics"... it abolished free will, gave out imperial crowns, encouraged envy, attracted the dictatorship of flies ... flies sticky with submissive blood and marmalade, drunken flies that buzz over the tombs of the people, circus flies, wise flies expert at tyranny.'

Pablo Neruda, 'The United Fruit Co.', 1950

It's hard to distinguish if it was the banana business or the Kennedys that had the better marketing campaign. They shared propaganda tactics and players and both spent millions of dollars in pursuit of power and control and benefited from the complicity of the carpetbaggers always tempted by opportunity.

Of which there were many, both in Massachusetts, in the well-heeled Brookline where JFK was born in 1917, and the Long Wharf of Boston port, where the business of tropical fruit had headquartered since the turn of the century. Again, they had similar needs, always requiring something fresh to offer the public, political reputations being as perishable as bananas.

Joe and Rose Kennedy's first 'family' home stood, appropriately enough for the purpose of metaphor, on Beals Street, named after a notorious land and commodities speculator in Brookline. By the time the couple's eldest son Joseph was born in the summer of

1915, the first of nine children, the Boston Fruit Company, after engaging in some inventive 'horse trading', was the United Fruit Company.

Two world wars later, both the Kennedy and United Fruit plans to conquer the globe were, after difficult moments, flourishing. Tragedy had interrupted Joe Kennedy's purpose when his first son Joe Jr, a Navy Bomber Pilot, was killed testing a secret drone aircraft in England on 12 August 1944. With his co-pilot, Lt Wilford J. Willy, he perished when the twenty-two thousand pounds of Torpex high explosives his experimental plane was carrying detonated about two thousand feet above Halesworth in north-east Suffolk in England; they were the only casualties.

Four years earlier, before America entered the Second World War, Joe Jr was a delegate at the Democratic National Convention and the plan was for him to get a seat in the US House of Representatives, en route to the White House. After his death, the details of which were kept secret for many years, patriarch Joe enlisted 'the spare' – JFK who he'd also been nurturing for a high-powered political career. Joe Kennedy Jr posthumously received the Navy Cross for his service. His father vainly solicited for the US Medal of Honor, the nation's highest military decoration.

His brother Jack was awarded the Navy and Marine Corps Medal for saving his fellow sailors after the sinking of his patrol torpedo boat PT-109 on 1 August 1943. When a Japanese destroyer crippled the boat in the Blackett Strait, south of Kolombangara in the Solomon Islands, Jack Kennedy swam his men – towing one with a belt clamped in his teeth – to the comparative safety of land patrolled by the enemy and his action, and their unexpected survival, made him a war hero. Asked for an explanation of his courage, he replied, 'It was involuntary. They sank my boat.'

The laconic attitude and colourful wartime adventure helped his run, as did financing from his father and prominent New England business interest 'angels', to encourage support of local political bosses, to win a House of Representatives seat which he took in 1947 representing Boston's needy 11th Congressional District. It was not a provisional step: there was nothing tentative about where JFK was being aimed and getting to that point is one of the great fascinations of our times. Within months another moment happened between two altogether different players, a meeting which would, in time, be a catalyst for events of such absurdity and brutality they would ricochet about history.

In New York, the most dapper Edward Bernays, a nephew of Sigmund Freud and the self-styled – he was his own spin doctor – father of modern public relations was engaged by the United Fruit Company. It followed his meeting with Sam Zemurray, a rough diamond desperately in need of polishing. Hesitant, until a hundred-thousand-dollar retainer was offered, Bernays, who'd find his skill leaned more toward propaganda, agreed to enhance the image of the company which had grown and prospered under the guidance of *Sam the Banana Man*. That kindly moniker disguised the nature of the tough, determined Zemurray who would as happily hold a worker's neck in his big hands as a bunch of bananas.

A Russian immigrant from Kishinev, today the capital of Moldova, and imposing, six foot and three inches tall in his jungle boots, Sam Zemurray might have stepped like Stewart Granger from the pages of Victorian novelist H. Rider Haggard's *King Solomon's Mines*, with its wild adventure and travel by oxcart through swamps and deserts in search of gold, diamonds, and ivory. The riches here were golden bananas which in 1893 the teenaged Zemurray first saw for sale on a street market stall in Selma, Alabama, and a little later as steamship cargo arriving at Mobile, busiest of the Gulf of Mexico ports.

He started out with a $150 stake moving ripe bananas cheap and conjured himself up to become one of America's richest men and one of emphatic and inflammatory influence throughout the Caribbean and Central and South America. On this journey, more of an entrepreneurial voyage, at gun- and knife-point, fighting bandits and business rivals, being eaten by mosquitos but escaping being lunch for cannibal-inclined indigenous settlements, and succumbing to fevers, he found time to make deals with dictators eager to sell their land and utilities for outrageous bribes and promises. The legacy of his success, eventually controlling more than ten million acres across ten countries, tens of thousands of workers and fleets of ships, warped the politics and lives of millions of people. By then United Fruit, *La Frutera*, was known, with disdain and dismay, as the Octopus. It was appropriate: the tactics, the skulduggery of United Fruit, reached everywhere in the search for profits throughout the central and south Americas. Zemurray insisted, in literal terms, on a cut-throat monopoly. His business plan was clear from 1910, when he bought land along the Cuyamel River in Honduras to expand his banana plantations. Frustrated by local politics, the national government displaying the effrontery to demand a say in the governance of their own land, by American trading terms, by rich importers with their idle promises, silk suits and diamond stick pins, he arranged a coup d'état. Zemurray considered his land as his fiefdom, blustering in anger at paying taxes and obeying Honduran law. He despised Presidente Miguel Dávila who he thought an idiot for imposing taxes on him and limiting how much land foreigners could own in Honduras. He wanted his own idiot, a useful one.

The White House of President William Taft wasn't that fond of President Dávila and predicted his liberal attitudes might have a domino effect throughout Central America, the people might begin to think independently and provoke unwanted nationalist movements, oppose the wishes of Washington. It was to become familiar twentieth-century thinking. Publicly, they opposed change, but if it happened there would only be faux outrage. Zemurray's choice for the new President of Honduras was the former President of Honduras, Manuel Bonilla, whom he spirited back to power from exile in New Orleans to the bewilderment of the US Secret Service, who were his 'minders'.

The easily led Bonilla, who'd been forced out of office in 1907, was happily spending much of his time at a renowned club-brothel on Basin Street and with his aide, Florian Dávadi, was smuggled to Bayou St John, where Zemurray's private yacht was docked, to begin his return to Honduras. It was a careful conspiracy with the yacht met across Lake Pontchartrain and the Mississippi Sound by an old Navy boat, the *Hornet*, filled with weapons and mercenaries led by General Lee Christmas, once an engineer on one of Zemurray's banana trains, and Guy 'Machine Gun' Molony. The adventurers and plot, both worthy of Alexandre Dumas, moved to the *Hornet*, on 23 December 1910, when they set off to start a revolution.

Lee Christmas, his uniform, bespoke in Paris, reflected him and his time and events rather well, a splendid example of faded grandeur. Molony was known as a renowned soldier of fortune, he'd go on to ride with Pancho Villa in 1916, and 'commander of the machine gun regiment'. On arrival the revolutionary force met reality, Molony was the regiment, his 'troops' an elderly burro, his weaponry his own hand-cranked Hotchkiss machine gun. The 'enemy' were possibly better equipped but had little enthusiasm for the conflict with the determined and hungry mercenary force. Zemurray had circulated financial 'gifts' to many of the Honduran politicians and military commanders before the action began. Internal and external politics were equally important weapons and assured the new presidency of Manuel Bonilla, a politician acutely aware of whom his benefactor was.

Sam Zemurray gloried in goodwill. President Bonilla gifted him twenty-five thousand acres of banana land in the north-east of the country and then another twenty-five thousand acres on the border with Guatemala. Sam the Banana Man then acquired a special permit allowing him to import *anything* duty-free and authorisation to get a loan – the equivalent of fifty million dollars, on behalf of the Honduran government – in payment for 'organising' the revolution. There was no question who the boss was or who and what was ripe, like the bananas, for exploitation. Zemurray pursued different Honduran presidents after Bonilla's death in 1913 and spread his interests throughout Central America and the Caribbean islands, owning lumber rights, railways and, most viably and controlling, the ports. United Fruit was the powerhouse and branded in one critical study as a business which 'throttled competitors, dominated governments, manacled railroads, ruined planters, choked cooperatives, domineered over workers, fought organised labour and exploited consumers.'

It was such harsh words, ugly noise for the Banana Man because of the subliminal commercial damage, which, in 1948, took Zemurray, by now a billionaire with interests from Honduras to Guatemala, Nicaragua, El Salvador, Ecuador, Costa Rica, Colombia and the Caribbean including huge sugar mills in Cuba, to the offices of Edward Bernays. On the United Fruit books there were earnings far exceeding those of most American and European companies. He explained to the public relations man his dilemma – everyone was bad-mouthing his business which, he believed, was bad for business. He told Bernays he was the marketing magician to resolve his problem. And he did, in a campaign which, on a mendacious Monopoly board, linked United Fruit to the Cold War, the CIA, the Kennedys and the White House and, by happenstance, to the Mafia godfather Joe Colombo. It was a world of money and wily political players, a constituency of those who peed iced water, the world of the Kennedys, where everyone believed what they needed to believe and did what needed to be done.

Bernays dealt in simplicity: tell the public, the people, what to think. He wasn't being sneaky, he'd laid out his methodology in his book *Propaganda* (1928), in which he wrote: 'The conscious and intelligent manipulation of the organised habits and opinions of the masses is an important element in democratic society. Those who manipulate this unseen mechanism of society constitute an invisible government which is the true ruling power of our country. We are governed ... our ideas suggested, largely by men we have never heard of … we are dominated by the relatively small number of persons … who understand the mental processes and social patterns of the masses. It is they who pull the wires which control the public mind.'

It was to be a lesson for all in manipulation, mostly the drafting of public perception; Bernays convinced Zemurray to spend to influence, to be 'modern' by introducing schools, hospitals and religion, priests and preachers, into and onto the plantations and townships, to be seen to be improving the lives of those whose toil was annually making him millions and millions of dollars. It was targeted philanthropy. Bernays, a Mad Man (Madison Avenue) pioneer, as if as a bonus ploy also boosted the sale of bananas throughout America. The message was bananas were good for you. It worked before; in 1929 he branded cigarettes as feminist *torches of freedom* to promote smoking to women and convinced the medical profession that a bacon-and-eggs breakfast was better for wellbeing and getting them to say so publicly for the good of his meat and dairy company clients. Now, his campaign was that this wonderful, worker-friendly company United Fruit was offering good health in the convenience of a banana. Bernays used Carmen Miranda, the Chiquita banana girl from Brazil who sang and danced wearing banana-bunch hats, to emphasise the message. It was, as ever, show business. The public side. There was much darker business going on behind closed doors where politics and sleaze so often share a bed. Intimate political shenanigans ricocheted as Bernays doubled down on the agenda he'd voiced in *Propaganda*: 'If you can influence the leaders, either with or without their conscious cooperation, you automatically influence the group which they sway.'

He persuaded Massachusetts Senator Henry Cabot Lodge Jr. to join the board of United Fruit, an appointment which severely tainted the otherwise exemplary record of the career politician and diplomat. Lodge, who had large stock holdings with United Fruit, was a Boston man, born in 1902 fifteen years before the banana business was at the Long Wharf. A Republican, his family friendly with the Kennedys although political rivals, Lodge was a triumph hire for United Fruit but was only part of the plot. John Foster Dulles, the US Secretary of State under Eisenhower, and his law firm Sullivan & Cromwell, worked for United Fruit and did the deals which gave away huge regions of Honduras and Guatemala to Zemurray. His brother, Allen Dulles, head of the CIA for Eisenhower and, initially, for President JFK, advised and carried out legal assignments for United Fruit and was a director. Ed Whitman, the public relations executive for United Fruit, was married to Ann Whitman, President Eisenhower's personal secretary.

If you can influence the leaders...

Contacts became indispensable when, after bumpy revolutionary years in Guatemala, with the Second World War ended, the Cold War begun and bogeyman Stalin all-powerful in Moscow, the Guatemala government started expropriating unused United Fruit Company land to the people, to the landless, hungry peasants. It followed some years of concern about the motives of the first freely elected leader, President Juan José Arévalo, who took power in 1945. He was acting in a most democratic way and that would not do as it was against the interests of United Fruit. The breaking point was when Arévalo brought in labour laws allowing workers and peasants to form unions. Aghast at this, Bernays himself went on a fact-finding trip to Guatemala and reported back. It was inconvenient material. The Russians Weren't Coming. Guatemala, he said, was not prime for a communist takeover, as a Soviet step into all Central America. The Panama Canal was safe. Yet, all this socialism stuff, labour laws, unions, was bad for United Fruit, so the public of America, and those around the world intent on freedom, must *think* that Uncle Joe Stalin is a threat. They must believe Guatemala is in imminent danger of communist infiltration.

Bernays advised the United Fruit board that everything Juan José Arévalo planned, albeit modelled on 'the American dream', was detrimental to business, especially an anti-monopoly law which would mean other companies could be in competition with them. Utter heresy.

The master manipulator went to work. Media outlets, television stations and newspapers, radio outlets and magazines, many of which had only a vague association of where Guatemala was, were drip-fed warnings of the impending doomsday in Central America. The red menace was at the door and scarily – according to Republican Senator Joseph McCarthy – already under America's beds. The Cold War political chill was as perfect for Edward Bernays as it was difficult for Jack Kennedy and his political allies. The rabid McCarthy, a supportive chorus for Bernays' dubious warnings of Soviet infiltration in Guatemala, was calling out communists from Washington to Hollywood and every which way and, by 1950, *McCarthyism* was coined and became shorthand for a political megaphone promoting reckless allegations. McCarthy, the Republican senator for, importantly in Kennedy land, Wisconsin, was the bullying, the vile side of 1950s' American politics. He was also a close friend of Joseph Kennedy, dated two of his daughters – Patricia and Eunice – and socialised with his sons. He was godfather to Robert Kennedy's first child, Kathleen, and young Bobby Kennedy acted as legal counsel for McCarthy's feared investigations committee for six months before quitting. He didn't like what he saw. Yet, the Roman Catholic Kennedy family stuck close to McCarthy, whose message of simplistic populism was applauded by the Catholic community which comprised one fifth of America's voters, an attractive chunk for any ambitious politician. The big, burly demagogue was a regular visitor to Kennedy HQ at Hyannis Port, Massachusetts, at a time when Jack Kennedy was preparing to fight Henry Cabot Lodge, the incumbent Republican senator for Massachusetts, in the 1952 general election. Acutely aware of anti-Catholic movements, Joseph Kennedy blatantly supported the popular McCarthy as a national Catholic politician hopeful that some of the stardust would sprinkle over his son's Senate campaign.

Joe Kennedy was crafty. As election prospects brightened, he sowed seeds, he put it about that it would be more difficult for his son to defeat Lodge than to win the Presidency. Yet, the elder Kennedy knew Lodge, although very much the favourite going into the race, had lost energy, having run Dwight Eisenhower's successful campaign for President that year. McCarthy did not campaign for his Republican colleague Lodge because of his loyalty to the Kennedys – and a fifty-thousand-dollar payoff from Joe Kennedy. Reviled by so many, McCarthy was never attacked by the future President who explained, 'Hell, half my voters in Massachusetts look on McCarthy as a hero.' When the Senate finally censured McCarthy, the only senator who did not vote was JFK, conveniently in hospital for treatment to his ongoing back problems. Oral histories at the John F. Kennedy Presidential Library in Boston, Massachusetts, indicate JFK was personally fond of McCarthy the man.

With Senator John Kennedy on the White House snakes and ladders board, 'Ike' Eisenhower was in the Oval Office pledging a harsh agenda on communism, a fanfare of happy sound for Edward Bernays who had regular contact with two of Eisenhower's most powerful staff, the brothers John Foster and Allen Dulles. The Dulles duo were prominent influencers on behalf of United Fruit, a company more and more under threat in modern times. When, in a landslide of a vote, Colonel Juan Jacobo Árbenz Guzmán became the second democratically elected President of Guatemala in March 1951 he delivered even more social reform. A more generous franchise for all and the encouraging of political diversity were irritating for United Fruit but the shocker was the increase of their huge land holdings being given to poor farm labourers. The propaganda war heated up. Guatemala began appearing in headlines with 'red alert'. The country, wrote *The New York Times* and *Washington Post*, was a growing threat to the free world. All the apparent egalitarian reform was a cover for communism. To prove it, Bernays hosted the world's news correspondents at the Hotel Panamerican in Guatemala City and provided manufactured 'evidence' in neat, ribbon-wrapped folders, of how Moscow planned to usurp America's wellbeing and interests throughout Latin America.

Publications ranging from the *Evening Standard* in London to *The Christian Science Monitor* reported what Bernays wanted them to report, his lively imagination turning conspiracy into reality. He planted 'news' wherever he could. One devoted ally of the Kennedy family cohort, Walter Winchell, devoted newspaper columns and radio broadcasting to events as dictated by Edward Bernays. One gloriously fanciful report by the United Press agency, written by Irishman and British magazine editor Kenneth de Courcy, a confidante of Joe Kennedy and the Duke of Windsor, was that Russia was building a submarine base in Guatemala. The gregarious de Courcy also plotted to establish the Duke of Windsor as regent in Britain rather than allow George VI's twenty-five-year-old daughter Elizabeth to ascend the throne after his death in February 1952.

This subversive onslaught on a central America hot spot was relentless and one story merged into another until, with McCarthyism sharing the screaming headlines, Eisenhower, urged on by the Dulles brothers and others, took action. The US Department of State and the CIA orchestrated the 1954 Guatemalan coup d'état and the repressive horror that was Colonel Carlos Castillo Armas became President. His elevation was an invitation to Joe Kennedy's old friends, the Mob, to introduce their gambling operations in Guatemala. Leading the invasion – the building of a casino with the enlistment of influential Army officers as partners – was the man who was eyewitness to the most reckless behaviour of the Kennedys. 'Handsome Johnny' Rosselli was an intimate of Joe Kennedy from their shared wild Hollywood days, when he was the Mafia's Mr Fixit. He also had something of that role in central

America and in Guatemala his priority was to make the new casino business prosper. He worked with agents from the Dominican Republic – rapacious characters operating solely in the interests of their despotic ruler, Rafael Trujillo – which also held an investment in the gambling. Close to United Fruit and friendly with CIA agents, Rosselli enjoyed extraordinary access to his host country and the American agencies posted there. When Carlos Armas became irritated with their arrangements and closed the casino, it was viewed as not just a nuisance but an act of disrespect, of betrayal.

For that, an assassination took place, an act which echoed.

Four days after the Lewin Casino was reluctantly shut down by the military, on 26 July 1957, Castillo Armas was shot dead in the *Casa Presidencial* in Guatemala City.

President Armas was walking to dinner. He had to cross a small garden area, with its lonely acacia tree, from his bedroom suites to the dining room, and he found himself in darkness. He heard no bustle of dining room staff. And where were the palace guards? Panicked, he'd left his gun on his nightstand, he turned and as he did so a rifle bullet hit him and he fell facedown. A second bullet in the back was needless insurance.

The casino closure was the trigger but the act premeditated, long in the planning, the cover-up fall guy picked and primed. As the shots were heard along the hallway off the garden, the light came on. And along the corridor from the President's prone body was the dead Romeo Vásquez Sánchez, one of his own personal guards. Instantly, the murder was solved: Sánchez killed himself with the same rifle he used to assassinate his President. Nothing quite added up but 'evidence' mounted before the news truly became known the following morning. Sánchez was presented as a lone fanatic, a communist; diaries and left-wing propaganda were found at his home. A supposed communiqué with Moscow was also 'discovered' on his body. His death, so convenient for the American gambling interests, for the new military powers, was neat. He was the scapegoat, the fall guy, a patsy to blame for eliminating a

President who interfered with the Mob making money. No need for investigations, for inquiries or commissions. It was open and shut.

Lone Gunman/Crazed Commie Kills President.

The killing was applauded by Carlos Marcello, the Mafia godfather of Louisiana, a gangster integral in the uncertain world of the Kennedys. Marcello was born in Tunisia of Sicilian parents; he'd joined the flow to America in 1910. Marcello used a fake Guatemalan birth certificate based on citizenship documents with the forged signature of the dead Castillo Armas. Indeed, future authoritarian Guatemalan leaders welcomed Marcello as a native son. As they did an American presence, the flag-waving encouragements of freedom, which helped keep them in power.

The United States policy was clear and contagious, so much better to have in charge a 'friendly' if despicable despot, one who could be told what to think and do, rather than some freewheeling do-gooder. It was an intrusive foreign policy of which JFK had first-hand recall when, not half a dozen years later, he had to joust with the revolutionary leader Fidel Castro who'd taken control in Cuba in 1959.

Much to the dismay of the overseas owners and powerful stockholders, Castro followed the mandate of José Arévalo and Jacobo Árbenz and expropriated United Fruit land and holdings, including the sugar mills in the Oriente area on the eastern side of the island. Answering the indignation and bluster, the threats of intervention and reprisals, of American business and politicians Castro warned JFK, 'Cuba is not another Guatemala.'

Which, with time, is a matter of interpretation.

Chapter Three

Capital Crimes

'Nobody's perfect.'
Osgood Fielding III (Joe E. Brown), *Some Like It Hot*, 1959

High risk doesn't begin to cover the behaviour of Kennedy & Sons in Hollywood and the idea that Joe Kennedy had a teenaged starlet murdered by cyanide poison in his early days in the film business reflects history is beginning to believe what he was capable of. His ruthless manner and never-ending sense of privilege suggest constant danger for victims of his greed and vanity.

As did the deadly love triangle between President Kennedy, his US Attorney General brother Bobby Kennedy and the tragic Marilyn Monroe, and the continual misadventures of their younger brother Teddy, 'banging every starlet in town', while the Los Angeles Police Department did all they could to cover up their excess.

Old Joe led the way, a true democrat, he'd screw anyone for pleasure or profit, cruising in his chauffeured Rolls-Royce around Beverly Hills, enjoying its avarice-driven crossword of streets, he gloried in nothing but opportunity. The Kennedy method, with business and women, was to get in first, plunder and be gone. Betty Lasky, daughter of Paramount Studios co-founder Jesse Lasky, appears in the Kennedy files saying, 'Joe always wore a wide grin on his face to camouflage the dollar sign imprinted on his heart.' A clinical sociopath, a man of zero empathy, he'd been told by his mobster associates that filmmaking was 'the new booze'. In 1926, tall – six-feet three-inches – with a Fifth Avenue wardrobe and a manicure, the would-be movie tycoon made an immediate impression on Hollywood. Here was not only a figure with energy but a man with money (most often other people's). One commentator allowed, 'He charmed people into trusting him and then took them for all they were worth.'

Yes, the charm, for some, more a satanic power, got him into many boardrooms and bedrooms, as he forged his place in the history of Hollywood. It was still the time of silent movies but the 'talkies' were only months away and the pragmatic Kennedy compared it to the telephone business: an investment for the future. Like America's robber barons, his friends the Boston carpetbaggers and the business moguls who would dominate the twentieth century, he realised that fortunes were made by taking control of the content – and the selling of it. He wanted to make movies in a studio he owned and screen them in cinema chains he controlled. He'd sell the popcorn too. Some schemes ended in lurid headlines. The Hollywood Pantages Theatre stands today on the tourist trail where Hollywood Boulevard meets Vine Street – Hollywood and Vine, the euphemistic centre of the film capital – and, when Joe Kennedy first saw it, the flagship of Alexander Pantages' eponymous chain of theatres. The second-largest independently owned group of theatres on the Coast and, as such, an attractive proposition.

Pantages himself was not so agreeable. He had the reputation of a Scrooge and was easily corruptible. The Greek-born businessman had turned himself into a multi-millionaire in America presenting vaudeville shows. He presented himself as poor in speaking and reading English but was sharply numerate in negotiations. Kennedy jousted with him; there would be an offer and a counter and then the claim that a third – or even fourth – party was making another offer. Kennedy pressed hard but Pantages held the leasehold on twenty-six theatres from San Francisco to San Diego and into central California and the going price at the start of 1929 was twenty million dollars. Other film companies became involved – stalemate. Kennedy did not like to be thwarted. When he wanted something, his power word was NOW. The weeks dragged on. Then on 9 August 1929, a seventeen-year-old dancer, Eunice Pringle, appeared in the lobby of the Pantages Theatre with her dress ripped and her eyes filled with tears, screaming that Alexander Pantages, sixty-two, had raped her. She'd gone to his offices looking for a job and he brutalised her, she told the cops. He was arrested for what was termed criminal assault and released on the then hefty bail of twenty-five thousand dollars. The headlines did the rest. Pringle was 'the sweetest teenager since Clara Bow', a Kennedy friend and 'It girl' of the Roarin' 1920s. Pantages was an unpleasant sex monster.

And that's the way it was played at his trial with Pantages' denials – he tearfully repeated, 'I did not, I did not' – lost by his portrayal as a predator. The Los Angeles District Attorney, the always perspiring Burton Fitts, took charge of the case and led the courtroom theatrics. Fitts was always chasing votes and a dollar – his office employed two of Lucky Luciano's Mafia henchmen – and watched over Kennedy interests. He charged the accused man's witnesses with perjury – for fifty dollars they said Pantages had paid them to lie for him – and the guilty verdict was the one sure thing in all their lives. Pantages was sent off for fifty years to San Quentin penitentiary, out by the Bay near San Francisco. He appealed and called in lawyer Jerry Giesler, who represented Charlie Chaplin and would act for Errol Flynn (underage sex) and Lana Turner (murder of her gangster lover Johnny Stompanato) and Marilyn Monroe (divorce from Joe DiMaggio) and he won an acquittal after an equally muck-raking retrial. With all the legal hysteria and his personal notoriety, Pantages sold out to Kennedy for a little more than a third of his original twenty-million-dollar plus asking price.

The contemporary story was that Kennedy had paid Eunice Pringle to set up Pantages on the rape charges, a situation supported by much circumstantial evidence. Joe Kennedy's image as a gangster in Hollywood was cemented when a much more damning version found its way into the pages of several mainstream books. This racy take was that Eunice had an attack of conscience and was threatening to tell all – which Marilyn Monroe would do with JFK three decades later – and that Joe Kennedy killed her; all was supposedly revealed by Eunice in a 'death bed confession' in 1933 when 'she was violently ill and red in colouring, the telltale signs of cyanide poisoning'. One author has Eunice being paid ten thousand dollars by Joe Kennedy and given his promise to make her a star. No one would ever know, he wrote, if Kennedy had poisoned her because there was no autopsy. Which, back in the real world, never happened because Eunice Pringle died, aged eighty-four and a grandmother, in 1996 of natural causes. Her 'death' was one sin of which Joe Kennedy was not guilty and it was an exception. Blackmail and threat were high on his skill set.

He engaged them and more in controlling three studios simultaneously as the 'talkies' began, a substantial achievement, not the mere flaunting of the peacock's tail feathers. Yet, recklessly, by taking what appeared absurd chances, he made more money than movie memories in his brief four years in town. Author Cari Beauchamp, who died in December 2023, using her skill and connections, gained access to Joseph P. Kennedy's Papers, held at the JFK Library but only available through family recommendation. In her meticulously researched and crafted *Joseph P. Kennedy's Hollywood Years* (Alfred A. Knopf, 2009), she estimates he made at least nine million dollars, adding to his fabulous fortune – what would be six hundred million dollars in 2024. Our new files show much of his financial success was having control of the unions, which was achieved with the help of the first person he had dinner with when he arrived in Los Angeles, the urbane Johnny Rosselli, the Mob's man in Hollywood. As much as Kennedy was *his* man.

The Kennedy relationship with Johnny Rosselli, seeping all the way to JFK's White House, remains one of the more important and the most overlooked of all the deals-with-the-devil which contrived to create the artefact of 'Camelot'.

Through it we see the perils of the intricate underworld web established by Joe Kennedy, associations constantly deployed to further the Kennedy cause. The gangsters involved were the crème de la crème and to understand them is to understand the Kennedy dynasty, how far they would go and what they would risk. New documents offer information which display staggering information, material which if known at the time would have brought shame and indictment and changed future history.

Rosselli knew Joe Kennedy's methods. He lived in Boston in 1918, when Kennedy crazily spread money around the city's Little Italy, hiring tough guys to encourage the vote for his father-in-law John Francis 'Honey Fitz' Fitzgerald. Rosselli knew a gangster when he saw one; he had Kennedy's measure and he didn't trust him. It was simply business. Rosselli's loyalty was forever to his Mafia masters and for their advantage he forever entangled the Kennedys with the Mob, with outrageous bandits, in an extraordinary story of sex and drugs, shakedowns and murder, corruption, racism and multiple malfeasance. Sordid, like the cast of characters with their terrifying antecedents.

Rosselli started life as Filippo Sacco, born on 5 June 1905 in the rural village of Esperia, just short of seventy miles to the southeast of Rome. He arrived in America illegally six years later. After his father Vincenzo died in the 1918 flu epidemic, he settled in the crowded tenement streets of East Boston with his mother Maria. Like many young immigrants, he was a teenage street kid and quick to see the chances of easy money operating for the neighbourhood Fagins. The youngsters acted as runners for the bookies and, more haphazardly, the dope peddlers. Drugs, morphine, heroin and cocaine were widely used and readily available. At a price. Even movie heroes were addicted. In 1916, Douglas Fairbanks, an athletic and high-fashioned Broadway actor-turned-Hollywood leading man, starred in *The Mystery of the Leaping Fish*. His character Coke Ennyday was billed as 'the world's greatest scientific detective'. This was a crime-fighter lauded in the film notes as 'gifted, with not only a brilliant mind and great deductive talents, but also the ability to consume huge doses of drug without any problem.' They continued, 'Ennyday's life wouldn't be the same without his constant injections of cocaine, as whenever he feels down or needs energy, his loyal syringes will get him high and laughing again.'

For Filippo Sacco, supplying drugs was shameless. Morphine was available legally on prescription, though its distribution by the street gangs was such a social problem that city hall had a police task force working to eradicate it. Of course, most of the cops on the beat looked the other way and got their dollars and drugs in return. Such was the corruption that Federal authorities were brought in. And it was to an undercover Federal informant called Fisher that the seventeen-year-old Filippo Sacco sold a quarter-ounce of morphine and found himself indicted on narcotics charges. He made bail and fled town before his court case. But only after making the informant Fisher vanish as well. Fisher's remains were never found. Filippo Sacco, who by now was Johnny Rosselli (after the Florentine painter Cosimo Rosselli), would go on to be charged with many crimes, but never murder. Having made his connections in New York, and then in Chicago, with brothel entrepreneur Johnny Torrio, Rosselli was soon mixing with rising Mafia stars such as Joe Kennedy's associate Frank Costello, Tony 'Joe Batters' Accardo and the subtly malevolent Paul 'the Waiter' Ricca.

Ricca was a teenage killer in Naples turned Chicago waiter at the Bella Napoli Café, where the owner, 'Diamond Joe' Esposito, introduced him to some guys from the old country. The always softly spoken and elegantly dressed Ricca became the Chicago outfit's strategist. It was a title Johnny Rosselli admired. Until his unnatural dying day, he carried business cards stating: 'Strategist'.

Rosselli had learned from all of them, especially Al Capone – before he became *Al Capone* – when he worked as Capone's driver, before Joe Kennedy arrived in Hollywood. The mobsters liked Rosselli and, because of all his coughing and spluttering, it was Capone who recommended he be sent from the wet and damp of Michigan out west and onto the high seas with Tony 'the Admiral' Cornero, who was associated with Joe Kennedy in the illegal booze business. With 840 miles of Californian coastline to navigate, the consignments of liquor from Mexico and Canada were offloaded at several key beaches, often just north of Santa Barbara, from where shipments could be trucked in customised compartments to San Francisco and Los Angeles. The 'Hooch Highway' stretched all the way from Tijuana to Vancouver. The drivers were given stimulants, including tiny packets of cocaine, to keep them alert for the journeys, which for some must have turned into quite a trip. The network was annually supplying more than four million illegal gallons of high-proof alcohol. It was rough stuff.

By the 1920s and the popularity of the movies in Hollywood, however, tastes had become more sophisticated: clients liked to keep the first drink down. Good Scotch, about 200,000 cases a year, with a mighty mark-up, was being imported, giving the Mafia bootleggers tremendous profits. The attractive booze business lured adventurers like Anthony Cornero, who was born in 1895 in a village on the outskirts of Milan. His farming family prospered until his gambling father lost his property and livelihood on the turn of a Queen of Clubs. The Cornero clan emigrated in 1904 and the youngster who'd become Tony 'the Hat' Cornero took to the streets of San Francisco. He was ambitious, but by age sixteen had received ten months in reform school for improving his spending habits by stealing. On release, he became a taxi driver in the city and got a taste of how the better-off lived, seeing the luxuries for which they'd casually pay well. He'd spend his lifetime providing pleasures until he himself had one drink too many.

He moved to Los Angeles in 1922 where the Hat reinvented himself as Tony 'the Admiral' Cornero, using Kennedy connections to smuggle quality whisky across the Canadian border and selling it to top-end Hollywood nightclubs and emerging 'star' spots, such as the Beverly Hills Hotel and the high-rollers of the fledgling film business. Cornero, like western movie star Tom Mix, sported a white Stetson, which he accentuated with cream gloves; his bodyguards carried the guns. Purportedly running a shrimping business, Cornero started with a fleet of small boats and ran rum from Mexico to Los Angeles, his freighters missed by the US coastguard, who were short-staffed and also paid to glance the other way. The waterline heightened with his enterprise and he bought the SS *Lily*, a merchant ship that could transport around four thousand crates of bonded Scotch a time to beyond the three-mile limit from Los Angeles's San Pedro harbour. The Scotch was then unloaded into speedboats, which delivered it to ever-changing coastal points. But it wasn't plain sailing for the Admiral. He was in at the deep end in the constant and often vicious struggle to be the Mr Big of the underworld. Across the spectrum, from the scallywags to the killers, there were no illusions. The most effective way to better your odds was to kill off your rivals. Criminality can't abide a vacuum.

Albert Marco, who'd arrived in America from Bolgliasco, near Genoa, through Ellis Island, was an accomplished pimp by the time he began working out of Seattle in Washington state, the jumping-off point for the 1898 Alaska gold rush. There he met Charles Crawford who, as a young man, set up a business providing 'home comforts' to the prospectors heading for the Klondike. Together they created the city's best prostitution network. City officials were bribed, and their business was more reliable than digging for gold. They extended themselves and blatantly leased a five-hundred 'crib' brothel to accommodate their around-the-clock teams of busy freelance girls, who themselves were paying ten dollars a week rent, which was collected for Crawford by the Seattle Police Department. Charlie 'the Wolf' Crawford got out of town with 'decent people' baying behind him and headed south to Los Angeles. His associate Marco slipped back into bootlegging and the backwaters.

Like Joe Kennedy, these men were American pioneers. They shared passion and tactics – and secrets. Crawford got himself the Maple Bar (drinking and plotting downstairs; girls and gambling one floor up), smack at the corner of Maple and 5th Street and a close association with the 'City Hall Gang', a bunch of corrupt officials operating with the collusion of the LAPD. The main player in this game was Ken Kane Parrot (he pronounced it '*Poirot*', as in Hercule), who had manipulated himself into being the indispensable chief of staff for Mayor George Cryer, himself a few pages short in the ethics handbook. With dry-cleaning and laundry shops throughout the city used as fronts for the illegal booze business – thus money being 'laundered' – Charlie Crawford masterminded supply along the Hooch Highway. But he used Albert Marco, who had grown into a wily and superbly connected Mafia operator. Through Crawford, the corporate-thinking Marco also partnered up with another bootlegger-gambler, the generous Milton B. 'Farmer' Page, who was known for buying associates a drink before killing them.

Tony Cornero found himself swimming in crowded waters. The Parrot-Crawford-Marco-Page combination used the LAPD to keep constant pressure on the self-styled Admiral, while they ran booze, the city and the newspapers. Kent Parrot was a charismatic character known as 'the boss'. He was a big man with lots of bulk on his six-foot two-inch frame and he used it to give presence to his point of view – lavishly underwritten, along with Mayor Cryer's political campaigns, by seemingly eternal bootlegging and prostitution profits. The Admiral first fought back in the quietly intelligent mafioso way – he tried to buy himself out of trouble. He invested a hundred thousand dollars in Mayor Cryer's second re-election campaign, but the City Hall Gang simply smiled, took the money and kept the pressure on. While they encouraged Farmer Page, they made Cornero's life and business more complicated – and deadly. The Cornero bootleggers were constantly being caught – not by the law but by rival booze runners, just as Meyer Lansky's gunmen attacked Joe Kennedy's booze trucks. Consignments would be hijacked at gunpoint, while his bodyguards and growing band of gunsels were regularly rousted by the cops.

In benevolent contrast, the City Hall's hard men were allowed to thieve and kill as they pleased. In April 1925, Albert Marco pistol-whipped an LAPD uniformed officer and was fined fifty dollars. Then was given his gun back. When he was arrested by a rookie patrolman, having 'marked up' a couple of his girls, two detectives got the charge down to disturbing the peace, although Marco was also carrying a revolver. He had a concealed weapons permit even though, as a non-citizen, was not entitled to it. Los Angeles County's longest-serving sheriff, Eugene Biscailuz, had granted the licence and argued that he deserved it. The Los Angeles City Prosecutor agreed.

Cornero's frustrations burst over the edges. A gambler like his father, he staked everything and retaliated in the summer of 1925 after a Page pirate crew rammed one of his ships at sea and stole 1,500 cases of rum. He ordered Johnny Rosselli to do what he did most every night in Hollywood – get a girl. As instructed, Rosselli talked a little too much and 'leaked' the time and place of Cornero's next booze shipment.

The set-up was arranged on the Pacific Coast at Wilmington, not far south from what would become Los Angeles International Airport. On 3 August 1925, all that was in the sky and on the wind in the late evening were seagulls and impending trouble. Seven hoodlums, three shotgun specialists and four henchmen with snub-nosed pistols were deployed by Page around the rum shipment's landing spot. A sedan was parked at a sharp angle on the access road to the marshy beach land. As the smug hitmen sat, anticipating their prey, Cornero's team opened up with Thompson submachine-guns from bushes behind them. The black sedan took eighty-eight bullets. A gunman called Jake Barrett was also riddled with them but, like the others, survived the haphazard hail of gunfire. The LAPD had Cornero brought in, but he shrugged off their accusations. No one was talking, but the Admiral was still plotting. Eight months later another Page henchman, the absurdly violent Walter Hesketh, was taken out at the corner of Spring Street in downtown Los Angeles. He was strolling back to his apartment when a black sedan swerved toward him and a fusillade of bullets put him to the ground. As the weeks went by, there were more street accidents in which bodies and bullets collided.

Cornero and Rosselli were hauled in for police questioning, but the Admiral was never detained. Rosselli spent only one night on the metal bench of a Central Jail cell in downtown Los Angeles, charges for holding two unregistered revolvers being dropped for no official reason. Someone in Chicago had 'spoken' with Kent Parrott about the future of the suave sociopath Rosselli – always 'Johnny Handsome' in the wonderland of Hollywood. Short in stature, at five feet eight inches, on account of his tuberculosis, he came across as quiet, respectful and neatly turned out. He never looked out of place at his dinners with Joe Kennedy and the added advantage for the fledgling Hollywood mogul was his associate Rosselli had the blessing of the Chicago outfit.

Tony Cornero was still being harassed in his bootlegging operations – even the US coastguard had rounded on him. He was aboard his yacht *Donnarsari* shortly before Christmas Day 1926, having offloaded two thousand cases of whisky from Canada into speedboats. Rosselli was at the wheel of one of them when he spotted the coastguard. He went for the shore and escaped. Meanwhile, Cornero was arrested, though he jumped bail and went into hiding until Rosselli delivered the profits from that particular smuggling operation. With the cash, the Admiral bribed his way into Canada, but the country quickly bored him. He paid Rosselli back by linking him with Kennedy's bootlegging partner Longie Zwillman, who was involved with Hollywood's tragic and turbulent 'blonde bombshell' Jean Harlow.

The mobsters and the business entrepreneurs were mirrors of each other.

By Joe Kennedy's time in Hollywood, Zwillman, along with Meyer Lansky and Lucky Luciano, had organised the 1929 Cleveland Conference, a thunder dome alliance of Jewish and Italian mobsters which, within two years, would become the infamous National Crime Syndicate, a.k.a. 'the Mob', 'the Outfit', 'the Syndicate'. 'The Syndicate' was the more accurate description, although in essence it remained the Mafia, but with an ethnic twist – of your neck, if you weren't careful. And part of it always had an appetite for glamour, as well as an unlimited capacity for cash. It was all very much cash-and-carry.

By 1929, Tony Cornero had decided he'd rather be in jail than in Canada. He walked into custody in Los Angeles and got a two-year federal prison term in McNeil Island penitentiary in Puget Sound in Washington State, where he contemplated what profits could be derived from the stock market crash. This left his seagoing sidekick Johnny Rosselli clear to join in with Jack Dragna, a nasty, calculated criminal who'd kill for a cigarette or a favour. Any timidity Dragna ever showed was for his own safety. Born in Corleone, Sicily, in 1891, Dragna always got a bad press for his inadequacies when compared with the activities of the Chicago and New York hoodlums, but he was a Hollywood survivor, as familiar with Sunset Boulevard as anyone.

For Johnny Rosselli – and many others – the arrival of 1931 was important. Cornero got out of jail that year and went into the gambling business, opening the Green Meadows casino out in Nevada at a place called Las Vegas. He offered good odds and waitresses who liked to be friendly. It was the beginning of a Kennedy love affair with the city which Joe Kennedy – and later JFK – wallowed in with its easily accessible cash and women.

Over in California, Joseph Ardizzone, the 'thought to be too old-fashioned' head of the Los Angeles crime family, was having discipline problems. His men had twice tried to assassinate him. He said he was retiring. They didn't believe him and on 15 October 1931, while out driving – a .41 revolver in his hand on the car's driving wheel – he disappeared. His body was never found. While Don Ardizzone's chair in his office around the corner from the Maple Bar was still warm, the rather bulkier Jack Dragna slipped into it. Dragna had been President of the Italian Protective League, which kept space on the eleventh floor of the Law Building downtown. Officially, it minded the interests of its own community; however, it made profits by exploiting them and running rackets.

It wasn't easy to operate the vice and drug rings; the City Hall Gang had a monopoly on the corruption of the cops. Still, some of the LAPD were happy to collect more than one pay-off. Dragna's Syndicate had a small blackmail and extortion racket going and were constantly making contacts in the labour unions. Dragna also had the actual and metaphorical muscle of Chicago working for him. His attraction for them was he always did as instructed, a soldier not a general in a business in which too much ambition could be fatal.

He was content to let others put on a show. Especially Rosselli, to whom Dragna delegated the movie business and community. Rosselli became Mr Hollywood. It was a ducks-to-water appointment. Rosselli (Cornero saw him as 'a rattlesnake in a box – don't put your hand in') encouraged Dragna to be more adventurous, to kill a few rivals and encroach into the City Hall Gang domain. It became easier. Local politics helped – Mayor Cryer stood down and Kent Parrott lost his power base to a new political machine. Charlie Crawford remained a buffer against the

Mob's ambition, but happenstance helped again. In the summer of that pivotal year, a corrupted assistant city attorney lost the plot ('couldn't take it any more') and shot down Crawford at his desk. There are some things you simply can't legislate for.

The combination was unlocked.

Hollywood and all around it were flooded with booze; a bootlegged sixty-dollar case was now going for a third of the price. Supply was more than meeting demand, even with the soaring thirst that Prohibition had increased tenfold. At the same time, those who'd worked in nightclubs and saloons were now 'in the movies' doing myriad jobs for money their talents wouldn't fetch elsewhere. Hollywood was living fast and easy. The sun came up day after day after day in this public relations man's fantasy, acreage that began as an apricot and fig ranch that a Mrs Wilcox from Kansas City took over and named 'Hollywood'. There was now much more than fruit to be picked. Joe Kennedy was ready to pick up anything and anyone, especially if he had an audience. He was very much in the show business.

Chapter Four

Hollywood Education

'I am big. It's the pictures that got small.'
Norma Desmond (Gloria Swanson), *Sunset Boulevard*, 1950

The world was watching as the first global moving picture stars were created. The assured Gloria Swanson went from Keystone Kops comedies to a Cecil B. DeMille leading lady at Paramount Studios, a Rudolph Valentino co-star and the mistress of the man she found *roguishly attractive*, Joe Kennedy. Swanson was star material. She was always ready for her close-up. The money shot was her wardrobe. She was tiny, a fringe over five feet tall and would happily be weighed down by lavish gowns and beads, all manner of parts of walking and flying wildlife decorating her, setting off her carousel of dazzling jewels. Off-screen she was just as calculated in emphasising the image.

A department store dress cost about twelve dollars, yet Swanson managed to spend upwards of $175,000 a year on clothes. She was photographed. She was copied. She was, for a time, when it really was something to say, the most famous woman in the world and superbly paid for being so.

Swanson suggested she tempted Joe Kennedy as a marital prospect, but for him she was a commodity, a good business trophy in Hollywood where she dominated the spotlight. Marriage was never in his plans. Instead, he ripped her off with the adroitness of a veteran pickpocket. She was oblivious. Kennedy enjoyed the reflective fame of being with Gloria Swanson, their four-year Hollywood affair never officially acknowledged or decried by Rose Kennedy, but was irritated that photographers and newsmen were always chasing her at events; he didn't like to be overlooked. He wanted to be a star. Still, their open relationship in Los Angeles gave him glamour, a naughty notoriety, as he became her business adviser, setting up her film production company. He was never shy in showing his intentions. He had made romantic overtures toward Swanson and that moved on to reckless abandon at her home in Beverly Hills. She recounts the moment in her autobiography, *Swanson on Swanson* (Random House, 1980) when Kennedy, as it were, sealed the deal.

She tells it with a titillating teen magazine build-up, Kennedy standing at her boudoir door wearing white flannels, an argyle sweater and two-tone shoes and staring at her before stepping in and closing the door behind him:

'He moved so quickly that his mouth was on mine before either of us could speak. With one hand he held the back of my head, with the other he stroked my body and pulled at my kimono. He kept insisting in a drawn-out moan, "No longer, no longer. Now." He was like a roped horse, rough, arduous, racing to be free. After a hasty climax he lay beside me, stroking my hair. Apart from his guilty, passionate mutterings, he had still said nothing cogent. I had said nothing at all. I had known this would happen. And I knew, as we lay there, that it would go on. Why? I thought. We were both happily married with children. We were ten years apart in age. He was a staunch Roman Catholic.'

Faith, like principle, was not an obstacle for lusty Joe. Swanson became financially dependent on Kennedy and, in doing so, unwisely invested in him emotionally. Reciprocation was not in his family nature. Instead, Kennedy was dependent on his Mob connections. He was one of the few – until a fatal lapse – involved with the Mob to realise that any person or project is instantly dispensable. The money-making machine was all that ever mattered. Whatever threatened profits was eradicated, be it star-makers or star-fuckers or the stars themselves. The Mob made and broke careers, destroyed lives and it was always business-related. People who stuck an elbow out of their allowed parameters became collateral damage. Watch and control was the Mafia way. Joe Kennedy was careful with his duplicity.

The gangsters shared his profits, Gloria Swanson was around $1.5 million in debt when their affair ended, and Kennedy, through his production company, many millions of dollars better off. When she assessed her life in 1980, Swanson compared Kennedy's operational tactics to Russian under Stalin: 'Their system was to write a letter to the files and then order the exact reverse on the phone.'

Every manoeuvre by Kennedy was to enhance himself, promote himself as a great man, a *real* man. Especially to his sons. Having a wife at home and mistresses in every town, like a sailor with a girl in every port, he believed he absolved his philandering by regularly going to Confession. Of the women throughout his life and times there is not much thought given, or predatory behaviour addressed, in the volumes of research and histories devoted to the Kennedy dynasty. Singled out was a thought from one of Kennedy's friends: '[A mistress] was another thing a rich man had, like caviar. It was part of the image, his idea of manliness.'

So much so that he'd flaunt it in front of the family, or to Lyndon Johnson, to show him what a real man was all about. Although hinted at amid his blatant and rampant infidelities and womanising, more recently disturbing stories of his sexual flamboyance emerged from his love life with Swanson. He planned that the schoolboy JFK could watch him and Swanson have sex. Within a decade, the voyeuristic sessions – his penchant for being seen having 'conquests' – would repeat with Marlene Dietrich, sexual abandon which would have its own squalid sequel in the JFK White House.

Swanson was promoting her successful 1929 film *The Trespasser* [producer, Joseph P. Kennedy] when he went full brass neck and invited her to stay with his family – for a week. He wanted to show her his new home, the compound with eleven large bedrooms in Hyannis Port, Massachusetts. The debate of the stay was whether Rose Kennedy or Swanson was the better actress. They both played their parts – the devoted wife and the glamorous 'business partner'. Kennedy was excited by the risk and was desperate to get Swanson to himself. He arranged for them to go out on his yacht, the *Rose Elizabeth*, and a twelve-year-old JFK was also on board. This did not deter Kennedy enthusiastically having sex with Swanson on the top deck. After watching them, JFK leaped off the yacht and swam for shore. Author Stephen Michael Shearer quotes Swanson (in *Gloria Swanson: The Ultimate Star*, Thomas Dunne Books, 2013) saying she was embarrassed: 'Joe wasn't upset. He just laughed. Then, he fished Jack out of the water.'

How often this sort of incident happened is not on any official record; most people were reticent to mention such dubious and flagrant behaviour, something which would echo through Joe Kennedy's life and JFK's time in the White House, but Shearer found testimony of another such encounter in the Swanson archive. He quotes her on being at the Kennedy home in Westchester, New York, and found *in flagrante delicto* by the now teenaged JFK. 'I automatically pushed myself away from Joe, but Joe pulled me back to him and kissed me more forcefully. He was doing it for Jack's benefit. Here was Joe putting on a show for his little boy. Jack stood there with no emotion registering on his face at all. [He] wandered off as if nothing unusual had happened.'

Now accessible archives show that Kennedy was being just as reckless with Swanson's money as his lover's privacy and dignity. He was more discreet as a thief. She didn't notice any problem at the time saying, in 1965, 'We were making more money than we ever dreamed existed and there was no reason to believe it would ever stop.' Not Hollywood's first million-dollar leading lady (that was Mary Pickford), Gloria Swanson was the first to spend that then all but pornographic amount in one year. As an original glamorous, box-office star, she was producing her own films, choosing her scripts, her leading men and projects, designing fashions and the adoring fanfare around herself. Suddenly, Kennedy arrived and took charge of all that.

They were a couple about town and Kennedy worked the contacts, befriending stars and powerful men like William Randolph Hearst, with whom he shared skeletons and an attraction for infidelity and power, but most of all political influence. Hearst, whom Kennedy's Syndicate had supplied with illegal booze, was to be an important ally in putting Kennedy's non-family choice in the White House. Kennedy chased success and successful contacts like London-born Charlie Chaplin, who started making movies in 1913 on $150 a week. Within two years, he was on ten thousand dollars a week. Within a decade, Hollywood was seeing the highest profits in America and paying wages to match. In 1927, as Kennedy watched, goggle-eyed, the 'film industry' – that is, all assets, from talent to studios – was valued at $1.5 billion. That year the talking pictures began with *The Jazz Singer* – the Al Jolson vehicle smashed every record ever thought of.

By 1930, Warner Brothers Studios alone was valued at $168 million, with the brothers holding the majority of the stock. Kennedy received funding via Johnny Rosselli and even he, not known for his humour, must have found a wry smile when Warner Brothers Studios began feeding the public fascination with gangsters. The films debuted in 1931, with the endlessly polite and patrician Edward G. Robinson as *Little Caesar* and the fast-talking James Cagney as *The Public Enemy*. Cagney co-starred with Jean Harlow, girlfriend of Longy Zwillman and it's the scene where he shoves a half grapefruit in Mae Clarke's face that's remained the most memorable.

Even fifty years later, when he made his last film appearance, in *Ragtime*, the citrus fruit remained a topic for him: 'It was based on a real-life incident involving Hymie Weiss.' Weiss was a renowned Chicago North Side gangster who shot up bootleg rivals, including Capone and Johnny Torrio, and originated the 'one-way ride', when he took a fellow gangster out for a drive and only he returned. Cagney put him in the movies: 'Hymie Weiss was listening to his girlfriend yakking away at breakfast. He didn't like it and he took an omelette she'd just prepared and shoved it in her face. Repeating this on screen would have been a shade too messy, so we used the grapefruit half. It sure was popular – especially with Monte Brice. He was Fanny Brice's brother and had just gone through an unpleasant divorce from Mae when the picture came out. Every time I pushed that grapefruit in Mae's face at the Strand Theatre, there was a guaranteed audience of one – Monte. He would come in just before that scene was shown, gloat over it, then leave.'

Although it took much flak for 'glorifying gangsters', the popularity of *The Public Enemy* made it the first film to earn more than a million dollars at the box office. The producers didn't have to wave a flag for the real-life mobsters to believe there was plenty of money to be made at the movies. Rosselli was under pressure to bring Hollywood into line. He liked the films and the movie crowd. He'd work as an extra for the quick pocket money and the gossip. But what Chicago wanted wasn't small talk – they wanted a studio, they wanted control. They wanted partnerships with people like Joe Kennedy. They wanted their hands on the money. But, as always, it was events that controlled the game plan. The Great Depression was biting.

It was tough in union-free Los Angeles, where wages were kept low – and bread lines became longer. There were as many soup kitchens as speakeasies. But money could be made on the turn of a card or chance played for five cents a time – 'nickel bingo' – in hastily erected tents: because it was as reliable as work, gambling was the one business that attracted everyone. Including Joe

Kennedy, who made early investments in 'carpet joints', more upmarket gambling outlets being pushed by Meyer Lansky along the East Coast, down to Florida and through the Midwest states out to the coast where there was much money to be made off-shore. The Mob made money from the needy and the desperate, as well as the flush, much of it with the help of Kennedy-Rosselli's ocean-going partner Tony Conero.

By then Conero's Green Meadows Casino, with its live entertainment and exotic interior, was a success, the model for all that would follow. Rosselli was allowed to use the place as his own. As could his friend's fleet of gambling ships moored beyond the three-mile limit off the California coast, which included the *Rex*, sitting in the water off Redondo Beach, with its $300,000 of luxury fittings. It had a crew of 350, always friendly, waiters and waitresses, cooks, a full orchestra and gunmen. The first-class dining room served French food only. Most evenings, around a couple of thousand onboard 'visitors' were accommodated, permitted to gamble, drink and dance as long as they pleased – or their money lasted. The *Rex* enterprise was a success, designed to lure an eclectic bunch of gamblers. After expenses, the operation was clearing $300,000 a night. Most often, it was the movie crowd who glamorously populated the tables. They had the money. And the excessive inclinations.

Drugs were a huge business and sex of every possible variety was something of an artistic licence. And not just on the casting couch, which became obligatory at every audition. The madcap Mack Sennett Studios – home of those fun guys, the Keystone Kops – had to be fumigated, plagued as they were by vast infections of venereal crabs. Mack Sennett Studios was also home to Hollywood's principal drug dealer; known as 'the Count', because he carried a cloak, heroin was his speciality.

Prohibition was truly an experiment in temptation and, as America continued to drink, imbibers concealed their tipples in prams, hot water bottles, garden hoses and coconut shells.

One enterprising individual who liked life sunny-side up went to work on an egg: half a dozen of them were drained and filled with booze. The Mack Sennet pusher had learned a few tricks, too. He provided bags of peanuts, the nuts having been removed and the shells filled with the drug of choice. The first bag was always free; after that users paid… and paid. *Dope* did just what it said: it made users pliable – but it could also make them capable of performing.

For the studio bosses like Kennedy, who required the cameras to keep rolling and the box office overloaded, anything that kept their stars – faces that became instant screen idols – happy and working was encouraged, prescribed by the studio doctors and dispatched from their lot dispensary, which was usually next to the canteen/coffee shop. The drugs were for 'nerves', or as a 'tonic' to make overworked performers lively in front of the cameras. The star crowd buzzed like bees and maybe some wondered, like Eugene Wrayburn did about the bees in Dickens's *Our Mutual Friend*, if possibly 'they over-do it'. Barbara La Marr, 'The Girl Who is too Beautiful', certainly did. Dope caught up with her before she'd reached thirty. She married five times, made dozens of films, and said she was able to do all of it because she slept only two hours a night. When she died the studios said she had been on too strict a diet.

Such explanations for appalling tragedies were a lesson to Joe Kennedy on how much the public could be made to believe. He saw if you camouflaged events in Hollywood with glitz and plausibility and presented it with a certain gravitas, then, in time, the razzmatazz would become the fact.

Simply, if you lied well enough, you could do anything you wanted.

Which is what he did and what he preached to his family as he flaunted Gloria Swanson's money in this new celebrity world, revolving around mansions and servants and just about anything you could gold-plate or diamond-stud; in the appropriately named

Tinseltown, bling was the thing. It was all about perception – what the public saw and what they believed they knew.

The Mob-mogul associations became so entrenched with the Hollywood authorities – the LAPD and the city prosecutor – that it appeared part of law enforcement policy to cover up any murder or dodgy death, even if a movie star wasn't involved. A star could be dropped from their contract if their sleeping around became public but if someone died, that was part of life's deal. It was a lesson he'd learned on an early trip to Hollywood.

William Desmond Taylor, fifty, a Paramount Studios director involved with young starlets, was discovered dead in his home study on 1 February 1922. When Taylor's butler found the body, he alerted a neighbour, who telephoned a doctor and Paramount Studios. The police were not alerted. Executives arrived and went through Taylor's home, supposedly removing coded love letters written by, among others, the twenty-year-old star Mary Miles Minter, who had made her first film, *Anne of Green Gables*, for Taylor. But news of the affair between the ingénue and the ageing director got out and Hollywood got more screeching headlines. What no one got was a killer. Taylor's death was initially ruled as being brought on by a heart attack. Later, a reluctantly performed medical examination showed two .38 bullets had gone through his back. Those had stopped his heart. There were suspects and suspicions; circumstantial evidence pointed to a Mob execution in return for Taylor's temerity to reject its financial investment in a movie – but there was never a conviction. Nor was there ever one in the shooting to death of Hollywood actor-director Thomas Harper Ince in 1924. It is one of the most remarkable incidents at a time when the powers of film and business were learning to live with organized crime and collaborate in what served the interests of both: none of that needless nonsense with police and arrests and trials. As the wheels of graft turned, everyone but the handsome Ince profited from his death. Press tycoon 'Citizen' Hearst certainly sold many more newspapers.

Hearst, a multimillionaire from his Press empire and silver mines, was keen to sign off on a film deal with Ince. To do so, he invited him to celebrate his forty-second birthday aboard his 280-foot yacht *Oneida*. Hearst, his mistress Marion Davies – for whom he'd created his film company Cosmopolitan Production Studios – and their guests, including Hearst's movie people, his local newspaper columnist Louella Parsons, Charlie Chaplin and Dr Daniel Carson Goodman, a physician turned screenwriter, were joined by Ince when the yacht anchored in San Diego harbour on 16 November. Marion Davies liked to drink, especially champagne, while Hearst was teetotal. So it was Davies who organized liquor, delivered to Hearst's San Simeon Castle up the coast from Santa Barbara by Mob distributors working for Hearst's friend Joe Kennedy. Hearst looked the other way to indulge his guests and Marion, who was allowed *almost* everything she wanted.

On the following evening, there was plenty of drink and food at Ince's birthday celebration. But his birthday went very wrong. The story, as it came out – in Hearst newspapers – was that Ince became ill and was taken ashore by water taxi. Dr Goodman went with him. From then, it is a confusion of accounts of events over whether Dr Goodman took Ince to a hotel or a hospital or to his Benedict Canyon home in the Hollywood Hills. That Ince was taken to his home and died there of heart failure was the Hearst line. It was endorsed by Ince's doctor, Ida Glasgow, who signed the death certificate. The Los Angeles District Attorney accepted it. There was just the bullet in Ince's head to be concerned about.

The *Los Angeles Times* – for one afternoon edition only – shouted the banner headline: MOVIE PRODUCER SHOT ON HEARST YACHT. Then the story was pulled. As did Ince's body.

At his wife Nell's request, he was cremated. Nell Ince was awarded a lifetime financial endowment by Hearst, who also helped others deal with the trauma of the death of their friend. Louella Parsons, who began her cruise on the *Oneida* as a columnist for one newspaper, left the vessel as a syndicated gossip star for every Hearst outlet. With all her fame, which made her the queen of newspaper malice in wonderland, she never found space to report on the events on the yacht. But then, how could she? She told the police and anyone else who asked that she wasn't aboard. The most popular version of events – official archives of the case do not exist – is that Hearst, a renowned sharp-shooter, shot Ince either by intention or mistaking him for his real target, Charlie Chaplin, who was a regular lover of Marion Davies. (Chaplin most certainly had a way with the ladies: actress Joan Barry once broke into his house at 1 a.m., lectured him at gunpoint for an hour about his morals and then slept with him.)

Hearst ignored Davies's dalliances with other men so long as it did not reflect on his dignity. She had apparently got a little too close to home with Chaplin and their friendliness, fuelled by champagne, had been much too obvious on the yacht. Chaplin and Ince were similar in look and hairstyle. Or maybe it was Ince and Davies who had turned Hearst into a jealous gunman with their impropriety. Only one thing is certain: Ince was dead and gone and William Randolph Hearst had the power to cover up the death. Not long afterwards, film pioneer D. W. Griffith was asked about the death of his friend. 'All you have to do to make Hearst turn white as a ghost is mention Ince's name,' he said. 'There's plenty wrong there, but Hearst's too big.' Which was what Hollywood had become. Too much for the wily Joe Kennedy who, true to form – take the money and run – saw opportunity afforded by the misery of the Depression and being based elsewhere. He remained invested through his Mob connections in profiting from Hollywood excess.

The Kennedy investments with Johnny Rosselli involved anywhere money was being spent, like the Clover Club, off Sunset Boulevard, a little west of the Chateau Marmont, which had a private, red-velvet gaming room on the second floor. On an evening of cards, usually poker, players could lose ten or twenty thousand dollars while outside people queued up for cups of watery soup. There were a string of more public places: the Cotton Cub in Culver City on Sunday night; Monday at the Cocoanut Grove; Tuesday at the Club Montmartre; the Roosevelt Hotel on Wednesday; Thursday driving out of town for 'weekend fun'. Resorts over the border in Tijuana became Hollywood getaways. The Agua Caliente offered twenty-hour-a-day gambling and *anything* else clients craved. There was a gold room with services for gourmet food and big gamblers. There was also a horse-racing track that hosted some of the richest races available. There were the odds at the Tijuana track… and the odds at the bookies. Johnny Rosselli took the bets from big players such as Joe Schenck who, with Darryl F. Zanuck, founded Twentieth Century Pictures. The extravagant wagering producer Harry Cohn of Columbia Pictures was both his and Joe Kennedy's new great friend, another grossly unsavoury character who would help a President be elected.

Kennedy was more business than show in Hollywood. His only considerations were himself and his family fortunes. He bled Swanson all but dry indulging her in projects like the 1928 film *Queen Kelly*, directed by Erich von Stroheim, Max the butler in *Sunset Boulevard*. For film producer Kennedy and star Swanson it was a miserable affair, echoing the end of their own, and the film plagued by stops and starts, Stroheim's bizarre requests and behaviour and star tantrums, was never released in America. Yet, the deals behind the movie deals saw Kennedy acquiring more and more assets. When he got out in 1931 before the Depression began to bite into film profits, he abandoned Swanson and all the loyal employees he'd gathered through his involvement with the film studios, investments he sold on for personal profit of more than twelve million dollars. He explained his decision as being because of 'health reasons'. Perception again.

Newspapers at the time applauded his triumph with archive articles – interestingly, held in FBI files – in *The Boston Globe* calling him 'the richest Irish-American in the world'. *The New York Times* reported that when he departed California, 'He already had so much money that making the rest of it, which must have been so many millions, was almost a routine affair.'

There had been many affairs in Hollywood and Joe Kennedy had been more tactful than usual in hiding them, not for the benefit of the mother of his eight children – Rose back in Boston – but from Swanson who, throughout their liaison, was married to her third husband, the constantly broke but titled Henry de La Falaise, Marquis de La Coudraye. Overshadowed for a time by the bullying Kennedy, she proved strong with a sixty-year career and admitted in 1980 that she was belittled and bamboozled by the Irishman, who overwhelmed her with his determination to get what he wanted, and to get it without objection or consideration of others. He was a selfish bastard.

In 1931, he went home to Cape Cod, relaxing by the ocean, on the beaches and in the arms once again of Rose. Their ninth child, Teddy Kennedy, was born on 22 February 1932.

That same year Joe Kennedy was actively involved in helping Franklin Delano Roosevelt (FDR) campaign to become the President. He was the money collector, the *bag man* in Mob patois. He raised $200,000 in itemised contributions and the same amount in cash from people who did not want to be identified. Like Kennedy, many of his associates liked anonymity while buying influence.

Chapter Five

Gamekeeper

'*Visiting* [Joe] *Kennedy in Florida is like staying with* [Nazi leader Hermann] *Göring.*'

Ed Murrow, CBS broadcaster/war correspondent, 1944

President Franklin D. Roosevelt considered Joe Kennedy a truly accomplished liar *and* a pivotal player in his 1932 landslide Presidential victory. His man had delivered not only financial clout but also, through his close connection with William Randolph Hearst, the endorsement of the nation's most powerful media organisation and the California vote.

There was no quarrel that Kennedy had delivered, yet Roosevelt's intimate advisers were wary of the confident-talking and deal-making political newcomer. Kennedy made it clear he expected a big job in return for helping FDR to such an impressive victory. When it was slow in appearing, he began grooming the President's son James 'Jimmy', who could be won over by a bottle of Haig & Haig whisky and some friendly girls, commodities Kennedy was expert in supplying. Dozens and dozens of documents show how much FDR – permanently paralysed from the waist down by polio in 1922 – mistrusted Joe Kennedy and it is a testament to the outrageous character of the man, his magical charm, that he finally joined the government.

FDR had tried to side-step him with offers of jobs in South America, with any assignment as far from Washington as possible, but Kennedy would not drift away that easily. As the months dragged, his patience ragged, he did what he did best – made money. He played the stock market using insider knowledge, betting on the ups and downs of Hollywood studios, especially Paramount, and knew early on that Christmas 1933 would be a bumper one with the end of Prohibition that December. Earlier in the year, using Jimmy Roosevelt to make the connections, he acquired two permits to import alcohol into America for 'medicinal purposes', putting him in pole position. The medical licence was a money-maker in itself but the potential of a thirsty America with Prohibition gone was a bonanza if he had the booze available when the cork legally came out of the bottle.

He'd paid for Jimmy Roosevelt to sail with him to the UK that autumn and, using the President's son as a talisman, negotiated the sale of almost all of Britain's export whisky – all the Haig & Haig and Dewar's and, for good measures, all the available supply of Gordon's gin. (Bottles of Haig Pinch were regular holiday gifts while JFK was President and Bobby Kennedy was Attorney General.)

After crossing the Atlantic, the high-quality booze was stockpiled in warehouses in important distribution locations so when bars and clubs officially opened for business it was Kennedy-imported brands the customers were drinking. He incorporated Somerset Importers Ltd., which became a political albatross.

In 1933, he had White House ambitions for himself, and it's important to stress how fabulously wealthy the Kennedy family were, when he bought two acres of ocean-front property in Palm Beach, an estate with seven bedrooms, a swimming pool and all the other Florida real estate trimmings along the already styled millionaires row. Coincidentally, Meyer Lansky and several of his prominent Syndicate colleagues also favoured the Florida climate and established homes and gambling 'carpet joints' in and around neighbouring Fort Lauderdale and along the Atlantic coast in Miami.

Kennedy did not look kindly to FDR and vice versa. FDR had a tricky job to offer Kennedy, that of Chairman of the newly formed Securities and Exchange Commission, which would oversee Wall Street and stop illegal trading – a Joe Kennedy speciality – among its members. Kennedy swore on his family's life that he was the most honest man the world had ever seen, unsparing of himself and dedicated to the enhancement, and the sensibilities, of his friends. FDR, who had some admiration for such ingenuity and the shameless concealment of his true character, appointed an original wolf of Wall Street as the nation's financial gamekeeper. The President knew what he was about and is quoted in the archive telling his advisers, 'It takes a thief to catch a thief.' Indeed, Kennedy – who, as a control freak, liked to boss people about – was splendid in policing others doing exactly what he'd been expert at – double dealing and dipping and insider trading.

His rigour surprised a Wall Street which held great suspicion about Joe Kennedy's Mob contacts and his mysteriously ever-increasing fortune. He bought himself a good press with the special help of Walter Winchell and the appropriately named journalist Arthur Krock. He was full of it. Plied with gifts and women, Krock, the Washington bureau chief of *The New York Times*, heralded Joe Kennedy as a man doing public service to give back for 'the debt he owed the country where he and his family have thrived so extraordinarily well'. Krock and others, charmed and developed by Kennedy, created a CV with a halo for the financial bandit guilty of everything but armed bank robbery. His personal life was presented as saintly but, in an odd twist on the future, America's President warned Kennedy about his philandering, especially taxpayer-funded employment of attractive members of his executive secretarial team. FDR, no hypocrite, did not tell Kennedy to stop, only to be more discreet, not so reckless. Kennedy paid no heed. Not for one moment. The accomplished financial poacher lasted fourteen months as chairman and did an applauded job in thwarting 'unethical business practices'. He'd already made his killing, now he'd be shocked to find gambling in a casino he owned.

As chairman of the SEC, Kennedy was a regular presence in the White House. There wasn't an assistant he didn't charm, a secretary bestowed an encouraging smile. He danced round with FDR, a tango of power and ambition, it being in their best interests not to step on each other's feet. Kennedy wanted FDR's job and the incumbent President was most aware he needed his to control his rival inside the political tent. Although his disillusioned friend William Randolph Hearst had abandoned FDR, Kennedy supported FDR's re-election in 1936, a landslide victory in better economic times and accepted the role of chairman of the Maritime Commission. In this position Kennedy's great triumph was to broker a deal between America's shipowners and the unions, an accomplishment much helped by his inside track with the union organisers who were beholden to the Mob. As always, it was who you knew. And who didn't know who you knew. Joe Kennedy's everlasting error was to believe he was invulnerable. Soon he got the job he dreamed of. It was to be a nightmare for the rest of his life.

He was appointed, aged forty-nine, United States Ambassador to the Court of St James's in 1938, the most prestigious and important posting in government and with Rose Kennedy he soared around the society circuit and spent a weekend at Windsor Castle with King George VI. Files now show he was also a very willing if unofficial FBI agent working for his friend J. Edgar Hoover. An unsealed Hoover memo to an agent (whose name is redacted) reads, 'In the event you feel that Mr Kennedy is in a position to offer active assistance to the Bureau such as is expected of Special Service Contacts, there is no objection to utilising him in this capacity. If he can be made use of as a Special Service Contact, the Bureau should be advised as to the nature of the information he is able to provide or the facilities he can offer for the Bureau's use. Every effort should be made to provide him with investigative assignments in keeping with his particular ability and the Bureau should be advised the nature of these assignments, together with the results obtained.'

British documents about Joe Kennedy's activities remain sealed while others are so heavily redacted as to contribute no decipherable detail. Yet, it is clear from oral histories that Ambassador Kennedy, viewed with suspicion, was watched by MI5: he was followed and his telephone tapped. This action followed the gathering of intelligence before he made his views so widely known. After he opened his mouth publicly, he was regarded as all but an enemy of a Britain preparing for the Second World War. In a first public appearance as Ambassador, at the Pilgrims Society in London in March 1938, he addressed a mix of influential businessmen and politicians. To their astonishment, he told them it was in America's best interests to stay neutral in British conflict with Germany and that the US would *not see eye to eye with Britain* as it had done in the past. It was a humdinger which bounced awkwardly back and forth across the Atlantic. He irritated the White House further by telling a London journalist that FDR would not win the 1940 election. Kennedy was furiously at odds with then backbencher MP Winston Churchill, and supported Prime Minister Neville Chamberlain in seeking appeasement. His pre-war statements – so astonishing seen from the present – made Kennedy a pariah for many. After only four months in London, he tried to arrange a meeting with Hitler through the German ambassador to Great Britain, Herbert von Dirksen. MI5 heard every word the two exchanged.

In these archive reports von Dirksen is quoted as saying Kennedy spelled out his personal animosity toward the Jewish people. He is quoted in discussing 'the Final Solution to the Jewish problem', telling von Dirksen that he believed, 'It was not so much the fact that we [Germany] wanted to get rid of the Jews that was so harmful to us, but rather the loud clamour with which we [Germany] accomplished this purpose.[Kennedy] himself fully understood our Jewish policy.'

In a now published letter to aviation pioneer and fellow appeaser Charles Lindbergh, he said that atrocities and open violence on Jews in Germany concerned him as it created bad publicity for the Nazis in America. Later in the year, he met German Foreign Minister Joachim von Ribbentrop in London. Shortly before the Blitz began in September 1940, Kennedy again attempted to privately meet Hitler – the US Department of State knew nothing of it – to 'bring about a better understanding between the United States and Germany.'

When the war began in September 1939, Kennedy's voracious support for American neutrality conflicted with FDR's efforts to support Britain. In a notorious newspaper interview Kennedy roared with reckless arrogance: 'It's all a question of what we do with the next six months. The whole reason for aiding England is to give us time ... As long as she is in there, we have time to prepare. It isn't that [Britain is] fighting for democracy. That's the bunk. She's fighting for self-preservation, just as we will if it comes to us. ... *I know more about the European situation than anybody else* [our italics] and it's up to me to see that the country gets it.' Intriguingly, an FBI memo dated 28 April 1947 – as 'reds under the beds' fears startled America – from J. Edgar Hoover to his personal aide, D. M. Ladd, reads: 'In June 1938, Special Agent [redacted] advised that he had received very cordial treatment from Ambassador Kennedy in London, while [redacted] was there visiting Scotland Yard. Kennedy's ambassadorship to Britain is widely regarded in the United States as demonstrating that Kennedy was an appeaser and believed that Britain would lose the war. His appointment during this period is thought to be important only as it throws light on his present views about Russia as reported by Mr Arthur Krock.

'Arthur Krock, of *The New York Times*, described Kennedy as spokesman for a group of industrialists and financiers, *who believe that Russia should not be opposed at any point.* All energies should be devoted to keeping America prosperous.'

The Soviet sentiment dismayed the FBI director, much as Kennedy's views infuriated Churchill who, when he took over as Prime Minister in May 1940, listed Joe Kennedy as a propaganda problem, one which – to Kennedy's dismay – he used in his campaign to get America to enter the war. At the same time, Kennedy continued to noisily shred his personal political prospects. Ed Murrow, the CBS TV newsman who throughout the war graphically reported to America the triumphs and horrors of the conflict and the tragic loss of lives, despised Kennedy for his views and his behaviour. When told a friend was going to stay with the Kennedy family in Florida, he remarked that would be 'like staying with Goering'. During the blitz, Kennedy left London with his family, prompting Churchill's son Randolph, when told they'd gone to the countryside to escape the bombing, to say, 'I thought my daffodils were yellow until I met Joe Kennedy.' Kennedy, never one for diplomatic platitudes, did not endear himself to the British by vocally admiring them for enduring the increasingly lethal Blitz while himself running from it. The Fleet Street newspapers called him *Jittery Joe.*

Unashamed, Joe Kennedy had no time for the underdog. He was convinced Germany would win any war and that America was well out of it. Magisterial historian Fredrik Logevall writes in the first volume of his biography *JFK*, Penguin-Viking, 2020, that the ambassador never understood that for the British fighting was about dignity, even at a most heavy price. He goes on, 'The concept of honour in international affairs was foreign to Kennedy; all that mattered was survival.' That attitude was displayed when he said Britain had no option 'but to concede to Hitler's control over eastern and central Europe'. When this was repeated at a dinner attended by Winston Churchill, he went on the attack, alternately jabbing in the air with his whisky glass and his cigar to punctuate his outrage: Kennedy was a timorous and naive man, an impediment to British-American co-operation. Britain would stoically endure and, whatever happened, Germany would eventually have to deal with America, the world's most powerful nation.

A British MP, Josiah Wedgwood, angrily denounced Kennedy: 'We have a rich man, untrained in diplomacy, unlearned in history and politics, who is a great publicity seeker and who apparently is ambitious to be the first Catholic President of the U.S.'

Indeed, such was Kennedy's reckless arrogance, his lack of self-awareness, he failed to see his defeatism put him outside those who made policy. He was dismissed as not worth listening to in London and in Washington. He was kept out of delicate talks and negotiations and left hugely humiliated. In the UK he was, and remains, despised for bemoaning British bravery in defying Hitler alone for so long that America joined the war – a war in which Joe Kennedy Jr and JFK both served with honour.

In October 1940, he relinquished his role as ambassador to the UK, his opportunity for achieving high political office ruined for the now and forever by, quite simply, his big mouth, a flaw continually damaging to his nearest and dearest. He'd only lasted as long as he had because FDR didn't want him involved in that year's Presidential campaign, one which he won with the reluctant support of Kennedy. He officially resigned in February 1941, a month into FDR's unprecedented third term in the White House. They were still dancing together: the Inland Revenue Service (IRS) paperwork is not readily available in government records but it is claimed that FDR got Kennedy on side by confronting his UK ambassador with an embarrassing past tax return indicating Kennedy had cheated the IRS, a felony which would see him in jail. Kennedy, wielding that incorrigible, tricky charm, still got something in return: FDR's promise to support Joseph Kennedy Jr in a run for Governor of Massachusetts in 1942. If he couldn't be America's first Catholic President, he was going to put his number one son, who he'd pushed on that political path as a delegate at the 1940 Democratic National Convention, in the White House. It was quite a coup given that Joe Jr had spoken against FDR's re-election at the convention. Now, he wanted a big win.

Not certain of getting FDR's promised support – the President could be tricky too – Kennedy enlisted the help of his old friends, the moneymaking men like Meyer Lansky and Santo Trafficante, boss of the Mob in Tampa, Florida, one of the most powerful crime families in America throughout the twentieth century. Gambling had superseded booze, although they continued to profitably mix for Kennedy and the Syndicate were all over Miami with new carpet joints, illegal but lavish upmarket casino-nightclubs with high stakes, doubtful odds, good lobster, shrimp and girls. Joe Kennedy invested with the Mafia, details of which have been conflated into his Wall Street chicanery, but recently available files show how truly he was in the business, in fact glued to them for almost all his life. Much of his investment, like that of others not wanting to broadcast their shared interests with organised crime, was through cutouts, front men.

They were often businessmen fearful of the gangsters and greedy or lawyers who could act with legal proxy, characters like Thomas Cassara who was the signatory and co-owner of high-end properties around Miami, hotels and nightclubs, spots where there would be action, usually illicit. It was in Florida that Cassara and Joe Kennedy connected. By then the lawyer's CV carried nervously earned enthusiastic references from Frank Costello and Longy Zwillman. Evidence of the connection between Kennedy and Cassara was heard from Capone thug Joey Fusco at the Kefauver hearings but for decades the implications for Kennedy – who is not listed in the official testimony index – were lost in the hundreds of brown boxes of transcripts. Evidence had him on record as working with the Mob. It was accurate. In 1943, he bought 17 per cent of the stock in the Hialeah horse-racing track in Miami, a controlling interest, with the rest held by members of America's Mafia Five Families. With *his* family, he spent days in Miami Beach and evenings playing roulette at the carpet joints; he always won. He was a fan of Carlos Marcello's Beverly Club with its crystal chandelier – and, yes, showgirls did swing from it – in Jefferson Parish outside New Orleans. He was also an early investor in Las Vegas, almost always, it appears, with the Mob as 'silent' partners, with suggestions in law enforcement files that he had around 10 per cent in a hotel-casino deal with Johnny Rosselli, Carlos Marcello and his longtime friend and admirer Frank Costello. The name of the property is not clear in the available paperwork.

It is suggested Kennedy had a financial investment in the Mob's Havana casinos, persistent gossip that the money was in the Tropicana Hotel-Casino, but there is nothing declassified in the archives to establish that. Yet it makes sense for someone with his business acumen, and fear of missing out, to want to share some of the astronomical profits coming out of Cuba, awed as he was by the daily flight from the island carrying packed suitcases of gangster cash. He did have a share of the Cal-Neva Hotel and Casino which would in the years that followed be the scene of atrocious behaviour involving Kennedy and his sons and their Mafia associates. Expensive prostitutes from across America and Europe – especially France for Joe Kennedy Sr – were flown in. Several Hollywood stars made their 'debut' at the Cal-Neva. According to Scott Lankford (*Tahoe Beneath the Surface*, Heyday Books, 1991), JFK enjoyed 'an endless series of extramarital affairs with wealthy divorcees and Tahoe's notoriously ubiquitous prostitutes' on the premises. From the moment it opened in July 1926, with its rooms and 116,000 square feet of gambling space split between California and Nevada, the Cal-Neva – which sits smack across Stateline Road – was a perilous place: an ongoing Damon Runyon show, a real-life *Guys and Dolls*, on the shores of Lake Tahoe. In the early days they said even the cigarette girls talked out of the side of their mouths. It was a world where dames were dames and men were whoever they said they were. The silent-film star Clara Bow – the movie star Joe Kennedy's friend Eunice Pringle was meant to be the image of – lost a fortune at the tables in 1930 and refused to pay, saying she thought the hundred-dollar chips she was flamboyantly playing were valued at fifty cents. Which was the going price for a couple of drinks. Judy Garland, aged thirteen, performed there in 1935, by which time Joe Kennedy had been an investor in the business eight years. He'd taken Gloria Swanson, among many, many others, there and thought of it as his more private retreat, hidden away as it is by the surrounding forest. Now it was another healthy source of funding to get Joe Jr on the campaign trail.

As his father profited and plotted his future with his hoodlum connections, Joe Jr was in Europe, fighting the war his father had worked so hard to stop America from joining. As we reported, JFK was in the Pacific where he 'died' for a week. In 1943 when his boat did not return from patrol his father was told funeral services were held for him and his thirteen men. Joe Kennedy kept the news to himself until he heard that JFK had survived – and the hoopla began with him insisting that everyone should know of his son's heroism. It was heavily featured in *The New Yorker* and published in an edited version in the mass market *Reader's Digest*. JFK was in the Chelsea Naval Hospital in Massachusetts in 1944 and Joe Jr, who'd remained in the UK for D-Day, was set to return to America after 'just one more mission', as he put it in a letter to his father who replied, in essence, with a don't-push-your-luck-too-much message. Joe Jr had flown nearly forty missions and he was full of confidence for this final one: the experimental plane was packed with explosives, squeezed in at the controls were Kennedy and his co-pilot, who were to parachute out having aimed and locked their flying bomb at an enemy target. As we've seen, the bomb went off over Suffolk, England, with their mission only just begun.

Joe Kennedy was bereft, in time burying his anger in business and the arms of actress Joan Fontaine, a new star as the leading lady of Alfred Hitchcock's *Rebecca* (with Laurence Olivier, 1940) and *Suspicion* (with Cary Grant, 1941).

Joe Kennedy's bitterness toward FDR never dissipated. He opposed FDR running yet again for President but supported Harry S. Truman as the Vice-Presidential nominee. Truman was campaigning and fund-raising in Boston when he was confronted by Kennedy. The man who went on to be America's thirty-third President recalled the meeting in an oral history held in the Harry S. Truman Library, Independence, Missouri, of his political career: 'Old man Kennedy started throwing rocks at Roosevelt, saying he'd caused the war and so on. And then he said: "Harry, what the hell are you doing campaigning for that crippled son of a bitch that killed my son Joe?" I stood it just as long as I could, and I said, "If you say another word about Roosevelt, I'm going to throw you out the window."

'And Bob [Hannegan, chairman of the Democratic National Committee] grabbed me by the arm and said, "Come out of here. I'm gonna get ten thousand dollars out of the old son-of-a-bitch for the Democratic Party." And he did.

'Old Joe Kennedy is as big a crook as we've got anywhere in the country.'

'Old Joe' corroborated President Harry Truman's remark in 1945 when, with the Second World War ended, he bought himself what was the headquarters of a den of thieves, the Merchandise Mart on East Chicago Avenue, north of the river and onetime home of Prohibition's biggest and most outrageous speakeasy. It was a world of pay-offs to the Mob. Police and political corruption were immense – almost every city official looked the other way. The Capone Mob, absent their syphilitic and dying leader, were the Syndicate power. Kennedy, who paid twelve million dollars in 1945 money was the landlord, largely an absentee one, and his investment soared in value as it gifted glorious returns which fed his refocused political ambitions.

Political plans could cope with hidden assets like the Merchandise Mart but the hugely lucrative Somerset Importers was a listed company and the liquor business still carried the taint of gangland. Something which was bloodily emphasised when Thomas Cassara, by then working full-time for Kennedy-Somerset Importers, was the target on 27 January 1946 of a gangland hit outside the Mob-owned Trade Winds on upmarket Rush Street in Chicago. For all his vulpine nonchalance, Kennedy could not ignore how it looked. Cassara survived a bullet in the head and went west to California where his legal expertise and signature began work for the boys operating in the sunshine. The LAPD's decade old Gangster Squad added 'Cassara, Thomas' to their surveillance list just above 'Cohen, Mickey' – the West Coast's most nefarious mobster, another acquaintance of Joe Kennedy. On 31 July 1946, the Somerset Importers business was sold for eight million dollars to a conglomerate headed by his longtime silent partner Longy Zwillman and including gangland kingpin Willie Moretti, the Mafia's first 'manager' of Frank Sinatra. It was some time before Sinatra became as embarrassing as the liquor business for the Kennedys. Old Joe was beginning to 'launder' the family image as he manoeuvred his second son toward the White House.

There was quite a deal of rewriting to do and, as well as the more immediate cover-up of JFK's reckless lechery, to most immediately obfuscate the mess still swirling around his son's pledge to marry a woman the FBI believed was a Nazi agent. There were to be many affairs across the political divide and it was easier to disguise when he bedded a communist spy. By then JFK was President.

Chapter Six

The Spy Who Loved Him?

'Everything is an illusion.'

Mata Hari, 1915

The beguiling Inga Arvad attended the 1936 Olympics with Hitler in Berlin and, five years later, fought off sexual advances by Joe Kennedy in Cape Cod. She was never quite certain which discomforted her most.

She most certainly discombobulated the Kennedys, father and son.

And the world's intelligence services.

JFK constantly feared their affair would wreck his career. For a time, his spurned father was furious that his son might ruin his life by marrying her.

Blue-eyed and blonde – her 'clean, pure' looks enamoured the Führer – Inga Marie Arvad Petersen was born in Copenhagen on 6 October 1913, a few years older than Jack Kennedy, whom she met in Washington where in 1941 he'd joined the Navy Reserve and been posted to the Office of Naval Intelligence. He did not have top secret clearance, but he had access. Despite JFK's all-but-daily womanising it was this affair which haunted him, for he knew the FBI had surveillance film – 'sex tapes' – and audio recordings of their encounters. And there were plenty of them.

They were kept by J. Edgar Hoover in his private 'blackmail' files – along with forty-seven others – until he died on 2 May 1972. Inga Arvad's individual file comprises 1,200 pages.

JFK's sister Kathleen 'Kick' Kennedy was working as a reporter at the *Washington Times-Herald*, an isolationist propaganda outlet favoured by Joe Kennedy, and introduced him to her columnist colleague Inga Arvad. She'd dropped the Petersen. Gorgeous and gregarious, Inga was swiftly part of their social circle and JFK was smitten as much by her exotic European antecedents as her sophistication and sexual magnetism. ('Jack's got a lot to learn and I'll be happy to teach him.') In the libraries of stories about JFK, pivotal women in his past are often given as much attention as he offered – 'We've got fifteen minutes', he'd tell lovers and keep an eye on his wristwatch – but there was more to Inga Arvad than many.

Nearly half a century ago, shortly after her death from cancer in Arizona in December 1973, Inga Arvad's son was tracked down to Carmel on the Pacific, a short drive south from San Francisco. With JFK and his mother dead, he decided to give information which has remained part of dusty archives. It provides remarkable insight into the woman for whom JFK was prepared to abandon his family for. He certainly told her he was. Her son, Ron, who wanted to stay out of the spotlight, nevertheless acted as his mother's proxy, documenting how she went from flirting with Hitler to sleeping with JFK.

She travelled widely with her own mother, Olga, after her father died when she was four years old, and as a seventeen-year-old won a beauty contest in Europe. She married Kemal Abdel Nabi, a member of what is now the Egyptian General Intelligence Directorate – he was 'ambassador' in Paris during the Suez Crisis in 1956 – and moved to Cairo. The marriage failed and through contacts she made a home in 1930s' Germany. Her beauty and personality fast-tracked her and through Danish diplomat friends she learned of the engagement of Hermann Göring, Luftwaffe

Commander-in-Chief, one of Hitler's most powerful lieutenants, to the actress Emmy Sonnemann. Friends won her an interview with Sonnemann who, acting as a hostess for Hitler, was known as the 'First Lady of the Third Reich'. Her profile, detailing the glamour, the Nazi salutes and 'never has the bride looked more enchanting', was published in Copenhagen's *Berlingske Tidende* newspaper and delighted her new friend who invited her to the wedding on 10 April 1935. There were about fifty guests and Hitler was the best man. Joseph Goebbels, the Minister of Propaganda, was quickly entranced by Inga. Could he do anything for her? She asked and got an interview with Hitler for *Berlingske Tidende*. Inga told her son that she and Hitler were alone, no aides, no guards and she asked him if he wore a bulletproof vest. He told her to frisk him, which she did, and there was no protective clothing. Hitler was enamoured; he arranged a specially prepared 'Danish lunch' for Inga, fluent in Danish, French, German and English, and granted her further interviews. 'You immediately like him. He seems lonely. The eyes, showing a kind heart, stare right at you. They sparkle with force,' she reported on 1 November 1935.

Hitler told her she was 'the perfect example of Nordic beauty' and to that end showed her off at the Berlin Olympics where she reported he was incensed by Jesse Owens, a 'non-Aryan' as a black American track and field star, winning four gold medals. She became a given in Berlin social circles and was lunched by Joe Kennedy's future friend in London, German foreign minister Joachim von Ribbentrop. Her son revealed that Ribbentrop suggested that Berlin would 'look after' her expenses if she moved to Paris or London and, in the vernacular, 'keep her ears' open on their behalf. Instead, she visited Copenhagen, married the older, by twenty years, Hungarian film director Paul Fejos and then moved to America, finding a place at the Columbia School of Journalism. There, in this small world, she met Arthur Krock of *The New York Times*, a man always keen to help young, attractive girls with their careers. He all but chased her around the lecture hall but even after his failed seduction he offered to find her a job in Washington.

As she began work on her social gossip column, 'Did You Happen to See?', she met Kathleen Kennedy and then onto JFK and created what the FBI believed was a straightforward, inviting, honeytrap for the randy twenty-four-year-old.

Inga described a self-centred lover, a young man insensitive to anyone but his own needs. She said JFK knew he could impress people, knew how to do it and could be anybody he believed his audience wanted him to be. It's the description of a good conman. Yet, in the archive, her son says the couple were much in love, their involvement 'awfully damned heavy'. The obstacles they faced are revealing: 'There were practical matters that just wouldn't work. One was the old man – Joseph Kennedy. The family was just an extension of the old man's hardline schizophrenic condition. She thought the Kennedy family were weird. The old man would push Jack, Jack would push Bobby, and Bobby would push Teddy and Teddy would fall on his ass. Jack was going through a hell of a crisis – she couldn't figure out how two people [Jack and Kathleen Kennedy] who were that bright could stand for all that bullshit. She thought they had to want the money badly. She thought old Joe was a real mean man. He could be charming but if Jack left the room he'd try and hop in the sack with her. He did that one weekend at Cape Cod. She thought there was something incestuous about the whole family.'

From FBI files and letters between the lovers, it's clear JFK was sexually besotted by Inga – he could not get enough of her – and this manifested in pledges of everlasting love and a determination that they should marry. A snag was she was still married to Paul Fejos, who had interesting associates, including Axel Wenner-Gren, a Swedish businessman and American dollar billionaire. With America very much in the war after the 7 December 1941 attack on Pearl Harbor, the links between the Nazi hierarchy and the fabulously rich arms dealer Wenner-Gren alarmed the FBI and US Naval Intelligence, who were monitoring his yacht the *Southern Cross*. The 320-foot yacht was lavish, boasting a crew of 315, sophisticated radio equipment and mounted machine-guns, vantage points for sharpshooters, and a system to refuel Nazi U-boats. US Naval Intelligence believed secret refuelling was going on around Guatemala. Wenner-Gren was a friend of the Duke of Windsor and post-war, the two men were subject to a quietly buried investigation by the IRS for breaching wartime currency control regulations. Wenner-Gren was also romantically linked to Inga Arvad. This was sensitive – she was having an affair with both a naval intelligence officer and the son of a recent American ambassador. There were also the politics of the President Roosevelt–Joe Kennedy antipathy. The FBI began watching, following and tapping the phone of Inga Arvad after being alerted to her associations in Germany, especially photographs of her with Hitler in his box at the Berlin Olympics. There are many versions of the tip-off, from a jealous fellow female reporter at the *Times-Herald* who had the hots for JFK or another journalist, Page Huidekoper, who previously was Press Assistant in London to Ambassador Kennedy. In fact, they were one and the same. Page Huidekoper, in FBI documents dated 12 December 1941 says she 'would not be surprised if Inga Arvad was a spy for some foreign power'. What immediately changed gear on the JFK-Nazi spy affair was the intervention of President Roosevelt. Astonishingly, the leader of the free world, in the wake of the Japanese attacking Hawaii, in the middle of a world war, took time to become involved in something which was comparatively small potatoes. What did he know? He wrote to J. Edgar Hoover: 'Inga Arvad in view of certain other circumstances which have been brought to my attention, I think she should be especially watched.'

Whether Roosevelt wanted the inside track on his nemesis Joe Kennedy's son or had information about Axel Wenner-Gren's connections, it put J. Edgar Hoover on high alert. The situation was sensitive, given Winston Churchill's problems in London dealing with the Nazi sympathies of the Duke of Windsor – the abdicated King Edward VIII – who he'd shoved sideways to be governor of the Bahamas in 1940. The result was Inga Arvad couldn't walk without a shadow, her mail was monitored and her fifth floor apartment at 1600 16th Street in Washington thoroughly bugged. It's hard to imagine today but the FBI agents failed to recognise the young Naval Officer in raglan-sleeved grey overcoat and matching tweed trousers who stayed the night. JFK was AWOL on these visits – he'd travelled up from Charleston, South Carolina, where he'd been transferred after the intervention of Joe Kennedy, who'd worked to divert his son from the ravishing temptation of Inga Arvad. Once more, Walter Winchell was the catalyst. Acknowledging the balance of power, Winchell did his unofficial master J. Edgar Hoover's bidding with a column item in 12 January 1942:

> '*One of ex-Ambassador Kennedy's eligible sons is the target of a Washington gal columnist's affections. So much so she has consulted her barrister about divorcing her exploring groom. Pa Kennedy no like.*'

On the warpath, Joe Kennedy immediately inveigled his son out of Washington to Charleston. JFK's superior officer, Captain Seymour A. D. Hunter, said the Navy viewed Arvad 'as similar to Mata Hari'. They thought she was using Ensign Kennedy to discover Navy Department secrets. Captain Howard Klingman, Assistant Director of the Office of Naval Intelligence, ordered Captain Hunter to throw JFK out of the service. Hunter explained the delicacy of him being a US ambassador's son 'and the young naval intelligence officer was not privy to information that would be more than a bit embarrassing'. Hunter advised that Kennedy be transferred to the Charleston seagoing unit.

The geography didn't bother JFK, who invited the woman he called *Inga Binga* to visit him in his new lodgings, which were also heavily bugged by the FBI. This 'total intervention' was Oval Office ordained. Their letters were intercepted. In the FBI files, on *Washington Times-Herald* letterhead notepaper, she'd typed: 'I have made up my mind to turn out a few stories – and when I get time a few babies – hope illegitimacy becomes a fadd [sic] after the war, as I only know one man worth reproducing a perfect copy of.' And: 'Remember to save this letter for defense against Inga-Binga in the Supreme Court of the US. I will be seeing you – here or there or somewhere in the world, and it will be the best or, rather, second-best moment in a lifetime. The best was when I met you.'

JFK was totally aware of the FBI surveillance and one report maintains he directly confronted J. Edgar Hoover, demanding a letter saying his lover was not a Nazi spy. Hoover demurred. If he did that and she turned around and began working for the enemy then his 'ass was on the line'.

Inga's espionage status not proven, JFK considered marriage, and seriously enough to get advice from the church about Lutheran Inga becoming a Roman Catholic and having her first two marriages annulled. It was all very Henry VIII but the Tudor king didn't have to get around Joe Kennedy, who continually told his son to finish the affair. With hindsight, it appears reckless that he did not. Especially, seeing the FBI transcript of one of their bugged telephone calls:

JFK: 'I heard you had a big orgy up in New York.'

Inga: 'I'll tell you about it. I'll tell you about it for a whole weekend if you would like to hear about it. My husband has his little spies out all over the place.' That revelation didn't seem to electrify JFK as might be imagined. What followed did. She then relates details of conversations between JFK and his father, talks in which he said he had no intention of marrying Inga, he wasn't that fond of her. There's a pause and to the unasked question she says: 'Somebody who knows your family well and also knows my husband but I don't know who it is. The person had known you since you were a child.'

He doesn't quiz her more about this information – who is bugging Joe Kennedy? – and leaves the question of his commitment to her in the air. The unasked and unanswered questions are a red flag. They met the weekend after that conversation, on 6 February 1942 – all documented by the FBI – at the Fort Sumter Hotel in Charleston, had dinner on the mezzanine floor and were back in her hotel room by 10.35 p.m., when their lovemaking was taped. Hoover and the FBI knew and heard all; they picked up that Inga Arvad during her affair with JFK was also sleeping with businessman Bernard Baruch, a man involved with early planning of a 'war ending' weapon, presumed to be the atomic bomb. Inga chose interesting lovers but escaped sanction for her dangerous liaison with JFK. His father had a gift for changing the past. Leading the overall inquiries into JFK and the Nazi spy was a Hoover man, the lawyer and former FBI agent James McInerney, who in 1942 was charged with overseeing national security for the Department of Justice. He controlled the case and a decade later helped Bobby Kennedy get a senior legal position. When he went into private legal practice in the capital, McInerney's most prestigious clients were Joe Kennedy and all his sons, boys constantly in need of a clean-up.

McInerney became the Kennedy laundromat.

Inga also developed more interesting connections and became engaged in 1945 to Bob Boothby, the British MP who would go on to cuckold UK Prime Minister Harold Macmillan and, share toy-boy lovers with London gangster Ronnie Kray. They didn't find lasting happiness. More comfortable in Hollywood, she met and, in 1946, married the Western star, Tim McCoy. No one mentioned Hitler at her interview to become a US citizen in downtown Los Angeles. Neither the Führer or JFK appeared on her immigration file. Some files have totally vanished, lost when Hoover died on 2 May 1972. The FBI director had in place initiatives for such 'influence files' to be removed by his secretary Helen Gandy. In turn, she chose her words with care when quizzed about the documents – said to include graphic evidence of the sexual adventures of JFK – specifying, 'All official files were left there [within FBI HQ].' Not another word.

Hoover's loyal deputy Clyde Tolson, the director's only love other than the FBI, was believed to have the files but he died on 14 April 1975 without producing them. His obituaries do not mention a flattering profile of him in the *Washington Times-Herald* on 30 October 1941, bylined Inga Arvad. As well as society in Washington, she covered all the bases.

Of all the women in JFK's short life – the short psychoanalysis is that, deprived of mother love, he needed to be loved and, in the moment, often believed he was in love – Inga held a memorial place, an everlasting sexual fascination. When he was demobbed from the Navy, after recovering from the drama of the PT-109 incident, in January 1944 JFK, weak and thin, was flown into San Francisco but immediately went to Los Angeles to meet up with Inga who was working as a syndicated Hollywood columnist. The couple, who had quietly kept in touch by letter during his wartime service, had a lost four days before JFK went east for more medical treatment. His health, then and previously, was a serious matter, in that Joe Kennedy wanted him alive but that no one should know how close to death he had often been and could be again. Of all the Kennedy illusions, the medical fitness of JFK to be President was the greatest magic trick. JFK's perilous health was continually covered up by his family. Only in recent years was it revealed that he suffered from venereal disease for thirty years, plagued by reinfection from his constant casual unprotected sex with prostitutes and whomever else took his fancy.

The war and the immediate aftermath, death, illness and distress, put pressure on the Kennedys. On 6 May 1944, Inga Arvad's journalist colleague and Washington roommate, Kathleen 'Kick' Kennedy, married William Cavendish, the Marquess of Hartington, heir to the Duke of Devonshire and to the utter dismay of Rose Kennedy, an Anglican. With total family upheaval over the religious divide, they married in a civil ceremony. Four months later, while serving in Belgium as a major in the Coldstream Guards he was killed in action. His widow, the Marchioness of Hartington, died in a plane crash in France four years later. These tragedies were the beginning of gossip about the *curse of the Kennedys* and then few knew all the horrors, some even the immediate family never knew the details of.

The family kept secret the plight of Rose Marie 'Rosemary' Kennedy, the eldest of Joe Kennedy's daughters who was twenty-three years old in 1941 when her father arranged for her to undergo a prefrontal lobotomy. Mentally slow and given to sudden seizures, Joe Kennedy was anxious for Rosemary not to embarrass him. He took the advice of doctors offering a new medical procedure which would transform patients 'who were problems to their families and nuisances to themselves into useful members of society'. The operation left her permanently incapacitated, unable to speak but a few unintelligible words and she was hidden away by Joe Kennedy. Initially, he placed her in Craig House, New York, known as the 'dumping ground' for the mentally ill and severely disabled members of rich families. Old Joe ruled that only he could visit Rosemary and be able to contact the staff to check on her health and happiness. Out of sight, out of mind. Later, Rosemary moved and served the rest of her life in Jefferson, Wisconsin, in a institution called St Coletta. The truth about her situation and whereabouts was kept secret for decades.

With the death of Joe Jr and his future aspirations riding on JFK, Joe Kennedy was becoming more and more fanatical about 'unhealthy focus' on what might be 'defects' in his family, anything which might default his and their ambitions. JFK's health was a priority for subterfuge. His father emphasised any fragility was a failure: JFK never complained, never apologised but the image of the action man all-American politician was a fraud.

Mike Rothmiller filed countless freedom of information requests about JFK's health. Under American social security guidelines, JFK as President could have claimed benefits for being disabled. Yet even in 2023, sixty years after his death, there was reluctance to provide explicit documentation. But there is enough evidence on file to help explain the staggering risk-taking. The perception, the 'idea' of Kennedy and Camelot, of an almost perfect person, of honour and heroism, a creation worthy of Edward Bernays at his most ambitious, is so embedded that acknowledgement, never mind endorsement, of flaws is anathema. Nothing prompts myth-making like the vacuum left by an untimely death. Time and a more considered attitude to power and those who hold it has offered clues to what often appeared as absurd and reckless undertakings. Risking all for a moment of fun. Maybe it was always a race against time, we can only ponder on that.

JFK was a sickly child from the first, a baby difficult to feed, and a collector of most of the childhood maladies, including a bout of scarlet fever which almost saw the end of him. He was in and out of sanatoriums and puzzled doctors and specialists with what was constantly afflicting him. Joe Kennedy did a good disguise job, one that's still working as seen here. In 2024, it is agreed in the medical community that JFK had autoimmune polyglandular syndrome type 2 with Addison's disease and hypothyroidism. He also had, from adolescence, gastrointestinal symptoms which go with coeliac disease, common with Irish ancestry. By talking to doctors and using the US Freedom of Information Act (FOIA), Mike Rothmiller reports:

'I have filed a FOIA request with the National Archives and the Kennedy Library to obtain his complete medical records and his prescribed drugs while serving as President. In theory, this should be a simple request but they have refused to release them. Kennedy was a federal employee, and taxpayers paid all his medical treatment and drugs. Considering he's been deceased for decades, this information should be available to the public, as are thousands

of records and gruesome photographs relating to his assassination and autopsy. But they are not. Why? What are they hiding? The US National Archives and the Kennedy Library informed me that President Kennedy's medical records are "donated" historical material, and therefore not subject to a FOIA. The donor's deed of gift controls access to those records. In the case of John F. Kennedy's medical records, access is by pre-approved permission only, with the final approval given by a senior Kennedy Library official. Although hundreds, if not thousands, of researchers, have requested access, I've been informed only a handful have been granted access. An additional requirement to be eligible for reviewing his medical records is that you must be a licenced medical doctor, a Ph.D. in a closely related medical field or have one accompany you at the scheduled time of an authorised review. Again, the researcher and the medical doctor must be approved in advance by the National Archives. To be considered, you must request the permission of the archives' director in writing; state your research topic and why a review of the records is necessary.

'You don't know which record is significant unless you examine all records. So, providing detailed information of what you seek is unreasonable. Even if you fulfil the requirement for review, it's likely access will be denied. On the surface, such a continuing blanket denial of access is a clear indicator that the individual(s) who deeded the records to the National Archives have and are engaging in a cover-up to protect President Kennedy's legacy and his public image. From statements of researchers who claim to have reviewed his medical history, I can reasonably conclude the following; most likely, they sought to conceal the President's chronic use and addiction to various prescribed narcotic drugs and his use of anti-depressants. I can also conclude his medical records would demonstrate he was the first President to serve while addicted to drugs. The implications are enormous, considering the state of world affairs during his presidency. As with many addicted to narcotic drugs, it appears he was able to function. I asked three medical doctors for their educated opinion on how the side-effects of Kennedy's drug use could have influenced his

cognitive functioning. They expressed concern that the narcotic drugs may, and probably did, have an adverse impact on his ability to reason rationally, especially during times of high stress or high drug usage. It was also the consensus that Kennedy was drug dependent and his physicians were irresponsible. They expressed surprise he didn't die from a drug overdose.

'*One of the consulted physicians provided a table of side-effects of the drugs used by Kennedy.*

'*There are two classes of drugs that are usually abused:*

'*1.   Tranquillisers such as Nembutal, phenobarbital, and Librium,*

'*2.   Opiates like Demerol/methadone and stimulants like amphetamine.*

'*President Kennedy was abusing both: the potential problems/ side-effects with those drugs include the following: barbiturates and tranquillisers: depression, mood swings, agitation, irritability, decreased anxiety, unusual excitement, slurred speech, decreased motor control, poor concentration, sluggishness, low blood pressure, dizziness, slow heartbeat, reduction in dream time, depression of breathing and cessation of breathing, visual problems, difficulty urinating, dilated pupils, tolerance, slowed brain function, confusion, impaired judgement, dependence, hallucinations, delusions and addiction.*

'*Addiction brings harmful behaviours and damage, including strained interpersonal relations, changes in alertness, decreased functioning, irritability, memory loss, liver damage, heart damage and brain damage, risky behaviour, seizures and coma/death. The opiates Kennedy was taking could cause depression, rapid decrease in blood pressure, disorientation or confusion in familiar surroundings, constipation, digestive difficulties, and shortness of breath.*

'*President Kennedy was a very sick man and a drug addict. Not by a desire to experiment with drugs or for a narcotic high; instead, he required the medications for his numerous maladies and continued addiction to prescribed drugs.*

'*Records we were able to access indicate that Kennedy was either injected or took oral medication for nearly every hour of the day and evening – primarily for pain. He required crutches when out of public view, was physically unable to climb stairs and almost always wore a back brace. In 1930 he was diagnosed with colitis. In 1947 he was diagnosed with Addison's disease and started daily treatment with corticosteroids, continuing until his death. Throughout his life, he underwent scores of multiple courses of antibiotics for urinary, skin, and lung infections.*

'His X-rays demonstrated a compression fracture of his lower back and osteoporosis. The records also confirm he underwent multiple back surgeries. The first was in 1944. The second was in 1954 when a metal plate was installed to stabilise the spine to reduce his severe back pain. That surgery became severely infected and in 1955 additional surgery was performed to remove the plate and further stabilise the spine. Both operations were considered failures, resulting in severe chronic back pain.

'In 1955, he started a regimen of chronic pain medication, which continued and increased for the remainder of his life. Beyond taking prescribed pain medication to address his back pain, it's reported the White House physician injected him six times a day; in six different locations of his back with Novocaine and procaine.

'In a White House telephone transcript, President Kennedy asked the White House physician for additional medication and those blue pills. This short conversation raises several troubling questions.

'Dr George Burkley tells the President he's already given additional medication to Kennedy's secretary, Evelyn Lincoln. This indicates that Kennedy had already requested additional drugs but may have forgotten his first request. Later, he again requests one of those blue pills. According to physicians and pharmacists I've interviewed, in the early 1960s, those blue pills were most likely Demerol, a Schedule II Controlled Substance opioid. It's in the same class as morphine, tramadol, hydromorphone and others. It's prescribed to mask severe pain.'

JFK's other pills, it's suggested, encouraged other activity, more possible explanation for his sexual recklessness. In a remarkable book, *A First-Rate Madness: Uncovering the Links Between Leadership and Mental Illness* (The Penguin Press, 2011), Professor Nassir Ghaemi of the Tufts Medical Center, Boston, revealed a study of what, in essence, made Kennedy sex-mad. Kennedy's hyper-sexuality was not limited to his Presidential years, but also occurred in his college and congressional years, before and after marriage. JFK always had a high sex drive, probably related to his hyperthymic temperament and later strengthened by libido-enhancing medications [anabolic steroids and amphetamines]. When Kennedy combined procaine [injections] with other agents that produced euphoria, like amphetamines and steroids, they all augmented one another, increasing his energy and libido further.

A First-Rate Madness reveals Kennedy's 'poorly controlled Addison's disease' and that he suffered 'the wayward psychiatric effects of anabolic steroid abuse'. He was pill-popping fluoxymesterone, an oral testosterone. It concludes that Kennedy used 'more drugs than he needed', which provided him with 'a manic-like enhancement of his physical and sexual energy'.

That's the scientific stuff. One of JFK's early girlfriends, Harriet Price, whom he dated during his time at California's Stanford University in 1940, was convinced the future President's womanising was him simply following his father's example. He thought he could get away with it, according to her testimony in Fredrik Logevall's *JFK*. She believed that Joe Kennedy's low opinion of his wife, Rose, and his mentally abusive treatment of her, warped JFK's character. Womanising was a sport encouraged by his philandering father.

Indeed, he'd witnessed his father in full sexual action with Gloria Swanson. Harriet Price, known to JFK as 'Flip', explained, 'He knew all about his father's infidelities. That denigration that came from the father, rubbed off on Jack.'

Post-war, in the turmoil of political and social change, for JFK the crazy confusion of the psychological and chemical took shape as he stepped carefully across a world of secrets and shadows, through halls of mirrors, and toward becoming the most powerful man in the world. A world unaware of how dangerously ill he had been – and was. Joan and Clay Blair were so astonished by what they discovered writing *The Search for JFK* (Berkley Publishing, 1977) that they abandoned including their work on the later years of JFK arguing, 'We learned many more fascinating facts, but our confidence in our understanding of the overall picture waned. The onset of Addison's disease in September 1947 had to be a profound turning point. It must have controlled or heavily influenced his major decisions. The Kennedys and Jack's close friends and political associates were then, as now [in 1976], engaged in a dogged, systematic cover-up. The official medical records are closed. In the official and personal correspondence of these years at the Kennedy Library, we could find no reference to it. This meant Jack never referred to the disease, or the library archivists are under instructions not to release letters of documents referring to it.' The Blairs say that when JFK became a congressman in 1946 the 'medical cover-up was simply too vast, too overwhelming' to track; their time and patience – and sympathy – ran out. Ominously, they suggested voters were 'woefully unwilling to consider human complexities in the very human beings who want to lead them'.

Or that a leading politician, as testified by the eminent psychiatrist Professor Ghaemi, was an unstable sex addict.

Chapter Seven

Sex and the Single Man

'*I think I was the only Hollywood star NOT to have slept with Jack Kennedy.*'

Arlene Dahl, 1996

JFK couldn't keep his pants on and his lifetime friend Kirk LeMoyne 'Lem' Billings was there when he first got into the habit. As teenagers they shared rooms at Choate Preparatory School in Wallingford, Connecticut, and established a relationship that survived all the turbulence of life with the Kennedy family.

Lem Billings should never have fitted in. He was gay ('What's that queer doing, hanging around here?' was Joe Kennedy's very vocal early days comment) in a social circle that wasn't welcoming to a lifestyle outside strict establishment parameters.

Anything which upset the trajectory toward popular endorsement and enhancement was off Joe Kennedy's agenda.

Still, despite the sincere and strong sexual element in Lem's attraction to JFK, the two young men formed a friendship which began in early 1933 and would, in time, grant Billings a permanent suite at the White House. First, they went together to a supposedly different sort of house, a brothel in New York's Harlem. It was 1934 and Kennedy, seventeen, and his eighteen-year-old friend dressed up in evening wear, dinner jackets, having planned, bewilderingly, to lose their virginity to the same woman that evening. JFK enthusiastically went for it but when it was Lem's turn, he uncomfortably paid for the girl's time but didn't have sex. JFK put it down to first-night nerves. Another explanation offered itself later that year when the besotted Lem sent an indiscreet note to his friend on toilet paper – a public-school tactic as the message could be easily flushed away or swallowed – to which JFK's reply was, 'I'm not that kind of boy.' What Lem's note said vanished with that piece of toilet paper as did any upset JFK may have had with it. For Lem Billings was his constant and closest friend, a man he talked to without fear of indiscretion or betrayal for all the rest of his life. JFK's loyalty to his friend – a commanding figure, blonde and striking, at 6-foot-2-inches tall a school sportsman – and Billings's devotion to him towered over what was acceptable to anyone or any institution around them.

Billings never came out as gay – it was illegal for much of his lifetime – but his love for JFK is abundantly clear in his oral history for the John F. Kennedy Library in Boston. That library reluctantly, after an FOIA request, released to us JFK's diary for 1 July to 3 September 1937, which he titled 'Trip to Europe'. Joe Kennedy, now fonder of his son's close friend, subsidised Billings's costs although Billings insisted on repaying him when he could. On their European travels, JFK has several encounters with girls but in his diary, he also notes about an outing in Venice: 'Went out in a gondola which would have been quite romantic except that as usual Billings managed to make a guy threesome. Billings objects to this most unjust statement as Billings is always [unclear] himself in.'

Billings was a good friend. He helped and encouraged his friend through his medical traumas, of which we noted were immense, and in his testimony recorded at the Kennedy Library, for the first time he broke his self-imposed silence: 'Jack never wanted us to talk about this but I think it really should be told… Jack Kennedy all during his life had few days when he wasn't in pain or sick in some way.' Billings was always present – like a parent offering unconditional love – providing a distraction to alleviate the agony. The permanent pain also accounts, along with his dysfunctional upbringing, for JFK's acute selfishness and his heedless daring. He had no brake when he truly desired something or someone.

J. Edgar Hoover, for obvious blackmail and leverage reasons regarding Joe Kennedy, opened a file on Lem Billings and his friendship with a Kennedy. Astonishingly – and more proof that America still 'cares' for its all but royal family – the FBI denied in 2023 having such a file. In August that year, Mike Rothmiller appealed an FOIA to the FBI when they claimed not to have any knowledge of Lem Billings. He reports: 'I received an answer to my appeal stating they have searched and the results were reviewed by their attorney. In short, they claimed to have nothing and told me to file suit against them. Advising me to file suit is always the feds' answer when they do not want to give you records. They know it will cost tens of thousands, drag on for years, then they may or may not provide anything.

'I've been down the road before and it always indicates they have records they *don't* want the public to see. Knowing J. Edgar Hoover, I have no doubt the FBI has an in-depth file on Billings and JFK – that is what Hoover always sought. Since the JFK Library has documents, the FBI must too. The secrets and lies around the Kennedy dynasty is America's greatest soap opera.'

Without FBI files, others have suggested that there was more of a physical relationship between the two men. They were constant companions*: 'I was three years old before it dawned

---

* Lem Billings often met with JFK during the Cuban Missile Crisis and was with him in Vienna when he tried to meet Nikita Khrushchev. The last time Billings saw his best friend was at a White House dinner with actress Greta Garbo on 10 November 1963. Billings and Greta Garbo knew each other from holidays on the Riviera and he'd boasted to JFK about it. JFK pranked his friend by asking Garbo just before Billings arrived to pretend she'd never met him. Garbo played the part, JFK delighted with his fun and kept Billings discomforted till they got to pudding.

on me that Lem wasn't one more older brother,' said Teddy Kennedy. Billings visited the White House for most weekends during the Kennedy administration. When the staff noted Billings was leaving his belongings in one of the third-floor guest rooms, First Lady Jackie replied, 'He's been my house guest since I was married.'

American author Lawrence J. Quirk (*The Kennedys in Hollywood*, Cooper Square Press, 2003) has said he met Billings when they were both working for JFK's congressional campaign. In the archive it reports that in 1946 Billings helped JFK start his political career and shared his Boston apartment. In a 2017 interview, Quirk claimed the relationship was sexual at some times. He said that he knew Billings was gay when he first met him in the 1940s and that Billings revealed to him that his JFK friendship 'included oral sex, with Jack always on the receiving end … Jack was in love with Lem being in love with him and considered him the ideal follower-adorer'.

Many in JFK's romantic life, close and casual, would identify with this; drawing on documented files and primary testimony, it's clear that JFK didn't like to make much of an effort in his love life, something Marilyn Monroe complained about in her diary (*Bombshell*, Ad Lib, 2021). It was often opportunistic and predatory. In the twenty-first century he'd have risked severe censure and punishment, derision from the #MeToo movement, but almost always he got what he wanted. His fellow sex enthusiast, Senator George Smathers, said JFK, 'just would not take "No" for an answer, and he kept it up until he wore them down'. JFK looked the part of a good lover. Perception again. By several accounts the terrific haircut and winning smiles promised more than he was prepared to deliver. He liked to chase women, slightly older, preferably married or contentedly divorced. The younger girls were always about from his Choate prep days onward and throughout the years those who did not vanish overnight reappeared in his life. Laura Bergquist Knebel, who worked for

America's *Look* magazine, was professionally close to JFK and in an oral history interview with the Kennedy Library in 1965 said, 'I don't think he regarded women for their brains – no, that sounds wrong. He was beguiled by women, he loved being around them. But when it came to serious talk, he preferred talking to the guys about politics or whatever. He was kind of a man's man. There are men who really like women or who think of women as equals, with ability. My editor was like that. I mean, whether you are male or female it doesn't matter so long as you do the job. But I don't think Kennedy was that way. He was very sexually oriented. "Sexually" maybe is the wrong word for it, but he was very male-female oriented. Oh, I think he liked pretty women, female, female women, clever women, but not somebody in the sense of an equal working partner.'

As we've seen, he learned by example, but even those awed by the Kennedys were dismayed in modern times as information became available about the incestuous pimping carried out within the family; daughters for father and brothers and vice versa. Intoxicated by self-acclaim, they were on a constant sexual carousel and the speed it spun increased with JFK's political fortunes. Consequences were never a deterrent, not given a thought, especially when Joe Kennedy took the 'troops' to the south of France as he did while ambassador to the UK. He hired an attractive French girl to 'take dictation' and got Rose and the family made comfortable in a villa on the grounds of the Hôtel du Cap-Eden-Roc, accommodation which by cost and reputation singled extraordinary status. Joe Kennedy proved yet again that the strongest currency on the Riviera, outbidding the dollar, the yen and most certainly the euro, is the rich man's whim.

It has been that way since the Cote d'Azur became a playground for kings and princes, jet set hedonists and international society. All elements which also attracted Marlene Dietrich, then aged thirty-seven and her party – her husband, the casting director Rudolf Sieber; their daughter Maria Sieber, thirteen; his lover and her man-of-the-moment, the German author Erich Maria Remarque (*All Quiet on the Western Front,* 1929). The passion for possession trumps prudence every time. Since the days of Scott and Zelda Fitzgerald – Scott the novelist, Zelda the novelty – the Cote d'Azur has been a magnet for the creative and self-destructive. Giant figures in twentieth-century art and literature – Picasso and Cole Porter, Stravinsky and Somerset Maugham, Matisse, Rudyard Kipling and Evelyn Waugh – were all awed by the magical enchantment, the magnificent 'silver clarity' of the light. The west side of the Cap d'Antibes has always been accepted by the cognoscenti as a richer venue than the east. It has to do with the view towards Cannes and the setting sun. This is what provided a bonus cachet for the visitors. The sun and the salt-water pool had invigorating effects for all.

Joe Kennedy swiftly became a regular at Dietrich's cabana. Neither of their separate groups appeared bothered by this. JFK was twenty-one years old and happily joined the 'families' at a summer gathering, an open-air ball, staged by the legendary American party giver and society columnist Elsa Maxwell, an ogre of a woman who was besotted with and friendly with the Duchess of Windsor. They fell out and Ms Maxwell lost her trump social card when it got out that she'd described the duchess as 'looking like cook on her night out'. Elsa was desperate for other royalty, like Dietrich and the Kennedy clans, remarkable menages, to make her look good.

At the summer ball everyone looked splendid. Maria Sieber wore her first evening gown – she said she looked like a sparkling mosquito tent – and JFK was in a white dinner jacket. Seeing Maria looking rather lost, and with some chivalry, he walked across the dance floor and asked her to dance. They did the popular 'The Lambeth Walk'. It was most innocent. Racier, was his dance with her mother to Cole Porter's 'Begin the Beguine'. Dietrich held him tightly close to her and 'she slipped her hand down my trousers,' reported JFK in a conversation with Frank Sinatra's butler George Jacobs. (*Mr S.: My Life with Frank Sinatra*, George Jacobs and

William Stadiem, 2003). JFK suggested his father may have 'put her up to it'. That's a father asking his lover to sexually arouse his son. JFK was neither angry or upset but recalled he liked Dietrich's perfume. It's an extraordinary defiance of anything resembling a moral code – a missing link in a family convinced they were born to rule, to do exactly what they wanted. These strange and bewildering, to those outside the Kennedy circle, dalliances were ongoing for the next decades.

All emphasised by the testimony of Mary Pitcairn who half a century ago provided revelatory words about the arrangements in conversations, often forgotten in the archives, with the thoroughly disillusioned authors Joan and Clay Blair. She was friends with JFK's sister Eunice Kennedy and said: 'He was flirtatious, if the lady or girl succumbed, that was it, he wasn't ready to commit.' It was Joe Kennedy who was creepy: 'Mr Kennedy always called up the girls Jack was taking out and asked them to dinner. He came down and took me to the Carleton Hotel, then the fanciest dining room in Washington. He was charming. He wanted to know his children's friends. He was very curious about my personal life. He really wanted to know. He asked a lot of personal questions – extraordinarily personal questions. And then, and I'll never forget this, he told me about Gloria Swanson, how wonderful she was and how he kept in touch with her. When he brought me home, he did something that I heard he did to everyone. After dinner he would take you home and kiss you goodnight as though you were a young so-and-so. One night I was visiting Eunice at the Cape and he came into my bedroom to kiss me goodnight! I was in my nightgown, ready for bed. Eunice was in her bedroom. We had an adjoining bath. The doors were open.

'He said, "I've come to say goodnight." And kissed me. *Really* kissed me. It was so silly. I remember thinking, How embarrassing for Eunice. But beyond that, nothing. Absolutely nothing. I think all this confused Jack. He was a sensitive man and I think it confused him. What kind of object is a woman? To be treated as his father treated them. And his father's behaviour that way was blatant. There was always a young, blonde, beautiful secretary around. I think it was very confusing to Jack. [Rose Kennedy] never saw things or acknowledged things she didn't want to. The children just totally ignored her. Daddy was it.'

It was 'daddy' who first connected with British tennis champion Kay Stammers, who met the 'nice looking' Joe Kennedy when he was Ambassador to London in 1939, the year she lost, to Alice Marble, the Women's Singles Championship at Wimbledon. His son made his move on the sportswoman, she had a racy reputation for wearing her tennis skirts and shorts four inches above the knee, in London in the summer of 1945, and she found him as attractive as his father. She had a caveat: 'He liked to enjoy himself but was unreliable.' The tennis champion, coached by Dan Maskell, in later years the BBC 'voice of Wimbledon', she was the number two female player in the world before war interrupted her career, and three years older than JFK and very much in his 'range' of the women he was drawn to; those who would be fun without complications. Kay Stammers thought JFK was spoiled by women – 'he was attractive and rich, a terrific catch. I wouldn't say I was in love with him but I was terribly attracted to him. We had great fun when we saw one another – it wasn't just a flash in the pan.' Yet, it so often was wham-bam-thank-you-mam and one girlfriend turned into an identikit of another.

JFK's wartime friend Paul 'Red' Fay Jr, who stayed overnight with JFK, recalled to researcher Joan Blair, 'I went to bed figuring this was the girl for the night. The next morning a completely different girl came wandering down for breakfast. They were a dime a dozen.' JFK couldn't take a flight without 'taking' an air hostess.

Despite his risky revolving bedroom door, JFK was careful not to get trapped in any serious situations which would require marriage. Benevolently, being from a supposedly devout Catholic family was protective, especially if he concentrated on divorcées, who were marital taboo.

Fashion journalist Florence Pritchett, a former New York model, met JFK in 1944, a year after her divorce from her very Catholic husband and a lifelong bond was established. It was not exclusive. Pritchett had affairs with 'wicked' Errol Flynn and other Hollywood stars. She worked for the *Gone with the Wind* producer David O. Selznick – as did JFK's other close friend, Inga Arvad – promoting the movie *Duel in the Sun*, which starred Selznick's wife Jennifer Jones. In 1947 she married the moneyman and diplomat Earl Smith, appointed US ambassador to Cuba in 1957 but continued contact with 'the divine' JFK. One of her letters to him, following her marriage, is filed with the Kennedy Presidential Papers and is suggestive: 'Instead of making history with the Knights of Columbus, why not make something of your nights. The summer will be long and hot. So, I think you should adjourn occasionally and help make it hotter. I hope you will be up this way again, and that when you do, we can play.'

Such a grown-up relationship was not so simple with the Hollywood beauty Gene Tierney, the lead in the celebrated film noir *Laura* (1944) which made her a star. In 1946 she was filming *Dragonwyck*, a melodrama with Vincent Price as her mentally imbalanced husband, and in an off-screen drama, divorcing fashion designer Oleg Cassini who was equally difficult. When JFK visited the film set at 20th Century Fox she said she thought he'd stepped from a romantic novel. Her reaction was that of a smitten heroine. Just like the movies – JFK found himself the love rival to Hollywood idol Tyrone Power who was furiously pursuing his co-star from *The Razor's Edge* (1946). Tierney, who had a nervous disposition, and would suffer severely from depression in later life, found JFK a welcome antidote to the intense actor.

Of course, that casual ploy was real. JFK was not that bothered to be squiring one of the world's most lusted after women.

Gene Tierney got sacks of fan mail every day including countless marriage proposals. Her new boyfriend wasn't that forthcoming, happy with the affair knowing the actress was divorcing, not someone who'd meet the family criteria for a bride.

If that romance was 'safe' another, more intense, affair tempted sinister consequences. Before he returned East to pursue his political fortunes, JFK ran around Hollywood with introductions by proxy of his father's friend, Johnny Rosselli. The mafioso was coming to the end of a prison term for running a Hollywood extortion scheme but, from behind bars, planned for the visitor to be entertained. One of Rosselli's former lovers was most obliging: Lana Turner was movie dynamite from her first two-minute screen stroll, bouncing along in a tight sweater. She'd been spotted, aged fifteen, skipping school in Currie's Ice Cream Parlour on Sunset Strip by Billy Wilkerson and *The Hollywood Reporter* owner had got her on the books of the Zeppo Marx talent agency. In turn, Zeppo had got her into Mervyn LeRoy's *They Won't Forget* (1937). They didn't. She made three more films in 1937 and the next year was working steadily, moving her way up the screen credits – and making herself well-known around town. She shocked many by eloping with bandleader Artie Shaw on her twentieth birthday, 8 February 1940. The whirlwind marriage lasted seventeen months. Lana Turner didn't like to be lonely. She danced many evenings at mobster Mickey Cohen's favourite, the Mocambo, and her friendship and reliance on the Los Angeles gangster-in-chief was ongoing as her turbulent love life got her into trouble. In 1946 she co-starred with John Garfield in the remarkable film version of James M. Cain's *The Postman Always Rings Twice*. When audiences watched her onscreen, many were only thinking about one thing: the way her wayward wife Cora Smith smiled was sinful. Some argued she shouldn't be allowed to say 'Hello' at the same time. It was scandalous. She seemed that way inclined herself and was involved with Frank Sinatra and JFK's love rival Tyrone Power. Another turbulent romance was with Howard Hughes – they flew from New York to Hollywood to marry but by the time the plane touched down he'd gone off the idea.

She married seven times – 'My dream was to have one husband and seven children but it went the other way around' – and was brutally honest about some relationships while discreet about others. Her friend and screen rival – it was a blonde v brunette casting conflict – was Yvonne De Carlo (Lily in *The Munsters* television series), who told Douglas Thompson that she and Lana Turner took turns in 'dating' JFK in Hollywood. In 1986, at her home in Solvang, California, De Carlo said, 'It was strictly fun but I think he got carried away with Lana; they all did, she was quite a handful.' Forty years on, she couldn't recall how often they saw JFK – 'it was always fun'.

He had more of what might be termed a romance with Gene Tierney, who wrote of him: 'He had the kind of bantering, unforced Irish charm that women so often find fatal. He asked questions about my work, the kind that revealed how well he already knew the subject. His father had once invested in the movies, he told me … Jack was partial to French restaurants. One night, at the Versailles, in New York, we listened to Edith Piaf sing the love songs that made her famous. I don't recall how many dates Jack and I had, not many, before I told my family and a few friends that I had met a young man who would be President someday.

'That was his goal. He talked about it in a way that was unself-conscious, as another might talk about going to work in his father's store. Jack was single and eligible and not yet a national figure. Still, we tried to keep our romance out of the gossip columns and for the most part we succeeded. I visited him once in Washington and sat quietly in the guest balcony while Congress was in session. A reporter spotted me and asked what I was doing there. Thinking quickly, I said that I was studying the government. "Oh, some kind of movie project?" he asked. I nodded. "Something like that." At that moment, Jack picked me out from the floor of the House, waved, and ruined my story. I just didn't think that dating an actress, at that point, would be very good for his career.'

It was, of course, profile. Here was a young, go-getter politician and one of the most famous actresses of the day – Walter Winchell was made aware – and it spoke to the health and energy and virility of the candidate: that very much was the fraud Joe Kennedy and JFK wanted to promote in the moment. In time, over lunch in New York, JFK told Gene Tierney their relationship was 'difficult'. She said the relationship ended as he left to catch a flight to Washington where he was more interested in his own stardom. Which, appropriately, got a boost from a renowned, if historic, sex scandal, yet another involving the Kennedy family.

Chapter Eight

The Candidate

'*The mind I sway by, and the heart I bear, shall never sag with doubt, nor shake with fear.*'

Macbeth, William Shakespeare, 1606

James Michael Curley, a vagabond of a politician, was a key player in JFK's path to the White House. His contribution was that, for money, he got out of the way. It was what the in-bred politics of Boston called a 'buy-in'. Joe Kennedy would privately joke that for the money he spent, 'I could have got my chauffeur elected.'

It was his second son who won the House of Representatives seat on 3 January 1947 and, for the Kennedys, there was a certain *schadenfreude*. In 1914, the big, tall and roguish Curley had blackmailed JFK's grandfather Honey Fitz Fitzgerald into not seeking re-election as mayor of Boston. He'd discovered that Fitzgerald was sleeping with a hotel bar cigarette girl named Elizabeth 'Toodles' Ryan. Curley's first threat to go public with the information did not deter JFK's maternal grandfather. What did it was Curley's announcement that he would present a lecture tour: 'Great Lovers in History: from Cleopatra to Toodles, from Henry VIII to the Present Day'.

Curley served multiple times as mayor and held myriad political office, all the time being investigated for financial and political malfeasance – he was the source of the shady Irish political boss in Edwin O'Connor's *The Last Hurrah*, played by Spencer Tracy in the Oscar-winning 1958 film adaptation – which saw him convicted of fraud in 1937. Yet, the voters loved the rascal and in 1942 he was free and elected as Congressman of the 11th District.

Curley was glued to the seat Joe Kennedy wanted for his son. He flattered Curley, who he knew was seriously in debt, with how good he'd been as Boston's mayor, and how much the city needed him once more at the helm. And don't be concerned about the money. Curly needed at least one hundred thousand dollars to run for mayor but that was just another small cheque for Joe Kennedy.

The offer you can't refuse was presented to Curley: free up the congressional seat for the nice, fresh-faced JFK and your debts are cleared, your mayor campaign funds met and a campaign manager's salary funded. Which was how it played out, with a pain-ridden and ailing JFK campaigning in a safe Democratic seat but, being an outsider, having to fight for it against nine other candidates in the primary election. With his father paying for and running his campaign under the slogan 'The New Generation Offers a Leader', the relentless electioneering, taking a strong anti-Moscow stand, comfortably won JFK his place in Congress alongside fellow newcomers Richard Nixon, Joseph McCarthy and George Smathers for Florida's Fourth Congressional District.

Smathers was as an incorrigible womaniser as his new colleague. He said in archive interviews that he 'clicked' with JFK in their recreational pursuits: 'Jack liked girls. He liked girls very much. He came by it naturally. His daddy liked girls. He was a great chaser. Jack liked girls and girls liked him. He just had a great way with women.' He remained involved with a circus of women, most young and intellectually clever but often bedazzled by what was and wasn't on offer from JFK. As his father continued to tell him, a candidate needed the 'correct' woman by his side.

As well as chasing women, he was chasing votes, which as it played out was something of the same thing. His father was a hound-dog on heat, at his heels, urging him on politically to the House of Representatives: he did the job but spent time in Massachusetts speaking to all interest groups and creating a clever index file system – modelled on the FBI's – of politically helpful contacts. He also got a health breakthrough, good news for a man who'd been given the last rites four times, for the ailment he and the family denied he ever had, Addison's. He was secretly diagnosed after private treatment in 1947 by Sir Daniel Davis at the London Clinic. In 1949, cortisone treatment was finally approved as positive treatment for sufferers. When the Mayo Clinic at Rochester, Minnesota, announced the discovery there were fears there would not be enough of the medicine to share fairly. Joe Kennedy resolved the problem with a 'You're all right, Jack' approach. The underhand way he did was hidden for forty years.

In her much applauded *The Fitzgeralds and the Kennedys*, 1987, Doris Kearns Goodwin told how the Kennedys bought up and stored cortisone supplies in bank safe deposit boxes so JFK would never be without: for the Kennedys 'the fix' was always in. There always seemed to be an edge for anything that was wanted, all flowing to Joe Kennedy.

JFK's campaign for national office began before the 1950s did. It was a family affair with his brother Bobby working as campaign manager and his other siblings behind the scenes and pushing the campaign slogan 'Kennedy Will Do *More* for Massachusetts' with prominent images of a smiling JFK. Joe Kennedy's plan was to sell his son like a Hollywood screen idol – not on what he said but on what he looked like. Perception again. In 1949 he was pimping him out politically as the *women's candidate* with afternoon teas and evening salons across Massachusetts, a long run-up to represent the state in Washington. As we've seen, Joe Kennedy played his cards well, using Joe McCarthy and the Catholic vote to boost chances in setting up JFK to beat three-term incumbent Senator Henry Cabot Lodge Jr, board member of United Fruit, and chief cheerleader for Eisenhower's Presidential campaign. In 1952, Republican cheerleader Eisenhower won Massachusetts by 208,000 votes but JFK sneaked a win by 70,000 votes over the patrician Cabot Lodge Jr.

JFK went to Washington in 1953 and later in the year, on 12 September, married Jacqueline Lee Bouvier. She most certainly looked the part and that was all that mattered: the marriage was a myth from the outset, an elegant veneer over a suitably agreeable arrangement.

Lyndon Johnson, the power of the US Senate, was not impressed by Senator Kennedy, seeing him as 'a playboy'. It was astute. That summer of 1953 he'd gone off to the Riviera and even his father saw the risks. JFK, aged thirty-six, took advantage of a twenty-one-year-old Swedish girl sent there by her wealthy parents to improve her French. JFK told Gunilla von Post what a smitten young girl wanted to hear. He adored her, his father had forced his forthcoming marriage on him and, if it was up to him, he'd call the whole thing off. Decades later she revealed that their affair began then – and continued after the wedding.

Archive documents show that on 28 June 1954, JFK wrote to her: 'Perhaps I'll get a boat and sail around the Mediterranean for two weeks, with you as my crew.' The trip was postponed because he suffered back problems and in November that year he wrote again, from his hospital bed in Manhattan: 'After two months I'm still here. I'm so disappointed as I had to cancel my trip to Europe in the last minute. Especially since you're now in Paris, and we could've had such a good time.' The summer after that, in 1955, they finally met in von Post's parents' summer house in Båstad, where she said that he enjoyed the Swedish summer, bathed and sang.

'We sat in a car, and he held his arm around me and we sang as we drove around Skåne. It was very beautiful. Like a dream. I was relatively inexperienced and Jack's tenderness was a revelation. He said: "Gunilla, we've waited two years for this. It seems almost too good to be true and I want to make you happy."' She said that he'd enjoyed their lovemaking so much he wanted to get a divorce when he returned to America. His father, he told her, would be the biggest obstacle, and he was.

The months passed, and Senator and Mrs Kennedy began to establish themselves as a political couple. Marriage did not slow up JFK's womanising, in fact he saw it as 'a cover' for his philandering. He was a regular in Hollywood – there was an affair with the bountifully promoted Jayne Mansfield who was an intimate contact with JFK's brother-in-law, the British-born actor Peter Lawford. That was ongoing for a few months at a beach home Mansfield had access to in Laguna Beach, California. JFK indicated he was going to see her by telling friends in Los Angeles, 'I'm going to drift down south for a couple of days.' Twice while leaving her home he encountered the singer Bing Crosby, whose wife Katharine had shared lodgings with Mansfield when the two were starlets in Texas. Mansfield, who died in a horrific car crash in 1967, was discreet, as were Hollywood columnists and journalists who regularly reported on her; although constantly pressed by editors for an excuse to run photographs of her on the front page, this affair was taboo, the 'fix' was in for JFK via the protection of Los Angeles Police Chief William Parker. It was Peter Lawford who introduced JFK to Mansfield's blonde-bombshell rival, Marilyn Monroe. By then, Chief Parker's personal spy force, the Organized Crime Intelligence Division of the LAPD, had bulging files on Lawford and his in-laws and the Hollywood and criminal 'stars' they encountered.

Lawford gloried in his role as matchmaker, he thought it gave him leverage. He had a confused and difficult childhood, nomadic but with money, from his aristocratic English heritage, the only son of the impressive soldier, Lieutenant General Sir Sydney Lawford and cantankerous Lady May Lawford.

Young Lawford wasn't decisive and he wasn't brave. He scared easily, which would play an important role in events. During the family wanderings they arrived in Los Angeles: 'My mother was very keen that I meet the right people, and movies seemed a logical way.'

He was young, good-looking and charming and of that trio it was his charm, a willingness to help, to be of service, that opened the doors. At fifteen, he landed his first credited role in *Lord Jeff* (1938). *Son of Lassie* (1945) made him a leading man ('The dog didn't like me') and a man-about-town. Hollywood was a village and Lawford got himself involved with Lana Turner, JFK's friend and that minx of a movie star who was also friendly with Mickey Cohen Inc. He had a more mature track record with his movies and the sixteen-year-old Elizabeth Taylor had seriously enjoyed her first screen kiss with him in *Julia Misbehaves* (1948). She admitted that Lawford was her first big crush. His marriage to Patricia Kennedy at St Thomas More church in Manhattan (the Kennedys could not use St Patrick's Cathedral as Lawford was not a Roman Catholic) was on 24 April 1954. Lawford had made many movies, but there was a noticeable absence of star names at his wedding. Actress Marion Davies, the lover of the late manipulative newspaper baron William Randolph Hearst, was there at the invite of her close friend Joseph Kennedy. The senior Kennedy had tried to sabotage his daughter marrying Lawford and told anyone who would listen: 'If there's anything I'd hate more for a son-in-law as an actor, it's a *English* actor as son-in-law.' That remark did not intimidate his daughter, but it did his new son-in-law. Whether it was awe at the money and power of simply feeling out of place, he was constantly fearful of and, to his everlasting shame, too obedient to the Kennedy men.

Weeks after his marriage, in July 1954, Peter Lawford 'connected' the elder of his new brothers-in-law with Marilyn Monroe at a party hosted by agent Charles Feldman. When she was introduced to Senator Kennedy, he employed a tired line: 'Haven't I met you someplace before?' She took the question at face value and said possibly she had, when he'd stayed out in Hollywood with the actor Robert (*The Untouchables*) Stack. Marilyn was there with her husband of six months, Joe DiMaggio, but the baseball hero was a reluctant guest. He didn't like Hollywood and he most certainly didn't like the Hollywood people who gathered around his wife. DiMaggio got more and more upset as JFK stared at his wife for much of the evening. The partygoers were intrigued, and the gossip was whispered but it roared around the room. It proved a volatile mix. Marilyn was delighted by the attention – 'He couldn't keep his eyes off me' – but DiMaggio kept urging her to leave, taking her by the elbow and leading her toward the door. Finally, and reluctantly, she went off with him leaving her smile and telephone number behind with Kennedy. He telephoned Marilyn the next day. Joe DiMaggio answered, heard Kennedy's voice and hung up on him. 'I guess I shouldn't call at certain times, huh?' Kennedy asked Marilyn the next time they met.

In October that year, regular visitors to his hospital room, where he was recovering from more spinal surgery, noticed a Marilyn Monroe poster. She was wearing blue shorts and standing with her legs spread well apart. The image was taped upside down on the wall above Kennedy's bed. Young women he called his 'cousins' paid visits and his wife Jackie was attentive. During his recuperation she invited Grace Kelly, late of *High Noon* (1952) and *Rear Window* (1954), to dress up as a nurse and feed him. He failed to recognise her and the future Princes Grace left, complaining, 'I must be losing it.' (That was rectified in Monaco some years later.) Marilyn's poster stayed in place.

And JFK's back got better, but not perfectly. He always wanted his lovers to be on top of him during sex, an arrangement which nearly killed 'the most beautiful woman in the world', Hedy Lamarr. In the Czech-Austrian romance *Ecstasy* in 1933, she appears nude and simulates what was supposedly the first female orgasm in a mainstream film. Predictably, Hitler outlawed the movie, not for the risqué content but because Lamarr was Jewish. Her looks wowed the comic book creators of *Batman* who modelled their *Catwoman* drawings on her. JFK was adventurous too – having selfish sex in a bathtub with Lamarr in their first, and last, encounter: 'In an impulsive move, he pushed me backward. My head was underwater, and I felt I was drowning. This caused a vaginal spasm. But he had his orgasm. That's all that mattered.'

Most of JFK's lovers who have been found or gone public themselves have talked of his 'difficult' back, at times a paralysing ailment which was kept too secret from America in general. JFK continued spinal operations and was often critically ill and away from the Senate, often out on the Coat. Columnist Earl Wilson quoted, posthumously, Marilyn Monroe: 'I think I made his back feel better.'

In 1956, while convalescing, he published *Profiles in Courage*, about politicians taking risks for their personal beliefs. It won the Pulitzer Prize for biography the following year. JFK's adviser and speechwriter Ted Sorensen finally admitted in 2008 that he had written the book – not just ghostwritten JFK's own words, but he was responsible for the total work. Of course, in the moment it was excellent profile builder. Less surprising were the hundreds of newspaper and magazine articles under JFK's name that were written by Joe Kennedy's paid assistants. The image of the charming, intelligent and potential Presidential candidate was all and much on display at the Democratic National Convention held on the south side of Chicago in August 1956. Governor Adlai Stevenson was the Presidential nominee and his running mate was Tennessee's Estes Kefauver, the Mafia's nemesis, who won a free vote – a historic three ballots had to be held – over JFK, gracious in narrow defeat. It was a shaky ticket to face the incumbent Eisenhower, such a famous figure from his role as military commander in the Second World War, and his Vice

President, Richard Nixon. On the floor of the convention, JFK enthusiastically made the endorsement, televised nationwide. TV politics took bite, viewers, a.k.a. voters, recalled the charmer even as Eisenhower and Nixon won the White House and power again on 6 November 1956.

Joe Kennedy encouraged JFK to prepare for *his* moment, four years was not far off. One hazard was his brother Bobby going after organised crime. As chief counsel for Senator John McClellan's committee, Bobby Kennedy was after the bad guys, gung-ho, he thought he was Eliot Ness. It's also clear from contemporary interviews and the historical archive that he had little idea of the extent of Joe Kennedy's personal and business entanglement with those who controlled organised crime in America. RFK's job was to erase racketeering among the nation's workforce, corruption in the Teamsters' Union being the prime target. In time, around 1,500 witnesses were ordered before the committee, including his father's associates, Johnny Rosselli, Carlos Marcello and the biggest villain of them all, Sam Giancana of Chicago.

Salvatore Sam Giancana, a.k.a. Sam Flood and most often, Sam Gold, was by 1955 America's top hoodlum, having assumed total control, a steel grip, on the Chicago Outfit, the city where Joe Kennedy still owned the Merchandise Mart. Giancana was a veteran of the St Valentine's Day Massacre and other prominent Prohibition atrocities and by Eisenhower's time the somewhat Jacobean figure was the controller of protection rackets, pinball betting, prostitution, numbers, narcotics, loan-sharking, extortion, counterfeiting and bookmaking. In achieving this power, he is said, in his FBI files, to have killed more than two hundred people, many of whom were tortured. It was never a good plan to piss off America's most powerful mobster, a hoodlum branded a *constitutional psychopath* by the 1943 American Army draft board when it rejected him for wartime soldiering for being too dangerous; some rather arrogant people never learned that. He was born in Chicago on 24 May 1908 and became a teenaged thug who became a leader in the Forty-Two Gang. By the late 1920s he was an experienced criminal and the gang itself was becoming more violent. They had gone from vandalism and stealing cars and horses to burglary, holding up nightclubs and robbery. As their robberies grew more violent victims began to die. The police took more of an interest when police officers and suspected informants started to die, too. Sam Giancana was arrested for murder in 1925 but wasn't prosecuted, the main witness being murdered. By 1931 more than thirty of the first forty-two members of the Forty-Two Gang were dead, seriously wounded or in prison.

This tearaway team kept going and Al Capone decided he could utilise them: he needed manpower to fuel his hundred-million-dollar yearly profit – and this is the 1920s – from his free enterprise gangsterism. The young gang were hired as drivers to move liquor around the city and Giancana – known as 'Momo' or 'Mooney', local slang for 'crazy', proved a good wheelman who stayed calm under pressure. In 1933, Giancana was made, inducted into the Mob and when he took the reins he developed political connections which brought him into contact with Joe Kennedy for whom he did an everlasting favour.

Foolishly, Joe Kennedy had failed to deliver on a promise to Frank Costello who, in a moment of anger – friendship was one thing, business quite another – put out a contract on him. Joe Kennedy asked Giancana to save his life. That was a big favour which would haunt the Kennedy dynasty forever. Giancana easily persuaded Costello to cancel the planned assassination in return for having influence and debts due; the street-smart Giancana argued to Costello that Kennedy's son JFK was a US Senator being written about as a Presidential candidate. It wasn't going to hurt to have a man in the White House.

Yet, it was painful to have the terribly eager Bobby Kennedy on the McClellan Committee, by then known as the Senate Rackets Committee. Indeed, eager doesn't cover his often unthinking performance, falling over his shrill questioning and abrasive manner. There was no dignity. Giancana wore an amused look as Bobby Kennedy quizzed him, much as if he knew much more than his inquisitor. This irritated Kennedy and the more it did, the more the mobster smiled and chuckled to himself as he repeatedly took the Fifth Amendment. 'I thought only little girls giggled, Mr Giancana.' He was equally imperious with Carlos Marcello who, in the Senate Hearing Room, with its echoing high ceiling, all but spat at him. He took the Fifth Amendment time after time.

What amplified the problem for the Kennedys was that JFK was one of the sitting senators on the committee trying to take down Old Joe's mobster pals, people who knew of the long-time associations. As did Jimmy Hoffa, the firebrand deputy leader of the International Brotherhood of Teamsters, who took the animosity from Bobby Kennedy personally. He voiced it: 'You take an industry and look at the problems they came into while building it up, how they did it, who they associated with, how they cut corners. The best example is Kennedy's old man – to hear Kennedy grandstanding you might have thought I was making as much out of the Teamsters' pension fund as the Kennedys made out of selling whisky.'

Joe Kennedy was aghast at the goings on. J. Edgar Hoover had insisted to America that no such thing as the Mafia, organised crime, existed. But here was this own son rattling the skeletons in his own family closet. And smack in the middle of the hearings, in November 1957, in Apalachin, a small community in upstate New York, a gathering of fifty-eight gangland figures was raided by police and some names, including Santo Trafficante Jr, were arrested. From there being 'no Mob' the next day's headlines mentioned many leading Mafia men with long histories of arrests for murder and extortion, gambling and prostitution – and for being pivotal in the emerging drugs business. The Mob existed very much for Bobby Kennedy and he branded it 'a conspiracy of evil'.

As he did that in public, Joe Kennedy – who abhorred the Kennedys being anywhere near the Rackets Committee and feared the backlash – was negotiating with this very Mafia to get JFK into the White House. JFK was doing his own negotiating, risking everything by seeking high-quality sex at a good price in Havana and bedding women from Washington to Los Angeles. JFK viewed Havana like Las Vegas – what happened there, stayed there. He was like a ridiculously indulged schoolboy, especially on his frequent trips with George Smathers, who was friends with Meyer Lansky and even closer to Santo Trafficante Jr with whom he was overly trusting and informative. The US senators ordered up hookers like junket gamblers, like the thousands of American tourists desperate for rum, rhumba and a riot of sexual gratification they were afraid to seek on the mainland. In JFK's case it was a busman's holiday. In December 1957 he and George Smathers were guests of Ambassador Earl Smith and his wife, and JFK's one-time lover, the always lively Florence Pritchett Smith; a couple close to the Cuban dictatorship.

That holiday month, on 10 December, the twenty-one storey Riviera Hotel-Casino, a pedestal to the Mob overlooking the Malecón, the brash sea wall boulevard along the Caribbean on the northern edge of the profit promise which was Havana, opened. It was the creation of the Mafia's most ambitious and ruthless – nothing ever stopped the taking of a dollar – financial genius and empire builder, Meyer Lansky. He disdained JFK and his like as pleasure-seekers, not serious people, who sunned and sailed and indulged with women, unaware or disinterested in the mutterings of rebellion in Cuba. Lansky was moving funds to Zurich while JFK idled in the Comodoro Hotel and Casino cocktail bar where he met professional girls arranged by Lansky and Trafficante Jr. The mobsters wanted to keep those with influence in Washington on their side and intervene to help if the rebels became a serious threat. It was part of the *kompromat* sought by Santo Trafficante Jr through the two-way mirror view of JFK and Smathers in action with their Mafia-paid companions. Lansky was pro-active. He had already dealt with what he regarded as another obstacle to his gambling empire in Havana – the *Lord High Executioner* Albert Anastasia – while Nat King Cole sang at JFK's favoured Tropicana nightclub and Ernest Hemingway, America's applauded author, entertained at his hilltop home above the city, Finca Vigia. United Fruit controlled the Oriente sugar plantations, indeed the huge majority, about 85 per cent, of the Cuban economy was controlled by the United States. The more recent corruption was almost all-American.

PART TWO

MARRIED TO THE MOB

'The flower may look different, but the roots are the same.'
Chicago Don Sam Giancana on the
Mafia and the Kennedys, 1960

Chapter Nine

Gangsterismo

'There are always two deaths, the real one and the one people know about.'

Jean Rhys, *Wide Sargasso Sea*, 1966

Only ninety miles from mainland America, Cuba, a tiny island on the world stage, scene of his more reckless behaviour, was the beginning of the end for JFK, as events he could control, and a greater number that he could not, conspired to ferment his denouement. We'll never know if his personal history with Havana informed his later actions or if he learned anything helpful from his frequent visits in the 1950s.

Cuba grew tobacco, sugar cane and, away from the serried ranks of slot machines and the perfumed factories of hookers, away from the hubris of Havana where the poor concerned themselves with surviving not pleasure, much dissent.

Yet, a little revolution, the occasional outrage, can be helpful, for it proves you need a strong man, a dictator, in charge. There is no black-and-white and even the grey is faded. That political philosophy, indigenous to Central America and throughout the Caribbean, tells that whomever is in power, in control of the Army, the security of the state, is open to private enterprise, often the highest bidder. It's a turbulent zone where individuals make events and not vice versa and Meyer Lansky did just that with nearly half a million American dollars.

With that cash comfortable in his private Geneva account in 1952 the President of Cuba, Carlos Prio Socarrás, opened the way for the return of Fulgencio 'Batista' y Zaldívar, the upwardly mobile soldier who, after running a series of token Presidents, elected himself President proper of Cuba in 1940. He'd left the country in 1944 and moved to America with its blessing. He'd left his countrymen to be robbed blind by someone else, the new members of the Auténtico Party. At the same time, the US government and the Mafia had no wish for incipient revolutionary forces or communist groups to become a unified force. The simple way was to assassinate the leaders of such groups which threatened the ambitions of imperialism or gangsterism. On all this former President Fulgencio Batista was most helpful.

In exile, he ran his life from a suite at the Waldorf Astoria in Manhattan and from his home in Daytona Beach where he lived with his second wife: he'd married a young lover, Marta Fernandez. The Florida hacienda was on a vast estate with an English garden and the Halifax River connected to it by its own pier. He kept a small boat on the river. He played tennis at the Daytona Beach, Bath and Tennis Club (he was very good) and went to the cinema a couple of times a week: he saw Cagney in *White Heat* three times and Sinatra and Gene Kelly in *On The Town* twice. He had twelve personal bodyguards. The US government also supplied an around-the-clock protection team of four agents on duty. Batista's mid-distance control of Cuba was aided by his loyal followers. They'd fly out of Havana on Expresso Interamericano. The Santo Trafficante family was welcome. He also hosted Lansky there and other members of the Syndicate, Cuban politicians and soldiers and undercover operatives from several governments as well as secret agents from America north and south and central. Some agents worked for the Syndicate and the US government. Batista, for all his airs and graces, did too. These agents were willing and able to contract out on special missions. Lansky ran Batista's life. They would meet in New York or at the Martinique Hotel in Miami Beach but crucial talks were usually held in outdoor conference along the Halifax River beside Batista's garden. Such was the Mafia control of Batista that he could have retaken power in Cuba at almost any moment of his self-imposed exile. Even so, he was a touch premature.

It was all going to be wonderfully democratic with a three-way election involving the former Army Sergeant and President, Roberto Agramonte of the Orthodox Party, and Dr Carlos Hevia running as the contender for the Authentic Party. Batista was appearing on behalf of the Mafia Party but that didn't show on his electioneering materials, which involved dollar bills clasped in fists attached to strong arms and voters could accept it any way they wanted. Still, this unswerving support for the return of the prodigal son did not enthuse the constituency and their man was third in the polls.

Even worse, the *orishas* of the Santeria, the spirits Batista worshipped, warn him he was not going to triumph and the impatient Batista brutally engaged his own enterprise on 10 March 1952, proclaiming the elections corrupt and himself President. He took over, with Army support, police and military commands and the radio and television stations. With his dictatorship resurrected, his rivals were buried in the jungle, hung from lampposts and sugar-cane trees. And his Mafia partners celebrated the return of Cuba as their exclusive *Treasure Island* for the ever enriching if violent and chaotic world of Batista was back – and the cult of the Santeria, the mystical force that protects believers or acts malevolently if called upon. Batista, an initiated Santero and son of Changó, the ruler of fire, lightning, thunder and war, had the Army and black magic on side. He always won at the Mafia's roulette tables, his good luck rigged by secular entities. Installed as President, he forced out Socarras, who left with a shrug as ineffectual as his self-enriching regime. With him went much money and his second wife, Maria Dolores Tarrero-Serrano and their two children, Maria Antonetta and Maria Elena, his foreign minister and his minister of the interior.

The group's departure is freeze-framed, a photograph shows Senora de Prio in a silk suit and hat with black fishnet veiling, gloves and earrings and immaculate make-up. Her husband, the President of Cuba earlier in the day, is in suit and tie carrying in his arms a briefcase and his youngest daughter Maria Elena. This scene in the Cuban opera appears as richly cordial as circumstances allowed. As was the returning of the gambling boom to Havana. Batista, the US acknowledged the legitimacy of his leadership within two weeks, appointed a Minister of Gambling with a stipend of twenty-five thousand American dollars a year. Meyer Lansky quietly accepted this non-cabinet post and in turn appointed his Mafia henchmen as his leading assistants. Never documented but rumoured was that Joe Kennedy had a solid percentage in the Riviera Hotel-Casino. Lansky and Co. washed out the grifters and conmen: some card sharps ended up in the Caribbean, others were shoved in the overcrowded disease-ridden jails or deported and an unequivocal warning was issued to the casino operators to run clean houses, straight games, or face the consequences. Those being talked to knew who they were being warned by.

Santo Trafficante Jr, who attracted gamblers seven miles out from Havana to his Sans Souci casino-club with headline attractions (Liberace for a week, Kennedy favourite Marlene Dietrich for another) was accommodated by Lansky for his dignified crookery, his power and powerful connections in Cuba. Trafficante Jr imported Old Joe's friend, Johnny Rosselli, to run the Sans Souci casino. Rosselli, dapper, debonair, the dedicated fortune hunter, in every sense, was a perfect fit for the role. He could deal with the customers, the stars and the gambling: he knew how they all worked. He had all the Tinseltown tactics and had produced two film noirs: *Canyon City* (1948) about a mass escape from Colorado state penitentiary and *He Walked by Night*

(1948) a murder hunt police procedural about a cop killer; the good guys triumphed in both films which was an outcome Rosselli only ever championed on celluloid. With Rosselli's connections the low-budget 'B' picture, which had the former serviceman killer hiding his rifle in a blanket, received the attention of a blockbuster including a huge picture spread in *Life* magazine. Away from the cameras, Rosselli also represented the interests of Sam Giancana in power sharing deals with Lansky and others. In exchange for this all-for-one-one-for-all arrangement, the Chicago machine operated in Florida and throughout the Caribbean as well as achieving an even higher grip on Hollywood. Which was why many stars flew down to entertain in Havana. For the tourists it all added to the fun in the sun.

The come on for Cuba, from the National Tourism Corporation set up by Batista, to the vast audience of America so few miles away, a thirty-nine dollar Pan Am roundtrip from Miami, was of value for money sun and beaches, incredible food, and drink, of sensational sights, of the *foreign* feel, the hogsheads of molasses and sugar, stalks of bananas and entertainment. Indeed, the subliminal message was all about United Fruit's favourite entertainer Carmen Miranda, with extra maracas; how sensational it all could be was up to the visitor to discover.

Havana has the smell of the southern states of America, a coffee aroma like New Orleans, but spiked with the Spanish, the *cafe cortado*, the scented air from the blended olive oil cooking the potato and onion omelettes and sizzling spicy sausage, flavouring the bread toasting on the grills. The street stall shrimp somersaulting on the trays of ice while their big brothers, *gambas, langostinos, cigalas, carabineros and santiaguinos* fought for space with soles and turbots and cod, short, silvery eels, blue-backed sea bass, oysters, crab, mussels and a catalogue of clams. The other charms of Cuban hospitality were as exotic. Visitors, fuelled by *Cuba libre* from the maestro Mr Bacardi and the indulgent Coca-Cola Company, were quick to take off their inhibitions and put on more racy outfits.

Which was where sex became instantly available. While Batista's appointed henchmen plundered the profits of that business, Lansky followed the big money.

In the not-too-distant past, there were signs on the dirt roads around Havana, sort of advance warnings from the highwaymen, reading: '*Money or Mutilation*'. The casinos of Havana had better public relations: credit. They also had Presidential approval stamped all over them. There were new laws to make casino construction easier, tax breaks were available on asking, visas waived, sins forgiven; Havana was the new Lourdes, miracles happened. The airlines increased schedules, cruise liners made Havana a regular stop and clever shipping companies began car-transport ferries from along the Florida coast: many crewcuts driving bulldog Buicks and brightly coloured and tail-finned Chevrolets, Oldsmobiles and Plymouths, rolled into Cuba and along the Malecón. There was a price, of course, for providing the temptation. Initially, it was upwards of fifty-thousand dollars for a gaming license for a mid-sized casino. Some managed to chisel officials down to twenty-five thousand dollars which fed the police and lower echelon government officers their bonuses. With the profits involved it was a financial flea bite. It got better for those with one million or more dollars to invest in a hotel or a quarter-of-a-million in a club. The operation licence was gratis. The government also provided matching funds, tax incentives and free import of construction equipment.

The tiger bite was later: a giant lump sum payback to Batista after construction and an ongoing percentage of profits. With Lansky, he was almost a full partner, getting 30 per cent, counted each evening and collected by Batista's bagman. There was plenty to go around. The slot machine money, about a million dollars annually, even the cash from the parking meters, went to Batista's brother-in-law. There was no need for skimming, this was as straightforward as printing money. Meyer Lansky went about his empire building. The Montmarte Club was close to the somewhat Moorish Hotel Nacional which was owned by the Cuban government. When a casino complex with cabaret room, the Club Parisien, and bar-restaurant was created within the walls of the Nacional, it was sublet to Lansky. Santo Trafficante's International Amusements Corporation (IAC) provided the entertainment and on opening night Eartha Kitt, at her feline prime as a sex kitten, was the star. The IAC fed talent to the casinos, Nat King Cole, Johnny Mathis and Ella Fitzgerald, the premier names of jazz and cool. Every which way, the boys were earning. It was exquisite daiquiri diplomacy. They had casinos attached to the Capri, the Sevilla-Biltmore, the Commodoro, the Deauville and the mobsters kept these oceanfront money machines in around-the-clock working order. They also ran the gambling at JFK's favoured Tropicana, which was a Busby Berkeley cabaret all by itself in the jungle on the outskirts of town: the showgirls were startling looking and the best dancers with endless legs and smiles. The high kicks invited vertigo. On offer at the 'Paradise Under the Stars' was an escape into fantasy, a world where, for a price, all desires could be met. Lewis McWillie, who'd dealt blackjack in Las Vegas and killed a few people back east, ran the high-roller gaming room. He was visited by his friend Jack Ruby, a rascal who owned a nightclub in Dallas. US official records show they both spent a short time in prison following Castro's 1959 coup.

You can't want to take over even a small portion of the world without a smattering of megalomania. It wouldn't have been right for Meyer Lansky not to want to; he so fitted the role of a little man grasping for the top, for his personal kingdom; it was uncanny natural casting. He saw his castle as the Riviera Hotel-Casino, a dream project which had taken him nearly two years to fulfil.

In 1955, Batista, safely in Lansky's back pocket and with the gangster's voice in his good right ear, introduced Hotel Law 2074 with which his government went into partnership with the boys. Lansky planned to build a monument to his ambition with the Riviera, floors of double-bedroom suites into the sky.

He saw the Riviera as a repayment for the messy enterprise in Las Vegas, when Bugsy Siegel overreached everyone's patience with his grandiose behaviour at the Flamingo Hotel and was shot dead because of it. Yet, Lansky was equally ambitious. This was to be a jewel, a monumental achievement, a reflection of elegant Monte Carlo and luxury Las Vegas, the most upmarket carpet joint of them all. Which was why all the 'fixes' at home and abroad had to be solid. Batista's contribution to the Riviera was around six million dollars. Lansky and his investors, *we're all going to make a profit*, plunged in another eleven million dollars. It was a big bet. Everything from the bedding to the food and especially the gambling had to be completely taken care of. He wanted good gaming professionals and Cuban croupiers and dealers for the foreign ambience and public relations for Batista. And nothing was to interfere with business.

Albert Anastasia was doing just that. The legendary *Lord High Executioner* of Murder, Inc. had retained his intemperate ways. He still liked killing people. He liked money almost as much and was disenchanted with the profits tumbling out of Cuba where he had no action. He complained in a serious way to Meyer Lansky. He would not be told that he must remain quiet, stay out of the way *and let things develop for a time.* The grand opening of the Riviera was set for 10 December 1957, just in time for the holidays. This parcel of razzmatazz was cheap and arrogant, all veneer, much like those that created it, much like Cuba's capital. Yet, thousands were expected to be flying down to Havana to see Ginger Rogers. Anastasia's timing was way out. He made the mistake of not only irritating Lansky and then upsetting Lansky but did the unforgivable and did not listen to Lansky. That was too much. Lansky told Anastasia that there was no room for him on the island. It got worse. Anastasia began talking to the Cuban developers of the Hilton Hotel being planned for Havana. He would partner with them. The Hilton's architectural drawings showed it had two hundred rooms more than Lansky's Riviera.

Albert Anastasia was splattered all over the barber shop of the Park Sheraton Hotel on New York's 55th Street shortly after 10 a.m. on 25 October 1957. He'd left the Warwick Hotel where he kept an apartment and been taken there by Gino Merico, his bodyguard-driver who dropped his boss off, parked in the hotel's underground garage and went for a convenient stroll. Regular customer and big tipper Anastasia, who was known to the understandably friendly barbers as 'Don Umberto', climbed into the chair for his regular wet shave and hair trim round the ears and nostrils. Into the hotel which many New Yorkers knew as the Park Central, where Arnold Rothstein took a bullet through his monogrammed shirt just short of three decades earlier, two gunmen strode through the double glass doors of the barber shop. They were most efficient. Anastasia, like a hibernating bear, was dozing in the leather barber chair, his eyes closed, as the masked men pushed Franco his barber out of the way and shot the man who himself had so often killed to order. The bullets didn't seem to fuss Anastasia and he got up and went for his attackers: he'd reached toward their image in the mirror, desperately trying to grab them. From behind his struggle came more gunfire from the assassins. The *Lord High Executioner* fell to the floor, as did a discarded handgun. The professional hit, of which Anastasia would have approved, was complete. The seven Italian barbers on duty couldn't help the police in any significant way with their inquiries.

Albert Anastasia had tried to cut in on Meyer Lansky's gambling plans and that was not something to be allowed. In his world anything remotely of that nature was not at all possible. Anastasia's underboss, the quiet and traditionalist executive hoodlum Carlo Gambino, was standing not far off this violent stage. Gambino was an important friend of Lansky's from the early days and was now only a murder or two from the top job. Santo Trafficante Jr was staying at the Warwick Hotel the evening prior to Anastasia's violent passing. He'd left early in the morning for Idlewild Airport and a flight south for the opening some weeks later of the Riviera where Lansky told him Ginger Rogers couldn't sing to save herself. Happily, she resurrected herself by *wiggling her ass real good*.

Entertainment stars of the moment came out every night at the Riviera's Copa Room. Santo Trafficante's company provided popular attractions from Abbott and Costello to the Mexican funnyman Cantinflas and star singers Vic Damone and Johnny Mathis. The gamblers could have been on the original Riviera, in the south of France, for this Riviera was the venue where the high rollers came out in their finery. The jewels would have made Raffles' eyes pop, the gowns from European design houses, the tuxedos bespoke, the patent evening shoes handmade. This Mob-operated hotel and casino was the most respectable of places. Everything, including the gambling, was straight. Yet, the cross-cultural immensity of Cuba couldn't be totally disguised. Visitors came to Havana for the lavish decadence. There were vast profits for Batista's henchmen in sex tourism. Taxi drivers would offer pre-teen virgins, cute little boys and the hookers were hanging out the windows or cantering around corners. The casinos would treat high rollers, politicians with the right connections like JFK and visiting, and friendly, mobsters to the alternative offerings. Or they could choose *à la carte*. For the casino VIPs and wealthy tourists, the more sophisticated sex was in nightclubs where customers could decide on any combination of men and women, boys and girls, to perform live sex acts; girl-on-girl action was always the most popular. Other than the legendary 'Superman' who boasted a fourteen-inch penis which he'd display alongside an extended row of a dozen silver dollars before showing that it worked. At the Shanghai nightclub where he was a headliner, if that's the correct term, the tall, lean Cuban was a curiosity for New York gangsters and little ladies from Milwaukee who'd heard the gossip over dinner at their hotel. Superman, *El Toro*, was a tourist must-see, and no one ever complained or mentioned trades description disappointment.

There were also efforts to make the sex into a show, into entertainment, and routines from stage shows and Hollywood movies were adapted. There was a Marx Brothers number in which Harpo played a magical waiter pulling tableware from thin air. In the Shanghai version a couple at a restaurant table order coffee. From nowhere cups and saucers and spoons appear and then a pot of black coffee is poured. 'Where is the cream?' the woman inquires. The waiter pulls out his penis and, with a little encouragement from the *señora*'s fingers and lips, ejaculates into the cup.

The casinos, nightclubs, sexual shenanigans, off and on stage, delivered golden results. The Mob hotels in Havana all made money. Charles 'Charlie the Blade' Tourine out of Miami came in to run the casino at the Hotel Capri. They had roarin' twenties' gangster chic there, with the hand-stitch-tailored George Raft superbly playing the part of a meeter-and-greeter. Raft, who'd been brought there by Santo Trafficante Jr, was a cool front man. He was a quiet operator, wanted his comforts and not to be bothered. He was a man who took his afternoon nap no matter what was happening. He didn't like or cater for surprises and said as much when he talked to you, always with his eyes on your eyes. He'd played it that way in Hollywood when any career stretch was too much to trouble with. He'd prospered, survived, by not rocking the boat. He rolled out the tuxedo and the patter, slicked back someone else's hair – it was a *natural* toupée – and put on the welcome smile, and went to work. For others, he was his own attraction at what was the world's most sought-after playground. It intrigued many: Sarah Vaughan, Tony Martin and Jose Greco sang, Errol Flynn was the debauched adventurer who flirted with the rebels, Marlon Brando the young actor who was going to be the best method man ever, Ava Garner and Elizabeth Taylor brought glamour and looked for fun and Graham Greene came for the cocaine, bordellos and material for *Our Man in Havana*. It's difficult to imagine that the burlesque of Havana kept anyone ignorant of the endemic corruption of Cuba unless it was purposely avoided. The exploitation of the nation is what Fidel Castro used in his campaign against Batista in the process of building his own legend. Batista couldn't see it; the ultimate capitalist thought that with so much money around, the bearded jungle habitué would have no appeal.

Batista put Castro in jail but freed him in a public relations manoeuvre to reflect his benevolent dictatorship. PR worked both ways. It was put around that Castro had died in a jungle shoot-out. His following interview and photograph on the front page of *The New York Times* pretty much rebutted that and fanned the growing myth of Fidel Castro, a.k.a. 'Messiah'. Ambassador Earl Smith was advising President Eisenhower that Castro had to be 'dealt with'. The guerrilla manifesto tilted against the *desfalcadores*, the embezzling carpet-baggers, chiefly Lansky and the boys, responsible for the vivisection of Cuba.

Castro was seriously outraged that the name of José Martí, nineteenth-century freedom fighter and Castro hero, was on a street corner strip club. Indeed, it was a malignant symbol of Cuba being stripped bare. The gap between the have and have-nots was a chasm and widening every day. Dissidents, non-believers in profit, casino skimmers, thieves, presumed hooligans of any hue, who affronted the easygoing notion of anything goes were swiftly moved out of the way. They became target practice or were squeezed into prisons and if there wasn't room just hung up from trees or lamp posts as behavioural instruction. Those who got lucky were simply killed and not tortured or barbecued for fun first. It was a rule of terror by the kleptocrats and did nothing but fuel the revolutionary zeal of Castro and his followers. Every Batista atrocity added more hate and discontent. That brought more torture, firing squad executions and myriad barbaric acts which were executions in all but government terminology. It was evil and so much so that even America could no longer look away from the brutality, could they? Still, amazingly, while outside Havana the dissent grew with the sugar cane in the fields and in the neighbouring villages, the casino Mob kept hitting the jackpot, a cavalcade of cash deposited and cheques clearing at their account holding branches in Miami Beach, Palm Beach and sometimes Fort Lauderdale. The FBI watched every Havana flight. People were working hard, the money had to do that too. When construction began in 1958 on the Miami International Airport Hotel the majority of the investment capital was skimmed gambling money from Havana and similar funds from the Sands Hotel and the Freemont Hotel in Las Vegas, in which Joe Kennedy had investments.

Other monies came from a group of Los Angeles lawyers and international entrepreneur Jack Cooper who held much stock in the West Flagler dog track in Miami and the baseball team the Miami Merlins; Cooper sold a squadron of P-51 jet fighters to the Dominican Republic and, courtesy of Generalissimo Rafael Trujillo, ran a casino at the Jaragua Hotel in Santo Domingo. J. Edgar Hoover and the powers of law and order watched the corporate structure being established in front of their binoculars.

The US government's concerns for Cuba were not righteous; they despised Batista but they feared Castro and that newly coined 'domino principle', flicking through the islands so close to their shores. It was not a domestic political issue for America: everybody who was anti-communist was a friend. The situation for President Eisenhower and those who sought ultimate power was mirroring what had gone before in Guatemala. The Mob were in with the gambling and the approval of the government, the despot government was in place with the approval of America and the scaffolding holding up all the arrangements was very shaky. Richard Nixon had toured the Caribbean in 1955. He laid it on: Batista was a reincarnation of Abraham Lincoln; Generalissimo Rafael Trujillo, the butcher who wept for the men he killed, was Nixon's best friend. In Haiti the hapless Nixon tried to be a man of the people. He talked to a peasant woman who snapped: '*Tell this coconut to get out of the way.*' This was translated as: *Nice to meet you.* Which was all the encouragement Nixon required: *What is the donkey called?* The reply: *He's crazy. It's called a donkey.* It was a trifle in the ongoing perils of diplomacy. The Mob were also being diplomatic: they took a financial interest in a casino in Port-au-Prince, an altogether different voodoo to that practised by madman François 'Papa Doc' Duvalier's Haiti, and won some casino concessions in next door Dominican Republic with the Marine-trained dictator's dictator Rafael Trujillo. The Mafia and the Kennedys would in short time be dealing and risk-taking with the same unsavoury characters. If needs must, there's no need for transparency.

Trujillo was evil, a twentieth-century Caligula. As an Army officer he had discovered a penchant for rape; when he took power in 1930 and became President he ordered a constant supply of virgins for his bedchamber. He would humiliate his government officers by demanding they sacrifice the virginity of their daughters. When people attacked or mildly criticised his regime they vanished. When he got angry at the President of Venezuela he didn't bother with letters of protest in the diplomatic pouch. He tried to blow him up. He broke off with the Vatican and got a Dominican sorcerer to attempt to kill the Pope with the *evil eye*. Yet, Trujillo ranted against the communists and cleverly advertised which side he supported in the Cold War. So, for America, he was politically acceptable, an *anti-communist* degenerate, with a member of the diplomatic corps explaining: *The fact that they murder their enemies or torture them doesn't usually come up over coffee cups.*

It was similar games in Cuba, where Batista had grown chubby, yet all that flesh couldn't conceal the horns, the satanic black holes where his eyes once were. He'd been dealing dirty with this country for such a long time. His Havana was comprised of streets driven by greed while all around the island so many more were in desperate need and had nothing to lose by taking up arms with Fidel Castro. Batista's secret police, the SIM, watched and murdered them. The CIA and FBI were monitoring it with haphazard vigilance. The revolution was the only movement with proper purpose. At least they knew something: they wanted change. The FBI surveillance noted many meetings and departures from Cuba. One of them was by George Raft; he was off too. He was going to film for sixteen weeks at Universal Studios in Los Angeles and on location a two-hour drive down Pacific Coast Highway, with a stop for coffee at Laguna Beach, at the Hotel del Coronado on Coronado Island across the curving high-wire act of a bridge from San Diego. It was a Billy Wilder picture called *Some Like It Hot*. His co-stars were Tony Curtis, Jack Lemmon and Marilyn Monroe. He returned to the Hotel Capri on Christmas Eve, 1958, and began playing George Raft. The act, the posture and silk tuxedo were impeccable. The timing was not.

Fifteen days earlier President Eisenhower's personal envoy had told Batista that if he stood down immediately there would be sanctuary for him back at his peaceful home by the Halifax River. A week before Christmas Day he was given another message from Eisenhower with somewhat more edge: America would no longer support his government or give him asylum. Meyer Lansky was in Florida at the time but with a black cat's timing he flew back for the noisy and boisterous New Year's Eve party at the Riviera. None of the revellers heard the news on Radio Rebelde that Castro and Che Guevara were doorstepping them.

President Batista knew. For his Hogmanay celebrations, Batista folded his dictator's hand, took the money – about three hundred million dollars – and ran. It was 2.44 a.m. on 1 January 1959 when Fulgenico Batista flew for the last time from Havana on an Aerovias Q Douglas DC4 to the Dominican Republic. He wore his uniform and the women with him wore the evening dresses they'd put on for a sumptuous sit-down New Year's Eve banquet. The flight from the military base Camp Columbia took Batista and his runaway entourage into the black night out over Cuba and to the east, beneath the clouds which could never hide the detritus of his years in power, of his lethal and louche legacy as *Presidente de la Republique de Cuba.* Four transport planes followed him bringing along the spoils of his dictatorship. On the ground the rebel forces were a few hundred miles from Havana where there was dancing the streets, a zany jubilation like no other for a long, long time. As the people celebrated and the absentee Batista's loyal Army tried to figure out what to do to the mobsters who'd played such a part in events, in the corruption which led to this moment, were considering how much it might cost to pay off this guy Fidel Castro. As that first day of 1959 moved on the charismatic Che Guevara led a rebel victory at the Battle of Santa Clara as Fidel Castro's 26 July Movement began to take power.

The rebel troops weren't so successful when they invaded the *Salon Rojo*, the Red Room, of the Hotel Capri. They met a tough guy in a tuxedo. The revolution interrupted George Raft's routine and his sex life. He didn't like that. He was just getting excited. As the New Year's Eve festivities had settled towards dawn he'd sent his lady for the evening, a former Cuban beauty queen, to his room. He'd given her a gentle kiss and told her to wait for him. She slid between silk sheets and when he got there the invitation to join her was enthusiastic. He was doing just that and whispered '*Feliz Ano Neuvo*' when machine-gun fire began rattling around the lobby of the hotel. He called the front desk but screams and shouts and gunfire deafened him. He did hear, *Mr Raft, the revolution is here.* Pioneering gangster Owen Madden's one-time associate and personal driver, George Ranft, took the time to put on his George Raft tuxedo uniform and headed for the trouble. He was greeted by shouts about bandits and madcap confusion. The gunfire in the streets was real and he saw people collapsing dead. A mob of youngsters rioting turned the hotel into a target for their bricks and bottle missiles. Next, the revolution was right in front of him with around one hundred Castro patriots charging into the hotel. One or two sprayed machine-gun bullets around the bar. George Raft knew the scene. He'd played variations of it. He climbed upon a table and cried at them to calm down. They did. In the silence a girl pointed at him: *It's George Raft the movie star.* It was a good day to find a fan. Raft, wishing he had a script to follow, said that he and the hotel were neutral and if everyone just behaved food and drink would be made available. It turned the revolutionaries quite docile. Some did what Raft thought of as *lightweight looting* but others quietly drank Coca-Cola and looked for bottles of Bacardi. He'd saved himself and the hotel. He went back to his routine and the former Miss Cuba, who happily found all the excitement *exciting.* The Riviera Hotel was not so lucky in its treatment. It became crowded by the people and their farm animals, and particularly messy were their pigs. It's a colourful incongruity, an *Animal Farm* image, the fat, pink animals freely indulging themselves amid all the shiny glass and marble and pretension of the hotel lobby, restaurants and the casino. Shit, of course, happens. Which the Mafia men were in and, quickly, they made sure the Kennedys were too. The price for the White House had gone up.

Chapter Ten

Candid Camera

'*Once you were in the sex compartment, you weren't a person anymore.*'

Diana de Vegh, 1997

JFK's sex life all but spoiled everything. Distraction was always a problem. He believed his brain worked better after he had sex. He often lied to himself as well as to so many others. He was being offered to America like some Hollywood idol and movie stars need to love themselves and need to be needed. The candidate sold as *handsome Jack Kennedy* was no different. He'd take chances as if he was Teflon-coated. It was decades after one of his most high-risk dalliances, with a teenaged student, before this particular indiscretion was exposed. It was wild and irrational. He was twice her age.

He was on the campaign trail for the Presidency and sleeping with Diana de Vegh, whom he first met in 1958, when she was starting at Radcliffe College, a women's liberal arts institution in Cambridge, Massachusetts. He gave a campaign speech in a Boston ballroom while running for re-election to the Senate. He appeared at her table, telling her date, 'Give me your seat, so a tired old man can sit next to a pretty girl.' He then invited her to an event the following week and soon their relationship began. 'I was twenty years old with a full supply of hormones and madly in love with this compelling man,' she testified in 2021. Yet, years earlier when she spoke anonymously to investigative reporter Seymour Hersh for his myth-busting *The Dark Side of Camelot* (Little, Brown, 1997) she said she was only nineteen at their first encounter, statutory rape since the age of consent at the time was twenty-one: 'There would be signs of special attention. Yes, in public. And that was very flattering. Somehow it didn't register with me at any deep level that what I was doing was absolutely immoral, absolutely atrocious behaviour,' she told Seymour Hersh.

De Vegh insisted to Hersh that those around JFK and most of the Press knew of the affair. How could they not? But he'd charmed them too. He could do no wrong. A quarter of a century on from the anonymous testimony we know more about what a sex predator he was.

She was picked up from her off-campus home by 'Dave', JFK's discreet driver, and taken to wherever he was campaigning. His political staff would call her 'sweetheart' and bring her coffee before he joined her for the drive home. 'You know I'm working pretty hard for just one vote here,' he flirted.

On the election trail, Joe Kennedy could not monitor his son, as his overbearing presence would have made for poor public relations. JFK had to be seen to be his own man. His sexual adventures – often, bizarrely, applauded as macho derring-do – were accepted as long as the women involved could not damage him politically. De Vegh said that the routine was *easy and emotionally convenient* because Jackie Kennedy did not get involved in suburban campaign events. The secret lovers would meet at his Boston apartment and the Carlyle Hotel, New York. Reflective in later life, she was blind and eighty-three when she spoke to the digital weekly *Air Mail* in 2021 saying: 'Young woman, great man. Predictable outcome: heartbreak for her, no consequences for him. He was still in the throes of the male mythology of his time: see a pretty woman, have a pretty woman.' She told friends that from the first rush of the affair, JFK maintained 'a hold over me' and explained that was because of his 'power'. He used that to persuade her to move to Washington when he was President. Indeed, the night before his inauguration, on the cold Washington day of 20 January 1961, she said they slept together at his family home in Georgetown where he lived with his wife and two children. She found out, as the world was to eventually discover, that she was only one of many women enchanted into his White House private quarters to have dinner before *retiring* to the Lincoln Bedroom. On inauguration eve, as they lay in bed together, she discovered something else – a chance remark revealed JFK had no idea that a man he was considering for a high-level job was her father. Or anything about her or her past and future hopes. She stuck it out for another two years, kept nearby with a 'make-work White House job dealing with international affairs'. Finally – and she explains always being 'available' for JFK down to a misplaced 'love' – the true sense of being used finally persuaded her to break off. ('The whole idea of conferred specialness – "You go to bed with me, I'll make you special" – we've seen a lot of that with Harvey Weinstein, the disgraced sex monster Hollywood mogul,' she said after going public.)

She told *Air Mail*: 'When I was twenty, John Kennedy had all the markers of a romantic hero. But this is not a romantic story. Back then I thought it was. Was I a dope? For sure, so what? Twenty-year-olds are not supposed to be wise. Ardent and hopeful, yes, heart on sleeve for sure. Underneath, fearful, unmoored. How much I did not know.' What we get from Diana Vegh's testimony is yet more evidence that the Kennedys fatally believed they could brazen their way through any situation, they were so special. As a very primary witness to JFK she offered a most telling remark: 'I think that somehow between his money, his position, his charm, his whatever, he was caught up in feeling that he was buffered. That people would take care of it. There is that feeling that you are not accountable; that the laws of the world do not apply to you. Laws had never been applied to his father and to him.'

She coloured the background of JFK as a feckless child of privilege and he most certainly went on endorsing that with his sexual addiction. In files finally available in the twenty-first century, there are constant references to his trysts, assignations and encounters, chance meetings, overnight stays, parties with 'hookers', all for the desk of J. Edgar Hoover. Some names and details are redacted but the unholy pattern is most clearly established. The list of women sneaking in and out of his homes and meeting up for quickies on the road is almost endless. This is a politician preparing for the Presidential elections in 1960. He's sleeping with Hollywood actresses including Marilyn Monroe, then the world's greatest sex symbol, and pursuing, it appears from the files, almost every woman he meets. Joe Kennedy made deals which highlight a lifetime of shabby hypocrisies. With hindsight, it all seems too astonishing to believe. The American media decided the best way to approach JFK's sex life – ignore it.

Pamela Turnure was gorgeous. A Georgetown girl, she worked in JFK's office as a receptionist and secretary from 1958 until his election when she became the first Press Secretary to a First Lady in American history, working for Jackie Kennedy. The gossip then was that JFK wanted her 'available' and his wife wanted to keep track of her whereabouts. Turnure died in May 2023, having observed a lifetime omertà over her relationship with JFK, yet several Kennedy authorities identified her as another JFK lover less than half his age. Following 2023 FOIA requests, the FBI denied keeping files on a little-known Washington landlady, Florence Kater, but other sources reveal more, including claims by Mrs Kater about Turnure, to whom she rented a Georgetown apartment. She told Federal agents that she had seen JFK leaving the apartment in the middle of the night and at breakfast time. She said she and her husband Leonard used two secret tape recorders to pick up sounds of the couple having sex. With her claims was a photograph she said she took of JFK leaving his lover's home at 3 a.m. one morning in 1958.

She said she and her husband first discovered the affair when they heard someone tossing pebbles at her second-floor window: 'We looked out and saw Senator Kennedy standing in our garden yelling, "If you don't come down, I'll climb up by your balcony."' She said in a letter that an angry JFK later confronted her and her husband in the street and told them to desist 'spreading lies'. She continued her campaign, writing to dozens of news outlets, all of which buried the allegations about the fresh-faced, charming politician running for the Presidency. Kennedy contacted the family's favourite lawyer – the man who'd coated a veneer over JFK's affair with the suspect German spy Inga Arvad – the Kennedy laundromat, James McInerney, to intervene. In the filed letter, Mrs Kater said she and her husband met seven times with McInerney. Whatever happened, the Press ignored the story and never published even a 'blind' item; *The Washington Star* newsroom which did investigate Mrs Kater's claims was swiftly warned off by the senior management. To publish and not be damned, a newspaper would need a journalist in, or at least under, the bed where JFK was in action. Even then the Kennedy influence was such that no derogatory scoop was likely to be printed. It remains sensitive.

Pam Turnure began working for the Kennedy White House in January 1961, days before the President's inauguration. She told Mrs Kennedy that her husband looked a little tired that day. Neither lady knew how busy he'd been with Diana de Vegh. Or noticed him flirting with one of his personally invited guests, the Hollywood actress Angie Dickinson, before he took the oath of office, at age forty-three, the youngest person ever elected President of the United States. Something that wouldn't have happened without the help of family friends.

Angie Dickinson had become another interest during Kennedy's campaign. By then, the unknown, to all but the cognoscenti, Judith Campbell Exner was very much a rival for John Kennedy's time. She grew up in Pacific Palisades, which looks south across Pacific Coast Highway to Peter Lawford's harem of a beach home. Aged eighteen in 1952, she married actor Bill Campbell, who said that his bride quickly came to believe she was 'missing out' by marrying so young. They separated in 1958 and a year later she began an affair with Frank Sinatra which ended, as had Sinatra's brief romance with Marilyn, when he tried to get her to take part in a threesome. Still, Exner remained part of his entourage. Which was startling eclectic. Only a few weeks before 2 January 1960 – when JFK formally announced his candidacy to be his nation's thirty-fifth President, his father invited Sinatra to lunch at Hyannis Port. He wanted Sinatra to engage the help of Sam Giancana in getting votes for his son in West Virginia against his rival for the nomination, Hubert Humphrey. JFK needed to show well there. He promised that Sinatra would be appointed ambassador to Rome. West Virginia wasn't just Protestant, but anti-Catholic and the labour unions backed Humphrey, angered at Bobby Kennedy's conduct during the McClellan hearings. The Kennedys needed to twist the odds.

In later years, Sinatra's daughter Tina said Joe Kennedy told her father, 'I think that you can help me in Illinois and West Virginia with our friends. You understand, Frank, I can't go. They're my friends, too, but I can't approach them. But you can.' She said her father met with Giancana on a golf course and said of Kennedy, 'I believe in this man and I think he's going to make us a good President, with your help.'

Sinatra, of course, had other friends. He introduced Judith Exner to JFK in Las Vegas in February 1960, at the Sands Hotel, where he was filming *Oceans 11* with a familiar selection of friends: Dean Martin, Sammy Davis Jr, Joey Bishop, Peter Lawford and Angie Dickinson. As Sinatra's guest, JFK stayed with his brother Teddy Kennedy at the Sands and each evening watched his host's 'Rat Pack' put on a show at the Summit Room. Sinatra picked him out of the audience: 'Ladies and gentlemen, Senator John F. Kennedy, from the great state of Massachusetts ... the next President of the United States.'

Exner said she and Kennedy 'clicked' and the only doubt she had in their sexual relationship was that he constantly demanded she 'service' him. Marilyn makes the same complaint in her diary.

Then, the Sicilian curved ball – Sinatra introduced Judith Exner to the psycho-Mafia man Sam Giancana. A tragic threesome was established. Exner was already acquainted with Handsome Johnny Rosselli, aware of the circles in which she was travelling. Los Angeles police chief William Parker's OCID monitored all the relationships but found it embarrassingly difficult to disguise JFK's behaviour. Many knew about Monroe and Kennedy and today it's all but impossible to imagine how such a relationship, America's screen goddess and the nation's golden boy politician could remain hidden from the public. The time, the atmosphere, the political climate and the Kennedy misogyny and money all played a role in runaway madness, opening JFK and his White House campaign to such vulnerability. Which was where Judith Exner and her other close friend, Sam Giancana, entered.

Tina Sinatra offered her analysis: 'The Mafia were very smart. They knew that power and control would keep this country together. My dad grew up with gangsters next door. He was living with them. They were his personal friends and he's not going to cast away a friend. It's very Italian and probably gave him a little more in common with the Mob types. These weren't people that Joe [Kennedy] didn't know. He had these relations as well. My grandmother called him "that son of a bitch". They did use the underworld to put their golden boy over the top. They [didn't] hesitate to ask for favours; the Kennedys were very able to ask for anything they needed. And I think they were accustomed to getting it. Everybody was duped.'

They were patient, as JFK went on the campaign trail through Illinois, Indiana, West Virginia, North Dakota, New Mexico and Nevada. In Las Vegas the Kennedy boys indulged themselves, seeking the Democratic Party nomination. Sam Giancana's brother Chuck and godson, also called Sam, in their book *Double Cross* (Skyhorse Publishing, 2016), replay Giancana's extortion expectations because of the Kennedy brothers' womanising: 'He'd learned they were not only adulterous but emotional and jealous, as well. It was no secret that Joe's sons had inherited their father's penchant for a good time. Mooney [Sam Giancana] said Joe had frequented the Cal-Neva, placed bets and banged his share of broads every chance he got. And in the early 1950s, Mooney confided, Jack had followed in his father's footsteps, secreting himself away in a discreet Cal-Neva chalet. Mooney himself had been at more than a few of the Kennedy Cal-Neva "parties". The men had sex with prostitutes – sometimes two or more at a time – in bathtubs, hallways, closets, on floors, almost everywhere but in a bed. The Kennedys liked the thrill that came with the kinky and clandestine. They liked to think they were above the morality of the "other classes". Mooney was convinced that if he could find the right woman, he might be able to put Jack Kennedy in a corner. Mooney knew a chink in the armour when he saw one.'

Chuck Giancana said his brother regularly met with Joe Kennedy and his Presidential candidate son during the primaries, in Florida, New York, Chicago, and at the Cal-Neva in Tahoe. He said he told him: 'Jack's worried about a few states. Mostly West Virginia, because of the Bible Belt there and the coal miners' union ... hell, the whole union vote back east is a problem. I told Skinny [D'Amato, an associate] to tell Joe [Kennedy] that I'll take care of West Virginia on one condition – that after Jack's President, Joe Adonis [Lucky Luciano's mobster friend thrown out of America in 1953] is allowed back in the country. The guys out east want Adonis back. Jack and his old man couldn't say "Yes" fast enough ... didn't have any problem at all bringing a deported gangster back into the country. So, we've got a deal for West Virginia.

'I did explain to them that once we get past the convention and start on the national campaign, the Teamsters can't come out publicly for Jack ... that would look pretty fishy given what the McClellan committee did to Hoffa and his boys ... let alone the stunts Bobby pulled. But behind the scenes, no problem ... I've already got it worked out with Jimmy [Hoffa] to skim a couple million out of the union for Jack's national campaign, based on Kennedy's agreement that Bobby will leave Hoffa and the Teamsters alone. The entire Kennedy family might appear to bring out the vote for Jack but Mooney said behind the scenes was where the vote would be won. He sent Skinny D'Amato to West Virginia with a suitcase full of money. Mooney confided that because the state was deemed so critical, he'd put in half a million of his own money: "Jesus, we even had to muscle the taverns to convince 'em to play Frank's song "High Hopes" on the jukeboxes. Those hillbillies hate the idea of an East Coast, Irish-Catholic President."'

Sam Giancana wanted JFK nominated, elected and then manipulated. By him. With his victory in West Virginia, beating Hubert Humphrey by a margin of 29 per cent, the Mafia's favoured candidate for President was on the way for the Democratic National Convention in Los Angeles, starting on 11 July 1960.

JFK had Judith Exner on his arm and, more of a difficulty, in his *and* Sam Giancana's bed. There's an amateur film of the fatal evening of 7 February 1960, when Judith Exner met JFK for the first time. It was at Frank Sinatra's table at the Sands Hotel lounge and with her under the dim lights were Peter Lawford, JFK and the equally sex-greedy Teddy Kennedy in the Garden Room. She'd already successfully fought off the twenty-eight-year-old Kennedy, who'd tried to seduce her in her hotel room. JFK addressed a meeting for nearly six hundred people in the city's convention centre and went on to a select cocktail party where several dozen wealthy Democrats – casino and hotel people – met him and wrote big cheques.

After the business, the dinner. While Sinatra sang for his supper, the Kennedy brothers sat down with Peter and Pat Lawford and Judith Exner. Teddy mauled her some more, his brother Kennedy fascinated her. He made her feel she was the only person in the room. The next day, at noon when she was still half asleep, the telephone by her bed rang: 'Hi ... this is Jack Kennedy. I'd very much like us to have lunch...'

Chapter Eleven

High Hopes

'Keep On Running.'
Jackie Edwards, 1965; the Spencer Davis Group, 1965

Most of the Hollywood crowd supported JFK for President. While the Mob saw money and influence, the stars confused charisma with competence, a bad habit in a town where celebrity equates achievement. Cash might be king but a shiny, impenetrable perception wins votes and the power follows. Nothing could be allowed to taint it. Kennedy aides and many, many associates, some looking for personal advancement, issued half-hearted warnings and were often engaged to make a potential *one-night stand* scandal vanish.

If the situation was more threatening, then proficient operators like Carmine Bellino, a former FBI agent and lawyer, working for Bobby Kennedy and a former 'personal secretary' to Joe Kennedy, would intervene. A trusted staff fixer, Bellini specialised in dealing with organised crime and corrupt trade union officials, knowing everything that was going on but closeting information and actions. He'd wiretapped one of his employers' political opponents who tried to expose JFK's relationship with Diana de Vegh.

Much of Bellini's job, for the moment, was covering up the constant, brief entanglements of JFK in Hollywood amid the malicious machinations of the town's onetime mogul Joe Kennedy. And controlling his ongoing affairs with Judith Exner and others, including one which continues to provoke conspiracy theories. JFK was involved with a carousel of women, most young and intellectually clever, but was besotted by Mary Pinchot Meyer who, in 1958, had divorced her husband Cord Meyer, a CIA agent. She had a colourful story, accused in 1953 by Joe McCarthy of being a communist, she socialised with such characters as James Jesus Angleton, the CIA's Witchfinder General and one-time close ally of Britain's great traitor, Kim Philby, but was defended by America's intelligence services controllers, Allen Dulles and, importantly, a man called Frank Wisner who watched over, with suspicion, many JFK affairs. The dangerous liaison with Mary Pinchot Meyer remains mysterious.

It was concurrent with many others but brought JFK even more directly into the spook community. If J. Edgar Hoover's FBI knew almost all, the CIA knew the rest, was how the spies thought in 1960 in Washington. 'That was a dangerous relationship. Jack was in love with Mary Meyer. He was certainly smitten with her, he was heavily smitten. He was very frank with me about it,' was how Charles Bartlett, a JFK intimate, recalled the affair in a 2008 interview. Yet, for all the 'love', she was only one of half a dozen women on the books at the time. Putting cynicism aside, in October 1963, JFK wrote an unsent letter, written on White House stationery and retained by his personal secretary Evelyn Lincoln: 'Why don't you leave suburbia for once – come and see me – either here – or at the Cape next week or in Boston the 19th. I know it is unwise, irrational, and that you may hate it – on the other hand you may not – and I will love it. You say that it is good for me not to get what I want. After all of these years – you should give me a more loving answer than that. Why don't you just say yes.' The letter is signed

'J'. Almost exactly one year after that letter was written Mary Pinchot Meyer was killed on a towpath along the Potomac River in Washington. The murder remains unsolved. Even those in the media and government agencies who knew of the JFK link were too intimidated to publicly make a connection.

It was to be Judith Exner who was the first to seriously disassemble the Kennedy/Camelot myth. She'd kept her secrets for sixteen years but was quizzed by the Senate Select Committee on Assassinations in 1975 and – on the betrayed assurance of anonymity – admitted she'd been the lover of JFK and of Johnny Rosselli and Sam Giancana. Frank Sinatra made the introductions. She was only identified as a *'close friend of President Kennedy [who] had frequent contact with the President'* in a report published on 20 November 1975. It was enough for her to go public especially with the report's zinger: *'FBI reports and testimony indicate that the President's friend was also a close friend of John Rosselli and Sam Giancana and saw them both during this same period.'*

Sitting on a yacht in San Pedro Harbour, Los Angeles, with her husband Dan Exner, this femme fatale didn't look like a femme fatale when Douglas Thompson met her in 1976. She was conservatively dressed in a white shirt and tailored, navy-blue slacks and carried a jacket with an expensive Beverly Hills department store, Bullocks Wilshire, label showing. She was forthright and assured. The purpose of the meeting was for her to elaborate on what she had written in *My Story*, her account of her time with President Kennedy and the Mafia; to explain such incredible circumstances where one young woman could find herself seduced and used by such powerful men, and become central to events which caused historical malfunction.

Exner presented herself as naive and unknowing, sticking closely to her account of events, with some variances on the murky theme of the JFK-Giancana illicit understanding. She maintained this until her death from breast cancer, aged sixty-five, in September 1999. But her relationships belied that innocence.

In her late teens, as Judith Immoor, she belonged to what her husband Bill Campbell said was 'the young Hollywood set', one around which Johnny Rosselli prowled. Their six-year marriage began in 1952 and by that time she knew many more people. Her husband was a talented actor. He could turn himself to all manner of roles, from co-starring and singing in Elvis's first movie *Love Me Tender* (1956) to appearing as a Klingon warrior in *Star Trek*. Through him his wife met stars like Presley and became friends with Angie Dickinson and Juliette Prowse; she liked to be part of show business, of Hollywood. But for Bill Campbell who died, aged eighty-seven, in April 2011, there was always a mystery: 'How she ever met the President, I don't know.' He was being kind. The meeting was orchestrated – it gave the Mob a contact within the immediate White House circle. And it gave the young Judith Exner more celebrity contact than she could have imagined. She was a bright, attractive young woman who easily mixed in powerful circles. She was a Californian 'party girl', a fine decoration in a glamorous world.

Exner had a perfect pedigree for this particular game. She was the daughter of Irish-American parents and her father, Frederick Immoor, earned well as the chief draughtsman for an architectural firm. He liked to spend and his daughter was brought up living a high life (at Frank Sinatra's Palm Springs home, she questioned why the singer owned such a 'small house'). She had a tutor and there was much help around the house. Robert Wagner also lived in the San Fernando Valley and they dated. He introduced her to Bill Campbell, who explained: 'They didn't want her to get married to me because Mama was a very pushy Hollywood mother who wanted her daughters [older sisters Joan and Jacqueline] to be movie stars. There is no way that she could have done so with Judith because Judith just didn't have the talent. Or the interest. But Mama felt that I would get in the way.' He had the opposite effect; they mixed with the ambitious young Hollywood group of actors and actresses. There were problems. 'She was a good-looking girl and there were plenty of guys paying attention to her. The divorce was pretty amiable. Judy was not a demanding girl. She didn't try to mangle me in terms of money. We were too immature for marriage. Judy's main concern was with her looks and her clothes. Nothing much beyond that interested her. I'm not saying she was dumb, but she was no great intellectual either.'

She had taste and elegance but the thought of work never occurred to her. She had alimony and a small private income. She was also a perfect, identikit mistress for JFK, an adventure easier to disguise than dalliances with Marilyn Monroe. In terms of exposure, of risk, Judith Exner was low for high returns. Supposedly, she could do no harm, she was discreet and had no strong political views. Her policy belief was in having a good time.

For J. Edgar Hoover she was yet another woman in his JFK file. The FBI director cross-linked her with Sam Giancana. His ever-watchful agents reported that little Judith would leave President Kennedy's bed and trip off to Chicago to meet with the Mafia boss. Hoover was delighted. This gave him wonderful leverage and he ordered a full-scale investigation into Judith Exner. He discovered quite a party going on. FBI agents, several sent from out-of-town offices, were soon working out of the Federal Building in Los Angeles. They'd meet for coffee at a doughnut shop across the street in Gayley Avenue in Westwood for unofficial briefings. They monitored flights to Las Vegas. Angie Dickinson was a regular, playing Sinatra's wife in *Ocean's 11*, as were the cast's friends visiting Vegas at weekends. Judith Exner was a regular for the downtime parties. Which led to that first, lazy lunch in the Nevada sunshine with JFK. He wanted to impress her and invited her to his Press Conference by the main swimming pool of the Sands Hotel. He was in mid-speech when she appeared and he stopped, looked at her and announced, 'Hi Judy, I'll be right with you when we finish.' It was audacious but he believed a safe way of operating with these extra women in his life. There were often more women than men in his audience and far more women than men in the groups of campaign workers pursuing his Presidential dream for him.

People and the Press, respectful, reticent and not too inquiring, were used to seeing him with smart, attractive females and never suspicious. He told Judith Exner he'd borrowed the patio of Frank Sinatra's suite, which was much more intimate than the restaurant and there they would be able to talk through lunch. He would persuade her to speak about herself, the Catholicism, the Irish blood which they shared. She whispered Hollywood secrets: 'He could never get enough gossip.' Or sex. JFK was enamoured and as his relationship with Judith Exner developed, she would become more than a casual fling.

That evening in Las Vegas, the Presidential hopeful's supporters staged a fanfare party. Gloria Cahn, the wife of songwriter Sammy Cahn, swooped on JFK like a mother hen. She gave Judith Exner the beady eye and led the candidate away to meet and greet the Democratic Party faithful. He was quickly back by the side of Judith Exner but for them the evening ended there.

The next day back in Beverly Hills a dozen red roses arrived from Kennedy. He telephoned in the evening. The calls began to be regular, from all over America where he was chasing votes. Judith Exner was flabbergasted and flattered to the point of exhilarating madness: in the middle of this great political battle the man who would be President stopped the action to telephone *her*. He told her how much he missed her. How much she interested him. He would say he was tired or elated depending on how that day's campaigning had gone. He told her how to find him any time of the night and day by routine calls through his secretary. Exactly one month after meeting in Las Vegas they became lovers in Room 1651 of the Plaza Hotel in New York. It was the eve of the New Hampshire primary in which JFK triumphed, a win which vastly improved his chances of being the Democratic Party's Presidential nominee.

Two weeks after that encounter, on 7 March 1960, Judith Exner went to Miami for the Rat Pack at the Fontainebleau

Hotel, where Meyer Lansky had regular meetings. She had a quiet drink with Sinatra and he introduced her to Joe 'Stingy' Fischetti whose brothers Charlie and Rocco were heavyweight members of Al Capone's outfit. Joe Fischetti was a Mafia minder for Sinatra and reported to Joe Kennedy's friend Frank Costello. An earlier minder had been Sam Giancana. Judith Exner met him at the Fontainebleau Hotel four days later. She went to a party and was called over by Sinatra who was sitting with Joe Fischetti and another man to whom she was introduced as Sam Flood. He took her hand and said: 'It's a great pleasure to meet you, Judy. A very real pleasure.' Smiling, he looked into her eyes:

'Do you mind if I say something to you, Judy?'

She didn't think that she really minded at all.

'You're far too beautiful to be wearing junk – excuse me – I mean costume jewellery. A beautiful girl like you should be wearing real pearls and diamonds and rubies.'

'A girl like me sometimes does.'

'No offence, please. Real pleasure meeting you. Hope to see you again soon.'

It was that sinister Sicilian courtesy you might hear in a Scorsese movie but Judith Exner reported that was how it went. By then, Sam Flood, Mr Gold and to his associates Mooney, Giancana was one of the most powerful gangsters in America. He had hoodlums, accountants, burglars, counterfeiters, hijackers, drug pushers, chemists, loan sharks, pimps, prostitutes, union bosses, businessmen, theatre and nightclub workers, bookmakers, crooked judges and police and Frank Sinatra under his control. The President of the United States would make a full deck. He was earning about a million dollars a week with his interests going all the way out to Hawaii and with the Yakuza in Japan, running at around two billion dollars a year. His patch stretched from Cleveland to Kansas City, from Hot Springs to New Orleans and the lucrative rackets in Florida, the West Indies, Arizona and the lively money-making territories of Nevada and California.

He quickly wooed and won Judith Exner. She said he fell in love with her but when Douglas Thompson asked her if there might be another motivation she nodded: 'At first he may have just wanted to use me but it became more than that.' It certainly did. She became the conduit between the Mafia and Kennedy. The narrative might be circumstantial but she met Giancana very shortly after she slept with Kennedy. Happenstance? Coincidence? For Giancana there was the prospect of influence whether Kennedy won or lost the race for the White House: he would remain a powerful person in American politics.

Giancana was a widower. For sexual companionship, he had as wide a choice as any man in America. For, in addition to drug trafficking, gambling and hijacking, he controlled a prostitution business, which provided exquisite beauties for some of the most important men in America. But the days of the gang molls were over. Giancana's respectability demanded a lady at his side, a 'classy dame' in his old days patois. Judith Exner filled both roles. Giancana was the opposite of the handsome Kennedy but he had power. He got Royal attention. If he went into a restaurant and wasn't pleased the unfortunate owners would know that their business was doomed. Deliveries would halt, unions would strike, customers would fade away and vandals would finally work things over so that nothing of value would be left. There was no one, in the world which Giancana dominated, who did not fear his power. Even the powerful names of show business. They all toed the line, some more than others.

Judith Exner discovered Giancana was poisoned with racial prejudice. He'd fought the upsurge of the 'Black Power' criminal gangs and regularly announced he 'hated all n******'. He always snubbed Sammy Davis Jr when he was around the Rat Pack. And elsewhere, as Judith Exner recounted about her experience at a cabaret show in Chicago: 'Sammy directed his performance to our table and Sam ignored him. This time, however, Sammy came to our table after the show. Sammy greeted us, a big smile on his face and Sam turned away from him. Sammy caught the movement and quickly turned his attention to me, asking me when I got in, where I was staying, how did I like Chicago? It was polite conversation but with a nervous edge as he kept glancing at Sam, who was impatiently drumming his fingers on the table. Sammy, turning his full attention to Sam, asked, "Would you good people join me and a few friends for a little soiree?"

'Sam abruptly stood up. "We don't have the time."

'"Well, I thought…"

'"Just forget it, OK? I told you, we don't have the time."

'Sammy gave me an anxious look and backed away. "Sure, OK, see you good people later."'

On the way back to their hotel Judith Exner remarked on the rudeness. Abruptly he told her: 'Don't worry about that n*****. He can take it.'

That evening Judith Exner received a phone call from a nervous and apparently frightened Sammy Davis Jr who asked her: 'Have I offended him?'

No one offended Sam Giancana. In April 1960, Judith Exner was all but living full time in the John Barrymore Suite of Chicago's Ambassador East Hotel. It was a vintage champagne lifestyle. Yet, the criminal empire was run from the Armory Lounge, a small bar and spaghetti restaurant in Forest Park, a Chicago suburb. There was a long bar down the narrow room and booths on the opposite wall. It had a jukebox and a coin telephone. And in the back there was a dining area, covered with bright checkered tablecloths and, behind that, the back room where fundamental decisions were made.

The Armory was run by Doris and Carmine Fanelli and they catered for regular customers as Giancana and his inner circle enjoyed pasta in the back. On FBI tapes you hear Giancana ordering a killing between spoonfuls of spaghetti. In the years of Giancana's rule, between 1958 and 1963, Chicago police recorded fifty-three Mob murders and twenty-four major bombing attacks.

The majority, the FBI believe, were conceived and planned in the Armory. Sam Giancana took Judith Exner to lunch at the Armory on 7 April 1960. He introduced her to his friends who talked among themselves in a language she could not understand. It was, explained Giancana, Sicilian. When she joked that she would go to a Berlitz language school to learn, 'he just about fell over laughing'. It is here that Judith Exner's version of their relationship clashes with credulity. She maintained that even then, in the heartland of the Mob, she still believed Giancana was 'Sam Flood'.

Arguably, more believable and conniving was Giancana's role as the 'other man' even given his savage, cruel temper. Although sharing a woman was totally alien to his position and background, he accepted it; as long as she saw him when she wasn't with JFK. Then, they could talk. An excited Judith Exner liked to do that, especially with a man who was friendly, sympathetic, the perfect listener. It was quite an act – some of those who met him say he smelled of evil. The way they tell it, he even had the look of Dorian Gray's picture, all that badness knotted up inside him reflected in his face and demeanour. But for the very Californian girl Judith Exner he was like a therapist. She told him the details of her love affair.

One day she left JFK's bed at his home in Georgetown, Washington, and joined Giancana in Chicago. She explained the risky liaison. Mrs Kennedy was away in New England at the time and after dinner with a political friend, JFK had taken Judith Exner on a tour of the house on N Street in Georgetown, the upmarket Washington DC suburb and eventually they made love in the master bedroom. Afterwards he offered to buy her a mink coat, or pay for the one she was wearing, which she had bought out of alimony payments. She later took two thousand dollars towards the price of the coat. Kennedy had made it plain that he wanted a long-term relationship. He couldn't wait to see her again and asked if she would come down to Miami, where he would be the following week.

Giancana listened and said he understood, so much so that he offered to fly her down to Miami: it just happened that he had to go down there on business. He took her to nightclubs and floorshows and to his summer home in Palm Beach, not too far from the Kennedy family's oceanfront Florida base. He bought her presents, not all of which she accepted. The days passed while she waited for her assignation with JFK. One present he bought her while she was standing in the same jeweller's shop. It was a turquoise and diamond earring and ring set. Delighted with her surprise he boasted, 'You never even saw me buy this and you were standing right beside me.' She smiled at that: 'It always delighted him to put something over on me.'

What the mobster had in play was the future of America. The Kennedy brothers had been campaigning on a law-and-order ticket and Bobby Kennedy had pledged to hound organised crime out of business. In answer, the Mob needed bargaining power. Which was when the aggressive CIA helped out: they wanted the Mob to kill Fidel Castro. President Eisenhower instigated plots to bring down Fidel Castro, whose communist takeover of Cuba, so close to the American mainland, was an ongoing embarrassment. 'Ike' had a reputation for taking down the bad boys. He was told the Mafia, hurting from the loss of their casino business, held sincere motivations and the Cuban Army connections to, with a little help from the government, help themselves and American interests. Operations which would haunt many future American administrations were given the green light. It was all done in such secrecy that the FBI was kept out of the loop. J. Edgar Hoover was aware, but played the information close to his chest for future leverage. He and his agents assigned to find Johnny Rosselli on racketeering charges kept failing. It was only when the LAPD's OCID recognised him arriving in Los Angeles on 26 October 1960 on a National Airlines flight from Miami that they traced him.

Oops: he was working for the CIA who were financing his lifestyle, suppling airline tickets, protected accommodation and a string of alternative identities. He'd been recruited by Howard Hughes's right-hand man and CIA part-timer Bob Maheu to knock off Castro, a calculated endeavour which began a world of crazy antics.

'Businessman' Bob Maheu was the perfect man to connect the agency to his pal Rosselli. He knew more secrets than most – his own agency was the inspiration in 1966 for the *Mission Impossible* television series – explaining: 'The CIA was my first steady client, giving me cut-out assignments [as a trusted Mr Fixit go-between], those jobs in which the agency could not officially be involved.'

Maheu contracted to work for billionaire Howard Hughes in 1955 – he never met him, all contact was by memo or taped messages – and through him had vast underworld contacts. Rosselli as Chicago's go-to man was one of the closest. Initially, he hid the identity of his employer and told Rosselli he was working for 'an international corporation'. He offered $150,000 to have Castro killed, but Rosselli wasn't interested in money. He brought in 'Sam Gold' and 'Joe' – Sam Giancana and Santo Trafficante Jr. They'd lost their gambling bonanza in Havana to Castro's coup and when the dictator turned sharp left, pro-Moscow, anti-Washington, they saw it as their patriotic duty – and an opportunity to retrieve their Havana casinos – by launching what was finally labelled 'Operation Mongoose'.

It was not only the fruit, rum and sugar interests that were hit when Castro imposed his Caribbean-style socialism. It was also the crime industry. Under the leadership of Santo Trafficante, father and son – in drug trafficking – and Meyer Lansky – in gambling – for three decades the Syndicate had run an illicit paradise; you could buy anything. The Mob owned the hotels, the gambling saloons, the bars and brothels, the boys and girls. Now all that was gone. But they still had their underworld infrastructure in Cuba, which was stronger than the CIA's underground political network. Signed off CIA documents show that by March 1960, the Eisenhower Administration had decided that Fidel Castro had to go. Fearful of a backlash from the United Nations, that elimination policy plan was kept top secret allowing *plausible deniability*. From them on that was all but official American foreign policy, clandestine activities with no strings, no paperwork or direct contact, between the players on the ground and the manager of the nasty game. Documents reveal that President Eisenhower blessed operations to 'develop a paramilitary force to be introduced into Cuba to organise, train and lead resistance groups against the Castro regime.' He did not want the details.

An Agency background boy had the idea that the Mafia were the way to make Castro disappear. For the thinkers in the Mafia, it was perhaps a way to legitimise more of their businesses and investments. It was positive to have cooperated with the government in an important overseas insurgency mission. Giancana was sceptical about any hit being a success. He says on tape that the idea was 'crazy'. But a favour was always repayable with another favour and the CIA could be welcome insurance he could cash in against a change of face in the White House. If they assassinated Castro, the CIA could help take Federal heat off the Mafia. And he had his personal conduit to JFK who was looking an even better bet to get the job as the most powerful man in the world. Whether he would *actually* be the most powerful man in the world was something Giancana was working on. JFK and Judith Exner were meeting as often as possible in private houses, in hotel rooms and they talked. There would be phone calls from Giancana after these meetings. 'Judy, I'm in New York. Why don't you come up and see me? I miss you.' And she would, for she liked flitting around America and the tickets were always first-class and she didn't know the company wasn't. When Sam called, she went. He was so undemanding and so understanding. She explained to him about JFK. *Of course*, it was confidential but she knew she could trust him. The absurdity of JFK's behaviour was that he didn't want others to cause upset.

That election year of 1960 Peter Falk, very prior to being that nice Lieutenant Columbo, appeared as the mad killer Abe 'Twist' Reles in the film *Murder, Inc.* That also starred Swedish actress May Britt, who caused controversy when it was announced she was to marry Sammy Davis Jr. Interracial marriage was illegal in thirty-one states. The Kennedy brothers told Sinatra to tell Davis to postpone his wedding until after the election. The prenuptial warnings were also issued by Sam Giancana. The manipulators were supposedly covering every angle. JFK was mounting the most professional political drive for the White House that America had seen since the days of Franklin Roosevelt. He was surrounded by a group of tough, hard young political organisers, the new breed in politics: men who could never be outsmarted. The supreme professionals all led by his brother Bobby. Their reputations, their incomes, their total futures depended on him winning. And to win there must be no slip-up. They had a motto: 'No risks'.

And yet, at this vital moment, Kennedy was totally vulnerable.

Some of the men around him were beginning to know about Judith Exner but not one of the supreme professionals checked her background and contacts out or asked, 'Is she a risk?' And the reason for this was the unwritten law around JFK. He had to have his fun – his girls. Then he could get out of bed and into politics. His reckless lifestyle became tolerated, accepted, even admired. It built a false confidence for not one person imagined such innocent, manly fun would harm JFK.

The advisers and guards asked themselves who could blame him for Marilyn Monroe. An even more lavish accoutrement for the Democratic National Convention. Bobby Kennedy had asked her to stay away. Not a chance. Even wild horses couldn't do that.

Chapter Twelve

New Frontiers

'Cheats never prosper but they have a big edge.'

Sydney Summers, bookmaker, 1955

Even a whisper of his sex life, and that one of his lovers was also sharing a bed with a psychopathic Mafia Don, would have ended it before the Democratic National Convention that July in Los Angeles 1960, but he got away with it and, maybe, it was the luck of the Irish. He certainly pushed that luck.

As throughout his Presidential bid he had help. For the convention, LAPD chief Bill Parker's intelligence squads had their own suites at the Biltmore Hotel to monitor and do their duty for the Kennedys. When several hundred supporters of Adlai Stevenson, the Democratic nominee in 1952 and 1956, tried to make their views heard at the LA Sports Arena where the convention was being staged, Parker's men swiftly stopped them. Still, Chief Parker was dismayed about what they were protecting. He was tentative about the Kennedy connection to Frank Sinatra – 'totally tied to the Mafia' – and upset by what he saw as immoral behaviour by JFK's dissolute brother-in-law Peter Lawford. Marilyn Monroe was bad for his blood pressure. She was in the Nevada desert filming *The Misfits*, the last movie she ever completed. Her marriage to Arthur Miller, who had written the script about a group of cowboys chasing Marilyn and mustangs, was a mess. She said her back was hurting to get away for the convention.

JFK had used his own bad back to get her sympathy and told her the family's other fantasy, that he'd damaged it playing American football. It was another whopper. He'd been born with one leg shorter than the other and that provoked back pain – aggravated when he'd tried to become intimate with a woman at a Californian swimming pool and she'd dodged his pass and he wrenched his already damaged back when he fell into the pool. The story, told by the distinguished journalist and expert on the American Presidency, Hugh Sidey, emerged in the mid-1990s after decades of discretion. He said no one would have been allowed to print such stories at the time. Or report a married Catholic, running for President, was seeing Marilyn Monroe. God forbid, teenaged girls.

Chief Parker knew but was loyal. He was an Eisenhower man and in any other circumstances would be supportive of the Republican Presidential nominee, Richard Nixon, with whom he shared friends and supporters. J. Edgar Hoover feared that if Nixon won the White House then he might replace him as the head of the FBI with Chief Parker. Hoover was aware that Parker was also threatening from another angle: his close association with Bobby Kennedy, who he'd helped with his organised crime investigations. That connection was heightened, cemented, when Parker put the LAPD and all its power and glory behind Kennedy at the convention.

For the opening Sunday reception on 11 July, Jacqueline Kennedy was heavily pregnant and not present, JFK, along with Bobby and his wife Ethel and Ted Kennedy and his wife Joan, were escorted by fifteen, white-helmeted 'perfect specimen' policemen. In turn this group was covered by thirty plain-clothes officers. The big Texan senator Lyndon Johnson and his wife Lady Bird and their two daughters were left to look after themselves.

It quickly became clear JFK needed support – he lost his suit jacket twice as adoring fans reached out to shake his hand or hug and simply tore the jackets from his shoulders and there were moments of extreme anxiety when moments of enthusiasm became bodily threats. Throughout the four-day political carousel an OCID team monitored JFK's movement from the Biltmore Hotel downtown over to the North Rossmore home of producer Jack Haley, son of the Tin Man in *The Wizard of Oz* (1939), near the private golf course, the Wilshire Country Club, in Hancock Park. It was where he had 'private meetings' with several women. Marilyn Monroe is not identified in the OCID files as having visited Kennedy at Jack Haley's home but she was with him during the first seventy-two hours of the convention. On the second evening, she had dinner with him at Puccini's in Beverly Hills, owned by Frank Sinatra and Peter Lawford. The next morning, 13 July, Marilyn and JFK were noted together, wet from the shower, at breakfast at Peter Lawford's house out on Palisades Beach Road.

It was a similarly well-scrubbed JFK, the clean-cut candidate, who accepted the Presidential nomination in front of a cheering and flag-waving crowd of supporters at the Coliseum. He also announced that Lyndon Johnson, the Senate majority leader, would be his running mate. After Johnson accepted the offer, Robert Kennedy went across Pershing Square to Johnson's downtown Biltmore Hotel suite to talk him out of the job. LBJ was offended and if anything, it made him more determined to stay on the ticket. It was the catalyst for a fierce feud between them which plagued Johnson's role as Vice-President. Johnson on the ticket was not what JFK wanted either. The Kennedys were put in a corner, trapped. JFK's personal secretary Evelyn Lincoln, who watched over him before and after his election, said she was with John and Robert Kennedy in a suite at the Biltmore Hotel when they agreed to accept Lyndon Johnson. She heard them say that Johnson had blackmailed JFK into offering him the nomination with evidence of his womanising provided by J. Edgar Hoover. They swore not to be compromised again, to be caught out by sexual adventures, by episodes like 'the Marilyn problem'.

Now, with the nomination won, any indiscretions, if made public, would sabotage a lifetime of family scheming to, in essence, take control of America.

Yet, for the sex-mad JFK, Marilyn remained a temptation. The 15 July night of his triumphant 'The New Frontier' acceptance speech – *We stand today on the edge of a new frontier – the frontier of the 1960s, the frontier of unknown opportunities and perils, the frontier of unfilled hopes and unfilled threats … The pioneers gave up their safety, their comfort, and sometimes their lives to build our new west* – a huge party was organised by Peter Lawford out at his beach house. It was a jubilant, summer, Friday night celebration – noisy, loud with squeals and slurred laughter, like kids on a spring break, with groups of party girls organised by Lawford. The next President of the United States and his global sex icon companion got lost in the crowd; most eyes were on the naked girls or searching for Ross Acuna the barman, hired expensively in from Romanoff's on Rodeo Drive, Beverly Hills.

Chief Parker's security squad protected the Kennedy celebration. OCID detectives Archie Case and James Ahearn were on hand and helped some revellers to their cars around 3 a.m. The team filed full reports which are in the OCID files. There is no notation saying JFK or Marilyn left 625 Palisades Beach Road. Chief Parker, the model for Mr Spock of *Star Trek*, must have pondered as he read the reports just where the final frontier might now be, especially with the OCID report from the Pink Palace, a.k.a. the Beverly Hills Hotel. It seemed that before JFK accepted the Democratic crown – Presidential candidates do not go to the convention until the nomination is settled – JFK had invited Monroe over to the Beverly Hills Hotel. When she got there, a wild, drinking party was going and she said JFK tried to get her into bed with another woman, 'a tall, thin secretary type', who left when she rebuffed the advances. It was a hiccup and by morning they were friends again. Monroe's friendship with Frank Sinatra drifted, although FBI records show they still talked – she telephoning him.

Sinatra was central to Giancana's manoeuvre, planting Judith Exner on JFK on behalf of the Mafia. He was one of the few people who knew the astounding secret, that the President's mistress was also sleeping with a Mafia chieftain – and he kept it. Johnny Rosselli knew the secrets too. He saw more of Judith Exner, as Giancana had a proper love interest, the singer Phyllis McGuire of the singing McGuire Sisters. She was a popular star and his long-time girlfriend and travelling companion. It had carried on during his 'romance' with Judith Exner which gave him an edge.

Their ideas might be weird but the CIA's electronic equipment impressed Giancana. He could use it for his personal affairs: with the time taken with Judith Exner and the CIA he was paranoid that his beloved Phyllis McGuire was lacking his attention – and getting someone else's. He had the tall, smug-smiled Dan Rowan half of the 'Rowan and Martin' duo in the frame as the other man. *Mission Impossible* agent-for-hire Robert Maheu lived in Las Vegas to be close to his major boss, Howard Hughes, and would have drinks with old connections. He died, aged ninety, in 2008, but 'never lost his marbles' according to one of his younger drinking buddies who likes to talk anonymously about 'the fun days'. Apparently, when a scheme went wrong Maheu was blamed and almost lost his life. Giancana, it seems, was a 'jealous bastard'.

There were a lot of dirty tricks going on and pivotal to so much investment was that the Kennedys *had* to win the White House.

On the day JFK became a Presidential candidate, in a moment of serendipity, it was made public that Frank Sinatra, Dean Martin, Hank Sanicola – a Sinatra friend and business partner – and the obsequious Skinny D'Amato had applied for permission from the state of Nevada to take over the Cal-Neva Lodge and Casino. Veteran gangster Elmer Renner out of San Francisco owned the Cal-Neva but owed $800,000 in tax. When hoodlum Bert Grober bought the place the tax man went after him too. Then Sinatra and his saviours rode into town. What wasn't announced was that Chicago Mob boss Sam Giancana had a big silent percentage in the

Cal-Neva and that he had persuaded 'Wingy' Grober to sell the property at an extremely undervalued quarter of a million dollars. The casino itself was no great moneymaker but it gave Giancana another hook in Sinatra who he wanted close to JFK. Sinatra had, for an often-drunk depressive, a rose-tinted view of this particular business. He was aware that Anthony 'Fat Tony' Salerno, the New York Mafia powerbroker, retained an 'interest' in the property. Giancana was putting up the money. That was pressure but Sinatra was certain that the seasonal resort could turn a healthy profit and that was how he'd sold it to Giancana.

Sinatra did have the contacts. On opening night, Joe Kennedy was there and for him it was déjà vu. The Cal-Neva was one of his love nests during his nine-year affair with his secretary Janet DesRosiers. He was sixty when he began 'dating' the green-eyed twenty-four-year-old who worked for him in Palm Beach, Florida. Now, he was with his Presidential candidate son and 'date' Marilyn Monroe, back at one of his favourite haunts. With them, a little out of the spotlight, were Johnny Rosselli and Sam Giancana. J. Edgar Hoover's FBI agents and OCID detectives were watching the Cal-Neva from Tahoe's famously heavily wooded hills. It didn't offer much of a view, even of a new frontier. If there was one, there were ambushes ahead. They arrived as quickly as events.

On 8 November 1960 America went to the polls, and JFK became President-Elect in the early hours of the next day, following what became known as the 'Campaign of the Century'. Marilyn Monroe had been indisposed, unable to vote. But it seemed Mickey Mouse and Donald Duck did vote, several times, especially in Texas and Illinois.

The Mafia helped JFK win but did they 'steal' the result from Richard Nixon who history has as the Dark Prince of American politics? Decades of study of the polling in the 1960 election have punctured myths. It's clear there was voter fraud, especially in Illinois, in a Chicago ruled by Sam Giancana and the corrupt Mayor Richard Daley. Judith Exner revealed that she had couriered election-related messages between JFK and Giancana and in later life, with a little remorse, bemoaned her own actions. Not acting as a go-between in election rigging but being involved with a married man: 'I always knew it was a mistake seeing Jack. The relationship absolutely was a mistake.' Yet, she added, on her spy-style role: 'I don't feel even today that I was making a mistake in taking those envelopes to Sam. If it was anybody's mistake, it was Jack's. I came to doubt his character.'

She acknowledged that Sam Giancana wasn't, in his patois, *pussy-whipped*: 'I'm not so naive that I don't think that his friendship with me and continued friendship wasn't very beneficial. He could use it to his advantage if need be ... [JFK also used] Sam for his own purpose. And Sam would naturally expect something for it. I don't like to think of friendship being used that way.

'Jack didn't play by our rules; Jack had his own rules. The father really set the pace for the boys. I used to say that the Kennedy men were morally bankrupt. And I still feel that way. It's a rather harsh judgment, but it's what I came to realise about Jack. No one wants to accept it, but there was a very cold inner core to him. He did what was right for Jack. And everybody let him do what was right for Jack. *Whatever* Jack wanted. I don't believe Jack should have been President. It's flaunting who you are and the power. And I think Jack did abuse the power.'

He certainly enjoyed pornographic wealth. Far richer than Nixon, who'd had earned this tough guy reputation as a ruthless politician by calling his congressional opponents communist sympathisers, he spread the cash about in 1960. The Mob influenced votes through payments and strong-arm tactics like those which won the primary election for JFK. In Texas, the fraud was more at the door of Lyndon Johnson's election teams, their manipulation of the voters and at the polling stations. There's no doubt Johnson carried Texas for JFK with the bonus of the influence of Santo Trafficante Jr and Carlos Marcello. Objective scholars and statisticians have weighed the racial element – the Republicans were better on civil rights – and the anti-Catholic brigade and outside, bad actors in their analysis, without a satisfactory verdict; like the election it's almost 50-50. Yes, there was voter fraud but did that tilt the vote for JFK? Did Nixon really lose? Because of lack of evidence – ballot papers were destroyed – it's impossible to say conclusively that Nixon was robbed; we do have questionable activity, unexplained big shifts in the proportion of votes between the two parties compared to past patterns, multiple polls in which the number of votes counted hugely trumped the number of registered voters (and where JFK always won big) and the instant vanishing of paperwork following recounts demanded by the courts. It's a given that JFK won the first television election, looking calmer and more authoritative than 'sweaty' Nixon. But did he win the real one? A pointer to the voter anomalies is that the party suffered significant losses in Congress, such a rare event it did not happen again until 2020, Joe Biden v Donald Trump. It was the first time the winner of the White House carried fewer states than the opponent; JFK won the reported national vote by 112,827 – that's 0.17 per cent – and the electoral college 303–219. JFK scored in the big cities like Carlos Marcello's New Orleans and, of course, Mob-friendly Chicago. JFK benefited from a favourable media which kept quiet, in some cases covered-up, the big fraud: that the clean-cut, healthy JFK was in fact a diseased and feckless philanderer.

Forgotten too is the business of politics and vice versa. The Nixon–JFK election is mythologised as good guy v bad guy. Yet, they were on friendly terms from their days as freshmen congressmen in 1947; in 1952, JFK sent Nixon a handwritten note congratulating him on being nominated for Vice President. As Vice President, Nixon's office in the Old Senate Office Building was across the hall from JFK's office and they often visited each other. Nixon's view: 'The test of democracy in action is our ability not to allow those differences to destroy friendly relations between members of the two parties.' The pre-Watergate Nixon refused to contest the Presidential election results and took the moral high ground despite the fraud in Illinois and Texas: 'The country can't afford the agony of a constitutional crisis – and I damn well will not be a party to creating one just to become President or anything else.'

With President Kennedy there'd be crisis enough. He had no intention of changing his ways. The evening before his inauguration there was a gala staged by Frank Sinatra at the National Guard Armory, with familiar names like Mafia-stooge Jimmy Durante, Gene Kelly, Shirley MacLaine, Ella Fitzgerald. The one sour note was the forced absence of Sammy Davis Jr, who had been banned from the proceedings on the orders of Joseph Kennedy because of the entertainer's marriage to May Britt.

The just-about-President went to Paul Young's, a newly popular restaurant, for a late-night dinner hosted by his father. Among the guests was Paul Fay Jr. In his memoir *The Pleasure of his Company*, Fay, who became Under-Secretary of the Navy, said his task that night was to escort Angie Dickinson; he recalled her 'wrapped in fur, standing all alone' to disguise Kennedy's 'early evening' date with Dickinson. The actress most politely brushed away talk of romance but of Paul Fay's remarks said: 'He shouldn't have written it. It was too personal. It's like having a broken wrist, an annoyance, but I have to live with it. They wouldn't believe me if I said it never happened.'

Chapter Thirteen

Foreign Policy

> *'The Party told you to reject the evidence of your eyes and ears. It was their final, most essential command.'*
>
> George Orwell, *1984*, 1949

On 20 January 1961, tall and erect in a smart tailcoat, and his canvas back brace with its tight metal stays, which his lover Diana de Vegh had helped him put on, President JFK, surrounded by crowds wrapped in winter coats on a snow blown day, appropriately offered a Cold War warning in his inaugural address:

> *'Let every nation know, whether it wishes us well or ill, that we shall pay any price, bear any burden, meet any hardship, support any friends, oppose any foe to assure the survival and success of liberty ... Let all of our neighbours know that we shall join with them to oppose aggression or subversion anywhere in the Americas. And let every other power know that this hemisphere intends to remain master of its own house.'*

With those words he had a full dance card. Stalin's successor, Nikita Khrushchev, had some disdain for the young President, whose KGB file closely matched that of the one held by Jesus Angleton of the CIA. Closer to home, across that narrow stretch of the

Atlantic, Fidel Castro was laughing at America. The day before the inauguration, President Eisenhower had conducted a long handover session with JFK in which Cuba – with which Eisenhower had severed diplomatic ties after Castro accurately called the American embassy a 'nest of spies' – was atop the agenda. Files show that the outgoing President told the incoming incumbent on Cuba: 'You cannot let the present government there go on.'

The JFK administration's secrets and lies began at the beginning. In other western capitals the election result was not always warmly welcomed. Richard Nixon had a track record and the thinking was 'Better the devil you know'. Nixon was also a 'conversationalist', in that policy could be debated with him. JFK was seen as more hawk-like, in that he'd campaigned on an anti-Soviet ticket and the false gap between America and Russia's nuclear capabilities. On the missile front, America was ahead ten to one. Fear was the vote winner – again, perception, this time of threat. The Action Man posture would play well.

Documents show that immediately, in late January 1961, the White House compelled the CIA to set up an 'executive action' capability – in truth an off-books assassination unit. The agency's existing arrangements with Johnny Rosselli, Sam Giancana and Meyer Lansky, impatient to get the gambling back in Havana, were lively. Such details were delicate, considering the attitude to the Mob of the nation's new Attorney General.

On winning the White House, JFK announced to public and even staffer surprise, that J. Edgar Hoover would stay in post as the director of the FBI. Hoover had too much on the Kennedys to be dismissed. Wily Joe Kennedy had a caveat, telling the President to appoint his brother Bobby as Attorney General and, as head of the Department of Justice, become Hoover's immediate boss. JFK reluctantly agreed and, in doing so, irritated Hoover even more. It was a clever move. There were still rumblings about election fraud and if there were investigations to contend with the files would all land on one desk – that of the Attorney General, who could block any further action. With Bobby Kennedy – now RFK to the world – in post, the case was closed. Chief William Parker in Los Angeles – his officers still watching over JFK's high-risk and ongoing Hollywood love affairs – sent his congratulations on the election victory and, privately, a warmer letter of applause to Bobby Kennedy.

Publicly he issued a statement: 'It has been the pleasure of my office to work closely with Bobby Kennedy during his period as counsel for the McClellan Committee. This opportunity to observe his philosophies in the law enforcement field has been most gratifying and I expect increased levels of support for law enforcement at all levels.'

Indeed, within days, the new Attorney General announced a war on the Mob. Privately, there was talk of Chief Parker leading a national task force against organised crime, but J. Edgar Hoover tied that particular policy parcel in red tape. Hoover held his public temper even when Bobby Kennedy insisted the FBI get Justice Department approval for all their directives and public relations announcements, but their animosity heightened.

Everyone had expectations but they were different expectations.

The entire American Mafia Syndicate would profit from Meyer Lansky's mission to get back into Cuba. This was where the Kennedy family were enraging the Mob: they wouldn't stay out of the picture. These people were cruel enemies to make. Promises had been made in the heat of the election – *promise her anything* moments – by Joe Kennedy and his enthusiastic son. But JFK was now President of the United States, champion of the free world.

When gangbuster politician RFK became US Attorney General in 1961, the Justice Department went after organised crime, indicting 116 members of the Mob. He increased Mob prosecutions more than a dozen times over the previous Eisenhower administration; he waged a personal vendetta against Jimmy Hoffa and pursued Carlos Marcello, who he knew was using a fake Guatemalan birth certificate; he had immigration agents place a protesting Marcello aboard a seventy-eight-seat jet as its only passenger and drop him off in Guatemala City. Marcello and his lawyer were later flown to El Salvador, where soldiers dumped the two bespoke-suited men in the wilderness. Marcello fainted three times and broke several ribs before finding his way to a small airport. Secretly back into New Orleans, he promised revenge against the Kennedy brothers. Angered by his more than one million dollars, and rising, legal bills fighting the Justice Department, he's on record talking to Ted Becker, a Las Vegas hotel flak, who naively mentions the grief Marcello is getting from Bobby Kennedy. In Sicilian, Marcello shouts: *'Livarsi "na pietra di la scarpa"' (Take the stone out of my shoe.)* He's warned about going after Bobby Kennedy but retorts: *'No – I'm not talking about that. You know what they say in Sicily: if you want to kill a dog, you don't cut off the tail, you cut off the head. The dog will keep biting you if you only cut off its tail, but if the dog's head is cut off the dog will die, tail and all.'* The Kennedy name was dirt – *Irish bastards* and worse, as RFK's anti-crime crusade emboldened hoodlums coast-to-coast and one tape on Sam Giancana's phone captured him saying: 'I never thought it would get this fucking rough when we put the brothers in there. This is murder.'

A more considered threat came from Santo Trafficante Jr: *Kennedy's not going to make it to the 1964 election – he's going to be hit.* For many years this captured remark was thought to refer to JFK but documents suggest that Trafficante was talking about Bobby Kennedy. Whatever is accurate, the Kennedy brothers were a target for what was seen as utter betrayal and, worse than anything, lack of respect in not knowing the rules.

Deported from Cuba in 1959, Trafficante established himself as Florida's most influential godfather and ruled from Tampa. However, he spent several days a week at his home near Biscayne Bay – with tragic irony a favourite haunt of Johnny Rosselli – and worked out of Miami using phone booths. Miami police records show he met regularly with Cuban gangsters, associates with whom he operated the Tropicana Casino, the Havana Hilton and the Hotel St John Casino. In Department of Justice files, it also shows that Eufemio Fernandez, chief of the Batista Secret Police (*Policia Secreta Nacional*) had financial interests, a modest percentage, in Trafficante's Sans Souci nightclub.

The Kennedys in the White House – RFK was all but Deputy President – knew all of those evil associations. Yet, on 13 March 1961 America's premier mobsters met with their CIA case officer, Jim O'Connell, a senior operative in the agency's Office of Security and the spook who recruited his friend Robert Maheu as the original operative for 'Castro's destruction'. Sam Giancana, Johnny Rosselli and Santo Trafficante Jr were supposedly in town for the third and final heavyweight boxing contest between Floyd Patterson and Ingemar Johansson, which Patterson won with a sixth-round KO. Sinatra, paying his dues to the Mafia men who helped his career, was making his regular appearance at the Fontainebleau Hotel and was noted by the FBI meeting the gangsters in the hotel's Boom Boom Room bar. He left before the CIA–Mafia plot to knock off Castro became the prime topic. The atmosphere was conducive. The anti-Castro stronghold was Miami and down in 'little Havana' Cuban refugees were protesting. The deal was done on the understanding that the authorities would 'look the other way' as events rolled out. Giancana was wary of RFK ever leaving them alone following his anti-crime pledges.

It all became, of course, a tragicomedy involving some of the more preposterous plots in the history of political murder. Rosselli was supplied with three capsules filled with poison, botulinum – pills developed by the CIA and told they 'would work anywhere and at any time with anything' (the CIA Inspector General J. S. Earman's *Report on Plots to Assassinate Fidel Castro*). From released CIA records, it's been established the agency had a wide variety of poisons in their arsenal to carry out assassinations to order. The CIA's 1962 'good stuff' (according, in 1975, to their chemist Dr Nathan Gordon) comprised shellfish toxins; a small dose is lethal. They kill by blocking the transmission of nervous system impulses.

One of the shellfish toxins was saxitoxin, perhaps the deadliest known to mankind. Just one to four milligrams will kill an average-sized person from respiratory failure within minutes (one milligram is equal to 0.0002 of a teaspoon). The same measure of sugar wouldn't sweeten a cup of tea and in dry form it would be smaller than a grain of sugar. It is instantly absorbed through the gastro-intestinal tract and passed in the urine. During the Second World War the British authorities had a poison, code name 'I', they intended to use to kill Hitler. It was also tasteless and odourless and, when added to a variety of drinks and food, did not advertise its presence. The CIA 'killer popper' was regarded as so quick-acting, so painless, that not long after its development it was supplied to Gary Powers, the U-2 spy pilot, for his flight over the Soviet Union in 1960; the fatal toxin was in a tiny poison needle concealed in a silver dollar. The idea was to provide Powers with *an option* if he was shot down. He was shot down but went for a different option.

Rosselli took the lead and was briefed on the *lethal material* and, with an Inspector Clouseau flourish, given the outlandish enterprise where anti-Castro Cuban politician Antonio Varona arranged for the poison to be put in Castro's meal at a favourite restaurant. The would-be assassins could never get close enough. Or explode his cigars.

It wasn't all a pantomime: there was talk of mining the Cuban harbour which, in essence, was an act of war, as it could destroy foreign shipping, including docked Soviet vessels.

The official unofficial hit list now included Castro's brother, Raúl, and Che Guevara. Varona was later supplied, through clandestine meetings in Miami overseen by Johnny Rosselli – always an attraction in his silk suits amid the bearded revolutionaries, with grown-up weaponry. Behind the bespoke image and quiet voice, the elegantly sipped, iced Smirnoff, he was tougher than the revolutionaries who dressed the part. He told Varona to hire a U-Haul truck and, when the Cuban arrived for a pick-up, waiting for him was thousands of dollars' worth of explosives, sniper rifles, handguns, and radar equipment.

The intent was always serious: it was dollars and cents business for the Mafia who were ambivalent about the dictators they manipulated. Rosselli ran a sniper training camp in the Florida Keys and plots evolved on and on. One particular CIA scheme involved putting a powdered drug into Castro's boots, which would work through the bloodstream and make his hair fall out. CIA psychiatrists reasoned that without his beard Castro would lose his political charisma. *Defoliate the sonofabitch and he'll never give you any trouble again.* Castro kept his beard and power despite the Mafia. And to their great anger, the Kennedy Administration. It resulted from the family's penchant for broken promises. There were ongoing communications between the JFK and Sam Giancana (the FBI found seventy registered phone calls from go-between Judith Exner to President Kennedy's secretary Evelyn Lincoln) that everything possible would be done to destroy Castro and return 'American business to Cuba'. That, to the mobsters, meant their livelihood, gambling and profitable assorted accoutrements.

Yet, JFK flunked at the first hurdle.

From the early weeks of the Kennedy administration, JFK wanted to put a man on the moon to win his space race with Moscow, but his main mission was to end the problem of Castro; for years Kennedy apologists angrily denied the brothers approved assassinations of foreign leaders but CIA executives and former White House staffers have reported that both the President and RFK were adamant about dealing with Castro by assassination. In two mentions in her diary, seen by Mike Rothmiller and reported in our *Bombshell* (Ad Lib, 2021), Marilyn Monroe writes of her pillow talk with the President: 'John told me about Castro and he must be stopped.' 'John does not like Fidel C and said he will be gone soon.'

We learned that a small contingent of approximately fifty US Marines had undergone secret training for an assault on Cuba.

They were to be covertly inserted into Cuba the day before the Bay of Pigs invasion. Their mission was to cut off incoming Cuban forces, allowing the others to establish a beachhead. However, the day before they were to embark for Cuba, their mission was quietly ordered to stand down. The Marines never received an answer to their primary question, 'Why was the mission scrubbed?'

CIA officers would testify and offer supporting memorandum that JFK indeed wanted to have *executive action capability* to deal with Castro and, by inference, any other foreign leader who was deemed worthy of murdering. Long before the Kennedy administration planned what became the botched invasion at the Bay of Pigs on the south coast of Cuba on 17 April 1961, killing Castro was a priority. It manifested from a Cold War mindset, a JFK obsession to look powerful, but Cuba was, as Castro had warned, 'not another Guatemala'.

The invasion of the island by a Cuban exile Army known as Brigade 2506 – financed and trained by the CIA and renegade secret agents, Army officers and 'patriotic' mobsters – was a disaster. The CIA underestimated Fidel Castro's power, both in popularity and, more importantly, militarily. Spearheaded from Guatemala, the haphazardly organised attack at the twelve-mile long bay, named for its wild pigs, was victim to failed CIA intelligence. Undetected coral reefs sank some ships as they pulled into shore. Backup paratroopers landed in the wrong place. Troops led by Castro trapped invading forces on the beach, and they surrendered within a day, with 114 killed and more than one thousand captured. As the enterprise crumbled, so did JFK.

The assault plan begun during Eisenhower's time and 'refined' by the Kennedy White House was devised to involve the support of the American Navy *and* Air Force without which the project was doomed. With the world watching this 'secret' invasion of a foreign country, JFK refused to order American fighter planes into action, enraging the military community, the Mafia and the anti-Castro forces. It was all over within three days, with the invaders surrendering to the Cuban Revolutionary Armed Forces (*Fuerzas Armadas Revolucionarias* – FAR) by 20 April.

British authorities had told the 'blinkered' White House and the CIA that the anti-Castro support was dismal but that was ignored. Cubans trained up by the CIA were no contest for Castro's men, who'd had years of revolutionary arms experience and up-to-date help from their Moscow friends. CIA Director Allen Dulles – he was gone by November – emphasised that CIA war-gamers believed JFK would authorise any action to prevent failure, as Eisenhower did in Guatemala in 1954 to remove an irritation, Colonel Juan Jacobo Árbenz Guzmán.

The fiasco was a huge embarrassment for JFK, a politician who had campaigned on military one-upmanship. It was also a lesson which he would need again in not too many months. In Presidential papers he said, 'The first advice I'm going to give my successor is to watch the generals and to avoid feeling that because they were military men their opinions on military matters were worth a damn.'

Bobby Kennedy was even more intent on 'getting rid' of Castro and applied supreme pressure to get that job accomplished. As such he came in contact with the experienced CIA agent William Harvey. Taking over the mission from Jim O'Connell, the podgy agent William Harvey, in look more Smiley than Bond, in purpose, deadlier than either, complained that getting into bed with the Mafia was creating 'a hand grenade waiting to explode'. He alerted his boss Richard Helms – who became CIA director in 1966 – that it could all end badly, with the agency being blackmailed. Despite this Harvey, who had a penchant for openly carrying a .45 Colt revolver and inhaling gin martinis, went at it with some enthusiasm. Veteran British intelligence agent and Witchfinder Peter Wright recounts in *Spycatcher*, his controversial 1987 revelatory book about his hunt for Moscow moles in British intelligence which the UK government tried to ban, that he was approached by Harvey at a secret conference in Maryland about 'the Cuban business'. He reported that Harvey wanted to discover improved 'delivery mechanisms' for poisons which would be deniable, a.k.a. undetectable. This was an almighty conflict of all interests: RFK was attempting to eradicate the gangsters the CIA wanted to pay suitcases of dollars to whack Castro with extreme prejudice (XPD), no questions asked; provide bank account number. At the same time the Mob wanted revenge on the Kennedy brothers.

Christopher Hitchens, the late and often contrarian author and journalist, picked up on this aspect of the Kennedy administration in the *London Review of Books* in February 1998: 'Having made or bought the friendship of mobsters like Sam Giancana and Johnny Rosselli, the Kennedys seem to have acquired quite a taste for the quick fix of murder. How closely this was related to their simultaneous pursuit of sexual thrill and cheap glamour is good material for speculation. That there was some connection is hard to doubt; Kennedy's best-documented affair was with Judith Campbell Exner, who was simultaneously entwined with the Mafia chief Sam Giancana, who was himself involved in the attempts to murder Fidel Castro.

'Ben Bradlee [the late editor of *The Washington Post* and *All The President's Men* alumnus] has told us of his horrified astonishment at finding that Ms Exner knew all of the secret telephone numbers for contacting the President out of hours. Anyway, orders were sent out from the Kennedy White House that Patrice Lumumba in the Congo, Rafael Trujillo in the Dominican Republic and Ngo Dinh Diem in South Vietnam were, with a bare minimum of *deniability*, to be taken off the chessboard. In some way, this was rationalised as a demonstration of manly toughness in a dangerous world. Both brothers were addicted to the accusation that anyone who had any scruples was inviting another *Munich* and one remembers the enthusiasm of their terrible father for that pact – not because he was pro-Chamberlain so much as because he was pro-Hitler.'

Of course, while this interest in world affairs was going on so was JFK's pursuit of his other abiding interest. The CIA's counter-intelligence obsessive leader, James Jesus Angleton, was as much concerned about what his President was disclosing in pillow talk as about whom he wanted eliminated. He 'listened in' to some 'escapades' through the wiretaps placed at the homes of Peter Lawford and Marilyn Monroe by Fred Otash, one of his many off-the-books assets. Otash worked for the CIA while officially employed by the LAPD and for many years afterwards. He wasn't the only detective following JFK's tail. J. Edgar Hoover had a burgeoning file, the LAPD's OCID a wall of tall file cabinets in a locked room devoted to the adventures, and the CIA maintained (through Otash) 'an overview'.

Not so hot on the case, as it turned out, were the Secret Service. It was, as we reported in *Bombshell*, the LAPD who had the best knowledge – which they kept confidential for decades – of JFK's sex life. In the OCID files he is cross-indexed with his brothers, Peter Lawford, Marilyn Monroe and many others, including a list of Mafia leaders throughout America. There are bundles of documents, some annotated, some with pencil marks, some with parts redacted – scribbled rather than blacked out – and a few with dates listed. Thousands of pages range from newspaper articles to private letters, CIA secret information and wiretap transcripts to covertly taken photographs including one, among others of the couple, of JFK and Marilyn Monroe in a warm private embrace. Many of the files were duplicated, sometimes triplicated, and held in different cabinet drawers or driven off the premises to storage units. The secret dossiers on the three Kennedy brothers contain paperwork covering every conceivable aspect of their public and personal lives, the assassinations and the reckless role of Senator Ted Kennedy in the death (18 July 1969) of Kennedy campaign worker Mary Jo Kopechne at Chappaquiddick. There are scores of classified intelligence reports garnered from the FBI, CIA and other

US government agencies and some from foreign intelligence services delving into the Kennedy brothers' sexual trysts, their bootlegger father's Mafia ties, and references to personal contacts with characters the FBI labelled as 'Communist or foreign spies'.

The OCID documents make it clear J. Edgar Hoover told Robert Kennedy that JFK was recorded on a wiretap speaking 'fondly' with Exner while she was at the Chicago home of Sam Giancana. That single piece of intelligence guaranteed Hoover would remain the director of the FBI throughout any Kennedy administration. What still astonishes is that when it came to arranging his secret sexual trysts with Exner and others, JFK behaved like a pubescent schoolboy: he wasn't temperate. He might have suspected that the FBI, CIA, his sworn enemy and Teamsters union boss Jimmy Hoffa, Giancana or a foreign intelligence service would be recording every call to any of his many lovers' phones. J. Edgar Hoover knew the high currency of obtaining the most intimate and damaging details of an aspiring President. As did LAPD chief William Parker and his protégé Daryl Gates, his one-time chauffeur and bodyguard, whom he would later appoint captain and leader of OCID. Often, OCID concentrated their focus on the kings and queens of Hollywood, but never closing their eyes and ears to potential scandals in Washington DC. The explosive triangle of President Kennedy, Attorney General Kennedy and Marilyn Monroe met all the criteria for LAPD spying. It was espionage to combat enemies but also to help friends; ultimately, the only cops who mattered knew almost every secret.

LAPD intelligence captain James Hamilton was an intimate friend of the Kennedys and regularly ran secret LAPD intelligence operations on their behalf. The tall, rugged Hamilton particularly bonded with Bobby Kennedy who, like Chief Parker, was a victim to bouts of depression that sometimes resulted in violence; 'Black Bobby' was a nickname JFK gave his younger brother. Parker, also a Roman Catholic, if Calvinistic, was a man who fought to control his thirst for whiskey, double shots of Bourbon de Luxe, *Parker specials*, and B&Bs (brandy and Bénédictine), was sympathetic to the perils of mood swings. Captain Hamilton regarded himself as the Kennedy 'protector'; OCID knew every time the Kennedys were in southern California and Captain Hamilton would serve as their bodyguard and chauffeur. Hamilton was also their concierge and would quietly assist both JFK and RFK during private visits to California by arranging accommodations under a banal alias or his own name. Hamilton personally handled their various requests with the cooperation of Chief Parker.

One OCID report details a sex party held at Frank Sinatra's secluded and recreational home in the San Fernando Valley, at the top of Winnetka Boulevard in Encino, where it dead-ends at the Santa Monica Mountains. Beyond a stable of active young women, there was unlimited alcohol and limited drugs (no one wanted overdosing starlets). The report identified some of the party guests included Sinatra, Dean Martin, Sammy Davis Jr, Peter Lawford and JFK – a Rat Pack with a plus-one. Captain James Hamilton and another OCID detective provided security at the party.

'Party girls' were checked for being wired to record indiscretions. If the media had shown interest or a curious neighbour had turned up, the moonlighting policemen would crush that interest. Then, before the days of chattering news helicopters and picture-snatching mobile phones, the cops had the power to remove anyone from an area. And they would. Forcibly. Potential intrusion and publicity were always prevented. For information on the Kennedys in Hollywood, the LAPD always had the big edge on the Feds.

Chief Parker was discomforted when he read the OCID reports and the transcript interpretations from the Fred Otash recordings. He knew he was not the only one seeing the information.

In the third week of November 1961 – the OCID files are not clear on the exact date – JFK attended a fundraising dinner in Los Angeles. He spent the night at his sister and Peter Lawford's beach house. Marilyn was there. Otash reported: 'Yes, we did have [Lawford's house] wired. Yes, I did hear a tape of Jack Kennedy fucking Monroe. But I don't want to get into the moans and groans of their relationship. They were having a sexual relationship, period.' This wasn't information America was ready for. No matter how brazen, it didn't fit the image. If you were a friend, Chief Parker, and Hamilton, and therefore the total power of the Los Angeles police, had your back, your total wellbeing, protected. They were the long arm of the law; there was nothing they couldn't or wouldn't do. Or wouldn't tell. Especially the delicate stuff.

When JFK visited Las Vegas, OCID, via its contacts in Nevada, learned the names of the women secretly brought to his hotel suite. All were high-priced prostitutes under the control of the Mafia. One of the OCID's most accomplished detectives, Con Keeler, recalled how the department looked after the welfare of JFK when it was Marilyn Monroe's Hollywood screen goddess rival Kim Novak who was his target: 'Parker was always fearful that something might happen in LA and embarrass the city. So, Kennedy himself comes to town, and they assign a car to watch him. I was like a supervisor then, and the guys are reporting to me. So, he [JFK] goes to the hotel where he checks into a bungalow and then they see him crawl out of a window and get a cab. A cab – the President of the United States... Oh, my... So, they call me.

'"What should we do?"

'"Follow him."

'So, they do... to Kim Novak's house. I call the Secret Service which is supposed to be protecting him: "Do you know where your man is?"

'"He's asleep."

'"You better check where..."'

The Secret Service would have many possible locations.

OCID files show JFK enjoyed a variety of interests, from the burlesque stripper Blaze Starr to the wives of prominent

Hollywood producers. One story was that a film executive was so honoured that the President was involved with his wife that he had the temperature of the family swimming pool increased to 'accommodate his comfort'.

With Cuba, putting a man on the moon, the Vietnam War, that accommodation always appeared as JFK's first principle, often involving the audacity of madness.

PART THREE

The Final Frontier

'Fly Me to The Moon'
> Bart Howard, 1954, *Might As Well Be Swing,*
> Frank Sinatra, 1964

Chapter Fourteen

Foreign Affairs

'Fleet Street can scent the possibilities of sex like a tile-tripping tomcat; and while sex – by which we mean, of course, extramarital or otherwise non-conformist sex – is not in itself enough to burn a minister at the stake, it makes excellent kindling.'

Julian Barnes, *Letters from London*, 1995

It was the British film and television producer Harry Alan Towers, the great roué whom J. Edgar Hoover called a KGB spy, who first confirmed Mariella Novotny's detailed story of how she played doctors and nurses with the President of the United States. Mariella, who wore a hat in all circumstances, happily put on a nurse's cap, and little else, to help JFK with his back problem.

That excursion in a bedroom off a suite in the Hampshire Hotel in Manhattan, embroiled Bobby Kennedy as America's Attorney General in an ongoing sex and security conspiracy which devotees continue to debate. In efforts to guard his brother, he worked with the FBI and the UK's MI5 in following what was called the 'Profumo Affair'. This went on through 1961–62 but did not become public until 1963. It was a security risk triangle involving UK Secretary of State for War John Profumo, model Christine Keeler and a Soviet spy, the burly GRU agent Eugene Ivanov.

Christine Keeler told the authors that, despite the many claims that she did, she never had sex with JFK on her visit to New York. She believed Novotny did and was told several girls from a London-based call girl service also performed for Senator and President JFK.

With the Cold War heating up, America's security services were utterly dismayed by what was going on in Britain. Spy scandals were like London buses, all arriving together. There were CIA agents all over the city and the US Embassy in Grosvenor Square was the only one in the world with FBI agents in permanent residence. They were Cambridge men, old school, pink-gin alcoholics and the network that gained its place in language in the mid-1950s, 'the establishment', mustered its ranks around them – and, of course, itself. The Kennedy brothers followed it all through FBI cables from London, paperwork which became the still harshly redacted Bowtie files.

Yet, there wasn't much intrigue involved to get JFK into a sexual fix with Mariella Novotny. That followed when the CIA enrolled her. It was a brave recruitment, for she played one against the other. Indeed, her original 'sugar daddy' American target was an equally rich man. She worked her schemes and her sexual adventures with her decades older, 'antiques dealer' husband Hod Dibben, whom she married at Caxton Hall, London, on 29 January 1960. Each presented varying stories of her background. She was Stella Capes, a.k.a. Mariella Capes, a.k.a. Maria Novotny, a.k.a. Henrietta Chapman, up there as a wonder of the world. She had a name for all seasons, a kink for all takers, an explanation for everything. She was a stripper to help her poor old mum; a dancer trying to make it in show business; a waitress trying to establish herself in the catering trade; a relative of the President of – take your choice – Czechoslovakia, Hungary, Manchuria and somewhere no one can remember how to spell.

Most of the crowd had no trouble recognising the name of George Huntington Hartford, one of the world's richest men and a fan of Hod Dibben's sex parties. Huntington Hartford was heir to the Great Atlantic and Pacific Tea Company, A&P, the largest supermarket chain in the world. A pleasure-seeker, he indulged his tastes in the Bahamas, where he created Paradise Island. It was all aesthetics – buildings painted strawberry ice-cream shades and many, many millions of dollars spent. In Huntingdon Hartford's home, some of the bedrooms were equipped with two-way mirrors. He created the island's Ocean Club, his own Xanadu, from monastic stones which William Randolph Hearst had been unable to use at his epic monument to himself, San Simeon on the California coast, but lovingly stored in a Florida warehouse. He knew Salvador Dalí, the Duke and Duchess of Windsor and Richard Nixon. He would spend time with heiresses Doris Duke and Barbara Hutton and movie stars – Marilyn Monroe ('too pushy, like a high-class hooker') and Lana Turner, despite saying the actress was 'past her prime' when he met her. The first of his four wives was Marjorie Steele, an aspiring actress. When they married in 1949, she was a teenager. Huntington Hartford found eighteen-year-old Mariella a little on the old side but his womanising friend Harry Alan Towers was smitten when he met her at one of Huntington Hartford's wild parties.

She was instantly invited for tea in London at suite twelve in Weymouth House in Hallam Street, a ten-minute walk towards Regent's Park from Oxford Circus. He promised to make Mariella a star. She didn't believe it for a moment but went around the next day, met Harry and his mother and went to bed with an American investor who appeared to believe that was what she was there for. She never had tea. Instead, the wily Harry produced his battered typewriter and punched out a one-page contract, no typos. He bought her a Pan Am economy ticket for New York. When Harry Alan Towers talked several times to Douglas Thompson about this, he said he had developed a relationship with Mariella in which they would enjoy sex together but as he would be busy with film contacts in New York, she could enjoy shopping at Bloomingdale's. Then he smiled: 'Hod did say she wanted to make a little money in New York, for expenses and such like, and I had no objections to that – it's what makes the world go round.' Towers confirmed Mariella's story that she had sex for money while they were both staying at the Meurice Hotel, near Times Square, though he dismissed the suggestion that he had provided or encouraged clients for her. He said they had a nasty row when he moved to a rented apartment on West 56th Street and that Mariella said he would be deported as she had contacts in the US government. A few days later he was arrested by New York vice squad detectives, charged with living off the immoral earnings of Mariella. She had given him, on two occasions, three hundred dollars towards their living expenses.

'That looked terrible but it was simply that: when she had a little money she pitched in – she was not a mean girl with anything. I know it sounds corny but I was typing up my TV shows when she was arrested by a policeman who was posing as a client. She was naked. I tried to stay out of the way, but they arrested me too.'

What Towers had missed was that Mariella was not alone in New York. Hod Dibben had followed her and, unbeknownst to anyone, had taken an apartment in the Essex House, a familiar place to British visitors to New York. Mariella also saw the actor Douglas Fairbanks Jr at his home 'for a merry time', like the threesome he enjoyed with Christine Keeler and her Profumo scandal roommate Mandy Rice-Davies. Fairbanks Jr was a sex devotee like his friend Harry Alan Towers.

Mariella and her husband also had four apartments taken in different names to run a prostitution service for 'party people' in New York: group sex parties, 'evenings for swingers' and sadomasochist specialities, all of which interested JFK's brother-in-law Peter Lawford. JFK himself had been elected President only a couple of weeks before Mariella landed in New York. She said she had sex with JFK before and after his inauguration. She said they played 'doctors and nurses' sex games with other prostitutes who were hired by Lawford. Kennedy had 'a nice haircut but a little cock'. Which he kept busy, as Harry Alan Towers languished in jail.

Initially, he couldn't raise his bail and was held in 'the Tombs', the Manhattan House of Detentions. With him were screaming and kicking prisoners, mostly drug addicts, and he said it was 'hell on Earth'. With wired money from film business 'associates', he said he made his ten-thousand-dollar bail, prompting District Attorney Alfred Donati to get it raised to twenty-five-thousand dollars, pleading that Towers would abscond and beginning decades of espionage allegations and conspiracy theories by saying: 'A large number of influential and wealthy persons involved in this case would like to see this defendant out of the country.'

The judge hearing the bail application didn't see the affable and Bristol-Cream-sherry-drinking Harry Alan Towers as a flight risk. Sprightly, for a portly man, he immediately jumped bail, drove into Canada, took a flight to Dublin, another to Copenhagen and then on to Moscow. For J. Edgar Hoover this was the final proof: Harry Alan Towers was a KGB agent and Mariella was a red Mata Hari. In reality, Towers was desperate to get financing for a movie deal and was smooching Russian investors. The problem for Hoover and his puritan policemen of the FBI was that this particular Mata Hari had seemingly had sex with their President. Quite often. And for another American official watching with an even more penetrative eye – focused obsessively on any connection to the Red Menace – the psychotic patriot of the CIA, Frank Wisner. He still held concerns over JFK's affair with Mary Pinchot Meyer who'd married into the CIA. He was a superstar of propaganda, maybe one of the best ever, and a master of covert action; a rival for Allen Dulles's chair as head of the CIA in 1959, he was conveniently appointed bureau chief of the CIA office in London. There he encountered the UK spy establishment, including the great traitor Kim Philby, whom he hadn't trusted when he was assigned to Washington and close to Jesus Angleton. They said Wisner didn't even trust himself. He was prone to deep depressions but also, savant-like, to the details of espionage puzzles, information and events which didn't fit either a pattern or themselves. His total belief was in the right of America to do what was right – how could it do anything else? No questions asked.

Eugene Ivanov had only been a note on his desk when the 'Mariella in New York' information began being fed via the FBI liaison at the embassy in Grosvenor Square. Hoover had linked it to all manner of sexual and political twists and turns and switchbacks. There was a Chinese-American woman called Suzy Chang (also known as 'Suzy Diamond') who, like the Duchess of Windsor, was renowned for a magical sexual gimmick, the so-called 'Singapore grip'. She had worked with a Hungarian madam and the President enjoyed her too, after meetings at the 21 Club in New York. Intelligence files show that 'Suzy Chang' was reported to have 'campaigned' with JFK around America before his election. They also suggest contact with Cold War enemies, more suspicion than facts.

That Communist country link sent Hoover round to see the Attorney General, the President's brother. Now, Frank Wisner was sifting through the memos, including one stating: *'The President himself has expressed concern'*. JFK was worried but not about spies, about details of his sex life being revealed. He wanted all cables about the case immediately presented to him. Another FBI memo noted the likelihood of 'an espionage-prostitution ring operating in England with American ramifications'. For Wisner, the President and a hooker was no big revelation whereas the President and Communist ladies of the night would be a story to tell. He and a Washington colleague dealt with Mariella first.

She was contacted by a female CIA agent in New York and given a walk-on ticket for RMS *Queen Mary*, which was sailing for Southampton on 31 May (the pass was for friends and relatives to say goodbye to passengers before sailing). Mariella stayed on board and by wonderful chance, a first-class cabin was available.

At the captain's table, she told her various versions of events without uttering one word of truth. Wisner was delighted with reports from the CIA agent 'Jennifer S.', who sailed with Mariella but the FBI were not in on this and alerted the British authorities that Mariella had gone.

Immigration was waiting at Southampton, but so too was Hod Dibben. Wisner had squared Mariella's arrival into Britain with the security services. What the master of propaganda hadn't figured on was the wiles of Mariella and her husband and their knowledge that greed could be rewarded in return for headlines. They sold their tale of high-level depravation and deviance at the height of American power to the *News of the World*. The crime reporter Peter Earle, a magnificent circus master of such material, left liver spots all over the copy. On publication it was about all that was left. The security services required the story to be 'edited' in such a way that it was a teenager's tame adventures in America: she didn't meet anyone or do anything interesting. Wisner kept the original copy in his desk file, the carbons were destroyed, detailing Mariella's revelations of Presidential naughtiness. It was only one of several careful, magenta ink-notated folders. There were also the details of Mariella – in her trademark hat and a dominatrix leather ensemble with spikes in her burgundy boots – hosting the infamous 'Man in the Mask' party, at which British notables were whipped and otherwise abused for their sexual pleasure. The sex parties were attended by so many senior politicians that she began to refer to herself as 'the government's chief whip'. Mariella shared, for some profit, details of the participants at her dinner party entertainments with her CIA handler. She also became a first-class informant for Scotland Yard's Frank Pulley, a much falsely maligned street copper who was one of a rare breed, an honest 1960s' Metropolitan Police detective. He worked closely with Special Branch and the

Home Office and investigated vice in London's West End, hence his keenness for Mariella's 'gossip', for she was also thoroughly well connected throughout London's underworld. She may have known – or told – too much.

The FBI case against Towers and Novotny was eventually dropped, for mysterious reasons. Mariella's death on 1 February 1983 – officially she died by choking on a custard pudding – has never been explained. There was much conspiracy talk of CIA and KGB involvement but Scotland Yard's Frank Pulley thought it was home-grown gangsters who found out she was a police informant.

In the Cold War, information was prized, a highly valuable commodity, yet Frank Wisner believed in direct intelligence from his agents in the field. The analysis by politicians was usually misdirected. Cynical and unstable, Wisner took everything personally but he was immensely powerful in the CIA, with its extraordinary budget and deep-penetration agents. He was also good at his job of spreading the American message: you don't stand on Superman's cape. Frank Wisner's mission was to save the world from communism. With 'Operation Mockingbird' he began to influence the American and international Press. One 'thinking' magazine in London, *Encounter*, was secretly funded by the CIA. It broadcast the views of, among others, Anthony Crosland, who had entered Parliament for the second time as MP for Grimsby in 1959. Along with Labour Party stalwarts Roy Jenkins and Denis Healey, he was a friend and protégé of their leader, Hugh Gaitskell. They were seen as modernisers and it was their lean to the right of the Labour Party that encouraged the CIA to entertain their thoughts. Jenkins, unsurprisingly, thought the magazine was funded by a kindly Cincinnati gin distiller; Crosland used it to promote his social democratic programme. The CIA knew all about the MP who, as Frank Wisner would point out, in theory they were paying. He had married Hilary Sarson in 1952, a marriage that had dissolved itself emotionally within a year and officially five years later. Crosland had girlfriends and one long-term romantic engagement was with the actress Shirley Anne Field, who died aged eighty-seven in December 2023 and who had links to the Profumo Affair through her friendship with the central figure in the scandal, the osteopath Stephen Ward.

Field described her relationship with Crosland: 'I was drawn to him not only because he was witty and confident but because he was committed politically. He told me all the policies he wished to instigate and, on some occasions, I went with him to his constituency in Grimsby. He was passionate about everything, not just his political beliefs. It's no wonder some politicians are in the headlines for private reasons as well as political ones.'

Ah, that political passion. With happenstance, she found that out firsthand once again – with JFK. Of course, Peter Lawford was involved. He was always happy to help, to tempt her into the arms of a President. Shirley Anne Field who was a most famous young actress – co-star, with Albert Finney of *Saturday Night and Sunday Morning* (1960), with Laurence Olivier in *The Entertainer* (1960) with Steve McQueen and Robert Wagner, a former boyfriend of Judith Exner, in *The War Lover* (1962). She was publicising *The War Lover* with an appearance on *The Johnny Carson Show* when the series was taped in New York. With her were Zsa Zsa Gabor and Mob comic Jimmy Durante and after the show she was told there had been a call from the White House asking about her. She thought it was a joke, her friend Dudley Moore playing a prank. It wasn't, as she found out a couple of weeks later when she had moved across America to Los Angeles. She'd been at an 'afternoon tea' with Charles Feldman (Peter Lawford's agent, who had hosted the party where JFK first met Marilyn Monroe) and told us: 'A day or so later, I received a call from Peter Lawford and he invited me to a party he was having at his beach home. He told me his party would be the one I'd always remember. Be sure to come, he said, because someone very special would be there. That was all he said, other than this special person would be the most attractive person I could ever hope to meet.

'I knew it wasn't just another Hollywood party when I was searched, frisked, by two security men. After an hour and quite suddenly without any fanfare President Kennedy was there. He walked over to me with two Marine guards on either side of him. He asked them to leave and we talked. He said I was a difficult person to meet and I remembered the call after the Carson show. Oh, yes, he was chatting me up. That's why I was there, I'd experienced enough of that to know what was happening. Of course, I was flattered.

'With him close-up he had a certain presence and he was very attractive and dynamic. I was a young girl, really, and in awe. He leaned over as he was speaking and his head was only inches from my face. He said it was more comfortable for him to stand like that as he had a bad back from a war injury [!]. He had to go, he said, but asked me to be a guest at a lunch party soon.

'On cue, the next day Peter Lawford called me and said I'd been a big hit with the President. There was going to be a big party the following month and he wanted me to be there and said the President would be. I was staying with a lawyer friend of my business manager in Malibu and he wasn't keen on me going to any Peter Lawford yacht parties with President Kennedy or anyone else: "You'd better take yourself seriously as an actress or you'll get a reputation as a party girl around town." I respected his advice.'

Frank Wisner didn't like coincidences, no matter how innocent the outcome. In the 1950s, he worked closely with Kim Philby and liked him, thought of him as a friend. He was aghast when he found evidence that made him suspect Philby was a traitor, a Soviet spy. Convinced but not convinced, he put his doubts to James Jesus Angleton who, after investigations, expelled Philby from America. Philby went back to work for the SIS in London with some of those he'd gone to school with.

Wisner never trusted Britain again. With JFK in the White House, he sat in his offices in London surrounded, it seemed, by spies, sex parties and secrets, and once again East–West tensions growing – the Cold War was driving him mad. And he didn't like having J. Edgar's boys in town.

The FBI in London were ordered by Hoover to discover any 'dirty detail of possible significance' on the social scene in Britain which, in reality, meant London where the Soviet spooks were walking around, looking like Savile Row suits on the wrong hangers.

Ironically, there was peril closer to home, in Washington. Mariella turned a turn at the Quorum Club, an amusingly described 'gentlemen's club', at the Carroll Arms Hotel in the American capital. It was founded by Bobby Baker, who became an influential 'page' in the US Senate and, in time, chief aide to Lyndon Johnson, called by *The New York Times*, 'One of the most influential non-elected men in the American government of the 1950s and early '60s.'

He also almost destroyed President JFK. The Quorum Club was a thinly disguised knocking shop for the politicians and their associates. Previously, Baker had provided his high-rise condominium for JFK's discreet use and now the President, who was close to Bobby Baker in his years as a senator, presumed he was safe to engage in regular dalliances at the Quorum. It offered food and drink and a constant turnover of beautiful women. The club was equipped with a buzzer that would alert the senators when they needed to run across the street for a vote at the adjacent Senate office building. Often it had to be sounded loudly. While Mariella visited, Suzy Chang and her colleagues were regular hostesses. New York born in 1934, Esther Sue Yan Chang worked in London as a 'model and actress' before taking to the more lucrative entertaining of America's distinguished decision makers. She had a good friend who looked like Elizabeth Taylor and caught the ever-roving eye of JFK. He didn't think for a moment she could be a spy from behind the Iron Curtain. Then, he wasn't introduced by Bobby Baker to Bertha Hildegard Elly but to the newly named statuesque East German-born former model, Ellen Rometsch. Modern available files tell the truth at last about the affair, the President, and the Communist spy. JFK was discreet in his approach using his close friend, Bill Thompson, to ask the twenty-seven-year-old at the Quorum Club if she would accompany him for dinner at the White House. Eager Bobby Baker arranged for Rometsch to be taken to Bill Thompson's apartment and onto the White House to have dinner with the President *on many occasions*. The authorities had no doubts Rometsch was a spy, and a good one. They'd singled out a group of attractive German women 'sleepers' who honey-trapped information posing as good-time girls to the movers and shakers inside and outside government. This Cold War covenant operated *by personal escapades, prostitution, partying, sex orgies*, and, according to the FBI files, 'so forth…'

Bobby Baker, who died in 2017, said the then Congressman and future President (1974–1977), Gerald Ford had a fond time with Ellen Rometsch. What level of information received is not recorded in the FBI files but she admitted sex affairs with influential politicians she met at the Quorum Club. And she'd visited the White House many times. As an East German, and not that long since American and Russian tanks had confronted each other at Checkpoint Charlie in divided Berlin, this remarkable-looking woman began a literal Red alert. Apparently, J. Edgar Hoover was so upset he wanted to impeach JFK. JFK's lover had worked for German Communist powerhouse Walter Ernst Paul Ulbricht. Rometsch was brought in for interrogation by the FBI but proved a difficult subject to grill. Nevertheless, with fears over the Profumo affair and JFK's links to that scandal, it was decided she should be deported. Yet, there were no official grounds to do that. The US State Department could not remove Rometsch without disclosing a specific reason to the West

German authorities. Discretion was again deployed to protect the President. The FBI inquiry evidence (a 478-page file with the code number 105-122316) was made available unofficially to the West German authorities. Hoover, as a favour to Bobby Kennedy played down the espionage angle with senators but gossiped – giving names – of the senators who had been 'entertained' by Rometsch and her friends. He also scored RFK points by avoiding mention of the German's sex sessions with JFK in investigations of Bobby Baker. Finally, on 21 August 1963, Rometsch was expelled from America and following events postponed further contemporary inquiries into a high-risk JFK sex scandal which could not be easily dismissed.

For Wisner and his CIA colleagues, President JFK posed other huge risks as the Space Age President intending to boldly go where Eisenhower had been careful. Meanwhile, the nuclear cloud kept on growing. In 1956, Eisenhower said he'd been advised that a Russian nuclear attack on America would eradicate 65 per cent of the population: 'It will literally be a business of digging ourselves out of the ashes, starting again.' Then in 1959, he declared: 'If nuclear war begins, you might as well go out and shoot everyone you see and then shoot yourself.' Throughout all these edge-of-holocaust moments, behind the scenes the American Joint Chiefs of Staff were set to blast away. Eisenhower resisted, there were no more skirmishes to be had; conflict was now an all-or-nothing option. And push-button technology is pugnacious.

In Moscow, they did not regard as 'an idle gesture' the newly instigated US programme of building nuclear fallout shelters in major cities. Inside the Kremlin, there was distrust and dismay: what if the Americans launched a pre-emptive nuclear attack? Khrushchev had much experience of Eisenhower but not the same comfort with JFK in the Oval Office. JFK presented a more defiant posture. And his generals were whispering the question, 'What's the point of all this military if we can't use it?'

There was a telephone conversation recorded at the White House between the President and his friend Paul Fay, America's Secretary of the Navy, who'd pretended to be Angie Dickinson's date at the inaugural.

'Have you got round to building that bomb shelter, yet?' JFK asked.

'No, I built a swimming pool instead.'

There was a pause on the telephone line.

'You made a mistake.'

Chapter Fifteen

Fear and Folly

'*There's no big apocalypse. Just an endless procession of little ones.*'
Neil Gaiman, *Signal to Noise*, 2007

Such were the Kennedy off-the-books high risk adventures that, in endeavours to contain their secrets and lies, cover-ups begat cover-ups, and throughout their enablers kept quiet. Irritable at deepening crises in personal, and world, affairs any dissent was dealt with by charm and promotion or menacing threat.

The Mob, never given to charm, were equally feisty. They needed to clone Cuba, move base to an equal opportunity dictatorship, preferably in the sunshine and not too far from America and potential money-spending junketeers. Central America was popular but lacked glamour and there were already more CIA agents there than tourists. The decision was the Dominican Republic, a fast boat from Havana, a semi-detached country sharing the island with next door voodoo-land Haiti, and close to Key West, just off the Florida coast. It fitted the bill exactly.

The obstacle in 1961 was the island's dictator, Raphael Trujillo, who made his neighbour Papa Doc Duvalier appear benevolent, and even given the competition, was arguably one of the most evil men of the twentieth century. He was a mad despot capable of deep-frying virgins. And just as the American Mafia needed his allegiance was hovering between the USA, who maintained financial and CIA support, and Moscow. Declassified documents show American policymaking and, from Eisenhower through JFK, the mantra was to keep even the deranged dictators happy if it kept out the communists, following on from Eisenhower's determination to overthrow the Cuban revolution in November 1959, the Bay of Pigs operation in April 1961 to the Kennedys' ever-ongoing Operation Mongoose of 1962.

Yet, Raphael Trujillo was a problem for those coupled American dynasties, the Mafia and the Kennedys. And, as always, JFK's sex life was in the middle of the action through his friendship with the killer, spy and legendary lover – the man acclaimed for his giant, and mostly permanent, erection – Porfirio Rubirosa.

From a military-diplomatic family, Rubirosa was, at age twenty, a captain in the Dominican Republic (DR) military before being assigned to collect Trujillo's daughter Flor de Oro from the airport. The next day Trujillo personally promoted him to be a lieutenant of his Presidential Guard: his protégé took the hint and in 1932, married de Oro. A roving diplomat, the striking Rubirosa represented the DR at the Berlin Olympics – as cosy with Hitler as JFK's lover Inga Arvad – and in Paris, Rome and Havana.

When the marriage ended after five years, Rubirosa remained close to Trujillo – *He is good at his job, because women like him and he is a wonderful liar* – for whom he'd murdered political opponents. He was questioned by American authorities over the kidnap and torture of his President's exiled opponents but never detained. Dissidents were whacked by the Mob or, and this was considered worse, put in the care of DR's secret police, the *Servicio Inteligencia Militar*, led by the evil Colonel John Abbes Garcia. *Johnny* Garcia got on well with Sam Giancana, they were both psychopathic killers. Rubirosa enjoyed their company. His love life disguised his work as an assassin. He married five times, including American tobacco heiress Doris Duke, in 1947, whose wedding-day gifts were a cheque for half a million dollars, a sports car and a converted

B-25 airplane. It kept the marriage going for thirteen months. In 1953, he married Woolworth heiress Barbara Hutton, previously married to Cary Grant – Cash and Cary – while he was involved with the equally marriage happy Zsa Zsa Gabor. Hutton gave him $3.5 million in cash and gifts during their fifty-three-day marriage. JFK somewhat hero-worshipped Rubirosa for his sexual prowess. Rubirosa endured priapism which kept him aroused but made it difficult for him to achieved orgasms. His renowned size convinced waiters at Maxim's in Paris to name their huge pepper mills *Rubirosas*. Still, it was Rubirosa's flexibility, politically, which attracted him to the Kennedys and the Mob. They wanted him to spy for them, discover that if President Trujillo, with CIA help, was removed from office if his son Ramfis, a general in name, but ruthless and spoiled like his friend and sometime brother-in-law Rubirosa, would stay loyal to America. That anti-communist stance would allow political comfort for JFK and open up casino society for the boys rather than being forced to find another country to corrupt.

Despite the lifelong help and support he'd received from Trujillo, he decided this was the best option. The deal was sealed at a little-known meeting he had with JFK aboard the Kennedy family yacht, Joe Kennedy's 92.3-feet-long, wooden and sleek seduction cruiser, *The Honey Fitz*. They sailed out of Cape Cod in early 1961 and spent nearly four hours planning the future of the DR and Rubirosa. To little grief, Raphael Trujillo was assassinated on 30 May 1962. With the end of three decades of almost constant terror, General Ramfis Trujillo took over with the support of his Secret Service monster Johnny Garcia who, as part of the smoke and mirrors surrounding the killing of President Raphael Trujillo, set about personally murdering 'suspects'. Ramfis Trujillo did not have Rubirosa's staying power and, fearful of dissent, abandoned the DR before the end of 1962 for the protection of Franco in Spain; he took with him his father's coffin, the remains comforted by American multi-denominational dollar bills the equivalent of thirty-five million dollars in 2024. He died after crashing his Ferrari sports car in 1969.

If you are known by the company you keep… behind closed doors in Washington many were aghast at JFK's personal, one-on-one dealings with rogues like Rubirosa and, by proxy, the mass-murdering Garcia. This whispering was exacerbated by the assassination of Patrice Lumumba, the first Prime Minister of the Congo, three days before JFK's inauguration in January 1961. JFK's apologists argue that as JFK was only President-Elect at the time of Lumumba's death, he couldn't have had any say. He, of course, was fully briefed after his election and during the transition period. US documents say CIA chief Allen Dulles ordered Lumumba's assassination as 'an urgent and prime objective'. Declassified CIA mission details indicate two plots to liquidate the African leader, one by shooting, the other by a poison created by the CIA's Sidney 'Dr Death' Gottlieb, a chemist and spymaster who took a vial to the Congo in September 1960. The plan was as absurd as some of the notions about killing Castro – the poison would be introduced on to Lumumba's toothbrush. The CIA station chief Larry Devlin admitted failures to do that. Instead, on 17 January 1961, 'contractors' from Belgium comprised a firing squad which shot dead the Congolese independence leader.

The contracted assassination solved the problem for Belgium and America and Britain who wanted Lumumba 'got rid of' as he threatened UK mining investments in the Katanga area of the Congo. Diplomat Howard Smith, later head of MI5, said in documents discovered decades later: 'I can see only two possible solutions to the problem. The first is the simple one of ensuring Lumumba's removal from the scene by killing him. This should solve the problem.' The second option is not explained but it was similar talk within the Kennedy White House and the gossip swirling about Washington which concerned JFK's admirers.

One of them was Laura Bergquist Knebel, a journalist for America's respected *Look* magazine, who reported on JFK in the Senate and as President. She had an easygoing, accessible relationship with JFK and he closely listened to her especially as she had interviewed Fidel Castro and Che Guvera. In 1965, she gave an oral history interview to the John F. Kennedy Library and in the buried away paperwork she talks of his risky contacts with characters like Porfirio Rubirosa. Before that she gives something of an explanation as to why he has such media protection before and after his death:

'Like any politician there were some journalists he liked better than others or trusted more – but almost every reporter I know who had had prolonged contact with Kennedy had the same experience. That he would divulge tremendously candid, unexpected, across-the-board facts, personal opinions, which would shake them up. It was miraculous to me that nobody seemed to break the trust or print these off-the-cuff remarks. I don't think he used candour as a technique, or perhaps he did, but just by his being so frank, you felt honour-bound not to use the confidence. Another thing, I felt I could talk as candidly with him. Working with other subjects who dropped casual remarks, well, you figure they knew you were a journalist, and you might go ahead and print same. But somehow you didn't often do it with Kennedy.

'An example: When Kennedy ran for the Senate, there was really no Massachusetts paper of any substance supporting him. Then suddenly, the Boston Post switched from endorsing [Henry Cabot] Lodge to Kennedy. It later came out publicly that the Boston Post had been lent money by Ambassador Joe Kennedy when it was in a precarious financial position.

'There was a certain assumption among pols [politicians] and the Press that there was a connection between the endorsement for Kennedy and the loan. Bearded about this rumour, [Kennedy] said: "Listen, that was an absolutely straight business transaction; I think you ought to get my father's side of the story.

'"You know . . . . . that paper." [Never reported at the time].

'Jack's father, of course, was then a very controversial issue. There was talk that old Joe was really running the show and buying his son's election and that he had great influence on Jack. A lot of important people I knew in Washington – political types or journalists – discounted Kennedy because they thought he was kind of a "golden boy" dominated by Big Daddy. I was very sceptical he would be elected President. I wasn't overwhelmed by him.

'I think he really got jolted by the Bay of Pigs fiasco and he certainly was up to his ears in the Dominican [Republic] mess. I also stewed about some of his buddies, his social companions, because I thought in terms of Latin America, for instance, his hanging around with Earl Smith [husband of JFK's lover Florence Pritchett Smith], who was probably one of the most stupid ambassadors to Cuba we ever had. Incredibly so; a great apologist for Batista. Then there was Senator George Smathers of Florida and playboy Porfirio Rubirosa. That bothered me because Rubi had been a henchman for dictator Trujillo and there he was, socialising at the Hyannis compound at a time when Trujillo's Dominican Republic had been expelled from the Organization of American States. I used to think, Kennedy is so smart about so many things, doesn't he realise the fact that Rubirosa is a guest at Hyannis, at a time of great turbulence in the Dominican Republic because this is when Ramfis, the dictator's son, had taken over and Porfirio was a Ramfis buddy and there were murders going on by the score, doesn't he realise that in Latin America this is going to have repercussions? OK, I was told by one Kennedy staffer, Rubi and Smathers were just social pals. But the Latins figure, "There Rubi is up at Hyannis, he has the President's ear." And this is going to nullify a great deal of the message Kennedy is trying to get across with the Alliance for Progress, for example. Who knows what Rubirosa tells him or what influence he has – or an Earl Smith or a George Smathers? The association was bad news.

'Once I talked to Ted Sorensen [JFK's adviser]. I think George Smathers had just gone to Mexico and made some idiot remark that enraged the Mexican government, and I went to talk to Ted and I said, "Doesn't the President realise what having buddies like Smathers around means to the Latins, what the repercussions are down there?"

'And Ted said, "Why don't you go tell him?"

'I said, "You're crazy. Why should I tell him, who am I to tell him that he can't hang around with George Smathers?"

'I mean, he and Smathers had been buddies for years, Smathers was an usher at his wedding. They were kind of young bucks in Congress together. Ted said, in effect, that if I told him, it might have more impact. I was coming from the outside, I'd heard the feedback. "You ought to go in and tell him what you think about his association with George Smathers." I gather Ted felt as I did.

'Another time I'd just done a piece on the post-Trujillo Dominican Republic; as it turned out, a number of prominent Americans had been on the take from Trujillo, including Smathers, and the Kennedy buddy Igor Cassini, the gossip columnist, who turned out to be an unregistered agent for the Dominican Republic. [By then Igor's brother, Oleg Cassini, Gene Tierney's former husband, had, in this small world, become Jackie Kennedy's favoured fashion designer]. I remarked how shocking it was that a character like Rubirosa, PR man for Trujillo, had been a guest of the Kennedys at Hyannis. I don't know how it ever got into Look magazine, but I also wrote about a dwarf named Snowball, of the Trujillo torture chambers, who specialised in biting off men's genitals. Anyway, I went to the White House to see Mrs Lincoln about something or other and the President popped out of his office. He said abruptly, "Read your piece on the Dominican Republic," which as usual startled me. Then he asked, "What's this about all those Americans being mixed up with Trujillo?"

'I said, "That's true, including some of your buddies."

'He said, "Well, let's talk about it," and then added offhand, "Hey, whatever happened to that dwarf?"

'When I was reporting on the Dominican Republic, I was horrified by what had gone on during the Trujillo regime. After Trujillo was murdered, a special mission went down to the Dominican Republic when Ramfis, Trujillo's son took over. This was a kind of fact-finding mission, at the behest of Ambassador Joe Kennedy or the President.

'And the whole point was that Igor was employed by Ramfis to clean him up, in a PR job, make him look like a respectable new strongman, friend of the US, and all that business. Igor Cassini denied everything, but he finally got indicted for being an unregistered agent.

'It bothered me plenty that the President of the US was somehow mixed up with sleazy characters like these.

'When I came back from the Dominican Republic, I called up Pierre Salinger [JFK's Press Secretary], once again steaming with indignation. Now why I felt so protective about Kennedy – not protective perhaps, but like, goddamn it, he should know about this dirty business and if he's involved knock it off – I said, "Listen, I've come back with material on Igor Cassini and Porfirio Rubirosa that will blow your mind. Believe me, this information is going to come out and it's not going to resound to the President's credit to be associated with these characters."

'Pierre got sore and said: "Rubirosa is not a friend of the President's. The President knocked him off a long time ago. They're not buddies anymore."

'I was then hooked on the subject of Rubi, because behind that playboy facade lurked such a gangster, he'd been a finger man in political murders. I was concerned, generally, with US involvement with Latin dictatorships.

'Cuba seemed a real obsession, problem, with him, especially in that first year or two of his Presidency. It had been a campaign issue; then came the Bay of Pigs and it was as critical and explosive an issue as Vietnam is now. It was Kennedy's first big political boo-boo as President and it rankled. Bobby especially; Cuba was one touchy *subject for the Kennedys. The fiasco was attributed to bad intelligence, but I also think it was bad intuition, judgment on Kennedy's part. He'd made a campaign promise, in a sense he'd implied he'd get rid of communist Cuba and he was stuck with that.'*

Laura Bergquist Knebel was candid throughout her contribution to the Kennedy Library and also talked about JFK's attitude to women. She saw it close up in the White House and wasn't impressed on the equality front:

'I think Kennedy liked women very much. He was very male, or what the Latins call "macho."

'I think, as he grew older, he probably would have gotten more like his father. He was getting more patriarchal, more familial. Maybe it was the Irish mick in him, but I don't think he took women seriously as human beings, for instance, that you work with casually, as I do in my business. The evidence is that in his administration there were really no important women. He married Jackie who had her own special kind of intelligence, but though she's very strong, as Bobby once said about her to me, that, "She's good for Jack because he knows she's not the kind of wife, when he comes home at night she's going to say, 'What's new in Laos?'"

'He liked pretty women, female, female women, clever women, but not somebody in the sense of an equal working partner in the business of government. I think, for instance, of that time when he accused me of having the "hots" for Che Guevara. What riled me was that he depreciated my appraisal of Che by that sexual remark. Now partly, he was giving me the needle, he knew I'd probably rise to the bait and give him a hard time or sputter or something. But that was the way his mind worked. For him, obviously, Che was this attractive character by whom I'd been beguiled and bedazzled. In essence, what I got mad about was that I was not to be taken seriously because I had let Che's male charm somehow befuddle my judgment.'

Which is, arguably what sometimes happened to a sex pest like JFK. He even admitted his problem to British Prime Minister Harold Macmillan, which was naughty, as he knew from intelligence reports that Macmillan's wife Dorothy was at the time having an affair with Bob Boothby, the Conservative MP and one-time fiancé of JFK's wartime lover Inga Arvad. 'I wonder how it is with you, Harold? If I don't have a woman for three days, I get a terrible headache,' he told Britain's last Edwardian-style Prime Minister.

Security, as always, was intense for these summit meetings but there were other safety concerns, when JFK and Jackie Kennedy attended a state banquet at Buckingham Palace in June 1961. Special Branch told Royal Protection Officers to alert the Queen and 'watch out for anything untoward' from the visiting President. This was confirmed by a top-ranking Scotland Yard detective and in 2023 a former protection squad officer said it was part of the force legend that the late Queen was amused at the thought of a JFK approach.

JFK never changed his voracious sexual pace when he travelled and in London he was helped in his needs by revolving 'secretaries'. He was fond of English women and Harry Allen Towers said the President was 'rather taken' by Pat 'Magic in an Angora Sweater' Marlowe who was also friendly with, among others, the late Duke of Edinburgh.

Christine Keeler talked about Pat, whom she liked: 'She was an Essex girl, Anita Wimble, and had the most amazing breasts; she went without a bra long before the Sixties got going. Pat wanted to become rich and famous so she went out with rich and famous men. She knew the Hollywood producer Mike Todd before he married Elizabeth Taylor.'

Harry Alan Towers was a great fan. He said JFK had seen her in New York and Los Angeles. He thought they also met in London but could not be certain. Pat Marlowe certainly got around.

She was 'mistress of ceremonies' for the British band leader Jack Hylton and his touring talent shows. It was a full-time job with Hylton. On her first night, Ben Warriss, half of the UK variety act Jewel and Warriss, sent her a congratulatory telegram signed by everyone she had slept with. Towers said, 'She shrugged it off. She was pragmatic. She was always in Monte Carlo or Paris and she loved the good life. She got involved with Jack Warner who ran Warner Brothers Studios in Hollywood. She was living in his house [on Angelino Drive, Beverly Hills] but they had a big argument and she moved to the Beverly Hilton Hotel. Jack Warner wanted to make up and invited her for lunch at the Hilton.

'"How had she spent the morning?" Jack asked her.

'"Shopping," she replied.

'Jack asked her what she had bought, pointing out that anything she'd got would be charged to her room for which he was paying.

'"Just a coat."

'"What colour?' he asked.

'"White," she said, getting up to leave for the airport, pausing, and with the farewell smile added: "Mink." Pat had charged a twenty-thousand-dollar mink to her room.

'She was a character but a lot of it was for show. She did get deeply involved with some of her men. She was with Jack Hylton for a long time. She had an affair with Max Bygraves; they met up in his dressing room at the London Palladium and she had a son, she called him Stephen, by him. He was brought up by an aunt. I don't think Max Bygraves ever acknowledged their son. She killed herself in August 1962 [acute barbiturate and promethazine poisoning] and her son was only about fifteen months old. She was pregnant when she died and I was told by those who would know that the father was ... but we'd better say a prominent royal. The story that was put about as to why she committed suicide, was that it was because she was despondent over the death of her friend Marilyn Monroe who she got on with.'

Pat Marlowe, aged twenty-eight, died on 6 August, her body discovered at her home in London's Mayfair two days after Marilyn Monroe's death. JFK was a link to both tragedies, a man personally besieged, with the spectre of nuclear destruction fast approaching.

Chapter Sixteen

Cliffhanging

'For the first time in his life Kennedy has met a man who is impervious to his charm.'

Prime Minister Harold Macmillan on JFK v Khrushchev, 1963

The world survived 1962 and, surprisingly, so did the Kennedy administration, if not some of the players in their lives.

It was a kind spring evening, 19 May 1962, at Madison Square Garden when Marilyn Monroe appeared in her moment of theatrical Viagra. She shrugged off her ermine wrap to reveal herself naked inside a skin-tight, rhinestone-encrusted gown and stepped up to the microphone and wished the President happy birthday in song, in a child-like, playful voice which has echoed her story and sadness ever since.

It was a blatant overture. The Jean Louis custom-made, sheer, flesh-coloured design, with more than 2,500 hand-stitched crystals, was so snug fitting that Marilyn Monroe was sewn into it. It was blatant. When she appeared, she wasn't the only one holding her breath. That evening should have had alarm bells.

JFK, and especially Bobby Kennedy, had heard them ringing in the preceding weeks and months. And throughout the months leading up to Marilyn's death there were constant displays of wild behaviour by JFK and his staff. It was becoming too much to ignore. But ignored it was. It wasn't until 1997 that it was reported in the American Press: 'The President did not simply have affairs. He had a taste for bimbos, girls brought in off the street by friends acting as procurers; that he liked cavorting naked with such women in the White House pool, that friends often joined him, and sometimes his brothers Bobby and Teddy as well.' Described were parties at Bing Crosby's estate in Palm Springs: 'The high point – or low point – of Presidential partying … Secret Service men described drunken debauchery when state policemen guarding the front of the house thought the wild cries coming from the pool might be an invasion of coyotes. The women were introduced as stewardesses from a European airline, but who they really were the Secret Service men had no idea.'

In *A First-Rate Madness*, Nassir Ghaemi of the Tufts Medical Center recounts how JFK used the White House swimming pool for sexual encounters including his ongoing affairs with Judith Exner and Mary Meyer, the sister-in-law of *Washington Post* editor Ben Bradlee, and two secretarial staff, the 'blondes' Priscilla Wear and Jill Cowan, nicknamed 'Fiddle' and 'Faddle'. He also reports that unknown women 'presumed to be prostitutes' were regulars at the White House pool which, for whatever reason, was filled in by Richard Nixon when he became President. Ghaemi forcefully suggests that Kennedy's drug use, and the control of it, led to distinctive episodes during his term in office, simply the good and the bad. The less successful was most certainly from 1961 to 1962 when, it is argued, his judgement was not at its best.

Among the White House staff at Bing Crosby's estate was yet another JFK conquest, Mimi Beardsley, an 'intern' and regular lover of the President. She became known as 'JFK's Monica Lewinsky' after she revealed details of her affair in a book, *Once Upon a Secret* (Hutchinson Radius, 2011) after the long-running relationship was discovered following more than four decades of secrecy. Under her married name, Mimi Alford, she described being told by the President to perform oral sex on one of his aides while he watched. He also asked her to *take care* of his younger brother Ted, which she refused to do. In the book she is pertinent about the atmosphere and situation during her weekend in the spring of 1962 in Palm Springs. And that she was not there to have sex with the President. That was Marilyn's chore.

'We headed out to Bing Crosby's house in Palm Springs, where a large festive crowd – many from the entertainment industry – had gathered to greet President Kennedy. I felt like I'd been admitted into some wonderful, secret club. But then the evening turned into a nightmare,' she writes in *Once Upon a Secret*. 'There was a large group of people, a fast Hollywood crowd, hovering around the President, who was, as always, the centre of attention. I was sitting next to him in the living room when a handful of yellow capsules – most likely amyl nitrite, commonly known then as poppers – was offered up by one of the guests.

'The President asked me if I wanted to try the drug, which stimulated the heart but also purportedly enhanced sex. I said, "No," but he just went ahead and popped the capsule and held it under my nose. For the first and only time since I met him, I was relieved not to see him – and fell asleep in one of the guest rooms.'

In one of the guest cottages, Marilyn was wide awake and, with the President lying in her bed, she called her friend, her masseur Ralph Roberts. Roberts explained in much later interviews that Marilyn said she was 'arguing with a friend' about the muscle system and put President Kennedy on the phone with him: 'I was listening to these familiar Boston tones. I told him about the muscles and he thanked me. I didn't reveal I knew who he was and he didn't say.'

Several people reported seeing the President and Marilyn as an intimate couple that weekend and many more kept quiet, for there were plenty of people around and there was no concerted effort to conceal the arrangement. There never appeared to be much effort to disguise such foolhardy behaviour. To American youth and the nation's liberals, from whom the hawk-like instincts were disguised, John Kennedy was something of a god: a contemporary newspaper report has one twenty-six-year-old man saying: 'We were so relieved to have a young, good-looking person in the White House after Eisenhower.'

The Kennedy brothers' infatuation with Marilyn Monroe was turning into a fear of the consequences. Bobby Kennedy was being pressured by senior politicians to cut her out. The stories of their sex lives might not be in the newspapers, but the Washington Press corps and the city's political constituency was speaking with some fluency about the goings-on. Strong pleas were made to keep her far away from what became a legendary if ultimately tragic gala evening held to celebrate JFK's forty-fifth birthday. Marilyn stood alone in a spotlight on a dark stage and the world watched her. Peter Lawford had got her there, Bobby Kennedy wasn't happy she was there and President Kennedy appeared guiltless.

The First Lady had absented herself, having heard a radio broadcast by columnist Dorothy Kilgallen that Marilyn and a stunning dress were going to be the highlight of the evening for the fifteen thousand specially invited guests.

A live event is nerve-stretching at best, but this was miracle working. Marilyn was surfing on champagne and coffee, preparing to present happy birthday, ten days early, to the President. Peter Lawford was aristocratic in his dinner jacket, looking off into the wings, waiting for a bright light, calling for Marilyn until at last he can welcome *the late Marilyn Monroe...*

When she came into the bright platinum spotlight her confidence was painted all over, much like her dress. What followed were televised moments of absurd recklessness. She surely knew what she was doing, she'd made love to the camera enough times. It was a premeditated marker, the dress her weapon of choice. It *was* titillating. Dorothy Kilgallen, who was present that evening, described Marilyn's performance *as making love to the President in the direct view of forty million Americans.* One of America's great golden era newspaper snoops, Dorothy Kilgallen also wrote in her notebook that Marilyn and Bobby Kennedy danced five times together; that was at a penthouse party held after the gala. There are no released files to corroborate how the evening ended but the consensus is that Marilyn left with President Kennedy and went to his suite at the Carlyle Hotel. As far as anyone alive knows she never saw President Kennedy again. On 24 May, only about one hundred hours since she breathily sang to him, she was back in California and telephoned by Peter Lawford at Hyannis Port. He had a message from the President. It was brutal and clear: she would never see and must never try to contact the President again. *Ever again.* It was a cruel letdown.

The Kennedys were doing what they did best, protecting themselves. It was brazen, behaviour provoked by the supreme pressure being applied by Marilyn herself with threats to go public about the dangerous liaisons. There were other problems. Dorothy Kilgallen is recorded telephoning the Justice Department and asking if Bobby Kennedy will confirm his affair with Marilyn. She was one of the most determined of the contemporary investigative journalists who simply didn't accept what they were told.

(Kilgallen applied the same pressure about the assassination of President Kennedy and was writing a tell-all book about it when she was found dead on 8 November 1965, in her Manhattan apartment from 'a drug and drink overdose'; there was no investigation despite a staged crime scene and her friends' suspicions she had been murdered because of what she knew and was about to publish. She died a year after the still unsolved murder of JFK's lover Mary Pinchot Meyer.)

Marilyn was dismayed by JFK's treatment of her. She called the White House, her 'access' was declined. It had been, she was told by the switchboard, cut off. What Peter Lawford had told her – 'Look, Marilyn, you've just been another of Jack's fucks' – was her nightmares of abandonment come true. It couldn't be. She wrote letters to the President and the Attorney General. She telephoned the Department of Justice but couldn't reach Bobby Kennedy.

Peter Lawford was her lifeline to the President and to Bobby Kennedy, to whom she had become most closely attached. Some of those around her during 1962 said she was *mesmerised* by him.

One of America's foremost newspaper columnists, Earl Wilson in his landmark biography *Sinatra* (W.H. Allen, 1976), admitted he had kept secret 'Jack and Bobby's sharing of Marilyn Monroe and other girls' and revealed just that. He was pressured by the Kennedy family but nothing official was ever done against him. Never seen until they were published in our *Bombshell* in 2021, extracts from Marilyn's diary, read and noted by Mike Rothmiller, simply confirm in Marilyn's own words what was known:

'*Bobby is gentle. He listens to me. He's nicer than John.*'

'*Bobby said he loves me and wants to marry me. I love him. John hasn't called. Bobby called. He's coming to California. He wants to see me.*'

There are records of person-to-person telephone calls made by Marilyn to Bobby Kennedy in Washington and at the St Francis Hotel, San Francisco.

Mike Rothmiller reports on what he read in her diary: 'The entries weren't dated, but they indicated when Robert Kennedy and Marilyn first had sex. Robert Kennedy was in Los Angeles and briefly stayed with the Lawfords. She had dinner with Peter and Robert; then Peter left for the evening. It was then she and Robert had sex for the first time. The entry read: "*Bobby and I made love at Peter's. He wants to see me again. This is our secret.*"

'One OCID report stated that Robert Kennedy impregnated Marilyn and shortly after the pregnancy was confirmed he pressured her to travel to Mexico under an assumed identity for an abortion. As on all OCID intelligence reports, the informant's credibility ranged from *reliable* to *unknown*. On this report, the informant was listed as *unknown*.' Between 19–21 July, 1962, Marilyn was in Cedars of Lebanon Hospital, Los Angeles, under an assumed name for a curettage or an abortion.

The Marilyn/Kennedys arrangement was *very* crowded. The evidence we present in *Bombshell* shows that Bobby Kennedy and

Peter Lawford were with Marilyn at her Spanish colonial home *Cursum Perficio*, Journey's End, in Brentwood in West Los Angeles when she died on 4 August 1962. And that RFK had direct responsibility for her malicious death and what became a sixty-year cover-up.

These were perilous times. Marilyn thought she was more important than government business. And, at times, it appears the Kennedy brothers thought the same. It was not a question of *if* but *when* it would all collapse into tragedy. That summer, as the administration puzzled over Vietnam, Bobby Kennedy, as Attorney General, attended a test in the Nevada desert of the H-bomb, the first try-out of a thermonuclear weapon in America proper. The *Sedan* nuclear device had an explosive power of 104 kilotons, the equivalent of eight Hiroshima bombs. This is the height of the Cold War.

One of the earliest and most influential accounts of the Cuban Missile Crisis was written by RFK, who was a member of the Executive Committee of the National Security Council (ExComm), the group swiftly formed to advise the President during the crisis. In his book, *Thirteen Days* (published posthumously in 1969 and never out of print), Bobby Kennedy portrays himself as playing a leading role in the deliberations. A White House aide, who read a manuscript version of the book in 1964, shortly after JFK's assassination, remarked: 'I thought Jack was President during the missile crisis.'

Bobby, who was then campaigning for the Senate, replied: 'He's not running, and I am.'

In death, the Kennedy brothers, especially JFK, achieved near-canonisation in a disproportionate weighing of legend and achievement. This has become more apparent with the release of classified information and previously unknown tape recordings of deliberations. Author Martin J. Sherwin, in *Gambling with Armageddon: Nuclear Roulette from Hiroshima to the Cuban Missile Crisis* (Knopf, 2020), highlights Bobby Kennedy's judgement, especially his lack of it in a crisis. Martin Sherwin debunks the official narrative of the thirteen days and the boasts that Bobby Kennedy and other members of ExComm, *through their careful consideration of the challenge, their firmness in the face of terrifying danger and their wise counsel, steered the world to a peaceful resolution of a potentially civilisation-ending conflict.*

'Nothing could be further from the truth,' writes Sherwin. 'The guidance JFK received was, for the most part, lousy. Some of it was loony. Had he heeded ExComm's "wise counsel", chances are I would not be writing this, or you reading it. As the President told a friend not long after the crisis ended, "You have no idea how much bad advice I had in those days."'

Most of that advice came from his brother. 'Oh, shit! Shit! Shit!' the 'levelheaded' Attorney General screamed when told Moscow was putting missiles in Cuba: '*Those sons of bitches Russians!*'

Another intriguing revelation from Sherwin questions Bobby Kennedy's prized moral high ground. On 16 October, day one of what the Americans call the 'Cuban Missile Crisis', Cubans call the 'October Crisis', and the Russians call the 'Caribbean Crisis', he suggested America should 'sink the *Maine* again or something' to give a pretext for invading Cuba. USS *Maine* was the Navy ship that sank in Havana Harbour in February 1898, a catalyst of the Spanish–American War that April. If truth is indeed the daughter of time, much of it has emerged, albeit sometimes in redacted form, over the years.

Following the Watergate scandal, with the focus so much on President Richard Nixon's 3,432 hours of secret White House tapes, it was discovered that JFK was there first. During his face-off with Nikita Khrushchev and amid the possibility of nuclear apocalypse, he'd secretly taped most of ExComm's deliberations with a recorder installed in the basement of the West Wing that he could discreetly activate by flipping a switch where he sat at the Cabinet Room table. Microphones secreted in the wall behind his chair picked-up the voices of everyone in the room. Only the Kennedy brothers and veteran Secret Service officers knew about the taping which JFK suddenly felt was necessary to protect his 'legacy'.

It was decades later that the explanation for his increasing paranoia about the politics of his own cabinet room emerged. It went back to President Eisenhower who didn't care for JFK and called him *Little Boy Blue* to his staff. Ike was convinced that *his* troops of Cuban exiles trained, at a cost of many millions of dollars in friendly Guatemala, would swiftly depose Castro. He wanted JFK to move forward with the mission plan and the new President was trapped into doing just that.

He'd attacked Richard Nixon – 'If you can't stand up to Castro, how can you be expected to stand up to Khrushchev?' – and was told by Eisenhower to make good on his pledge – 'whatever is necessary' – which forced him into the disastrous Bay of Pigs. When colleagues began denying involvement in the debacle, JFK decided to bug the West Wing VIP meeting room.

The finally declassified tapes and information released following the break-up of the Soviet Union offered details highlighting that just about everything anyone has claimed about his own conduct can be questioned. As the twenty-first century moves on, more and more insight is becoming available to counteract the rose-tinted recollections of Camelot, the often intuitive myth-making created by the vacuum left by untimely death.

The resolution of the Cuban Missile Crisis – days during which there was a real possibility of nuclear war creating a world of famine and fallout – is sometimes portrayed as super-intelligent brinkmanship by JFK and equally wily and clever moves by Khrushchev. It's painted as a chess game when it was political poker where neither player had a clue what was in the other's hand. What was regarded as statesmanship is now seen, by drawing on new documentary evidence, as days of second-guessing, fingers-crossing and, in several cases, dumb luck with egos and national pride in the ascending. There are remarkable moments at the very beginning for the crisis when you must wonder if JFK truly knew anything.

On tape he says Khrushchev's motives for placing missiles in Cuba are a mystery and asks: 'Why does he put these in there? What is the advantage of that? It's just as if we began to put a major number of MRBMs [medium-range ballistic missiles] in Turkey. Now that'd be goddamn dangerous, I would think.'

One of the advisers points out, 'Well, we did it, Mr President.'

There's a moment's silence on the tape and then JFK moves on to other aspects of the business tormenting the world.

New evidence, most of it sanctified by being locked away inside filing cabinets in dusty basement rooms, is gradually emerging. It includes audio tape surveillance of Civil Rights champion Martin Luther King secretly authorised by RFK. The Kennedy brothers were publicly portrayed as heroes and protectors of black Americans but when J. Edgar Hoover discreetly asked Attorney General RFK to approve 'technical surveillance' of Martin Luther King's Southern Christian Leadership Conference headquarters he signed off on it.

Hoover was asking to clandestinely install wiretaps on the telephones and microphones within various offices. Why? What Federal criminal activity was King and his associates suspected of plotting or committing? Hoover answers the question himself, none. Hoover just states that King is an associate of Stanley Levison, a 'concealed' member of the Communist Party. In law enforcement intelligence circles, *concealed* means there's no evidence to substantiate the allegation, but you need legal cover to conduct the operation. Hoover held a burning hatred for Martin Luther King and used the immense power of the FBI to destroy the man. The Attorney General's approval provided Hoover legal authority and, more importantly, cover for Hoover if the operation was discovered. In the 1963 memo, it is clear RFK agreed to sign off – for thirty days when evidence would

be evaluated for the mission to be re-authorised, which it was –
only after assurances that the FBI dirty tricks operation would
stay secret. Hoover's ambition was to take King down publicly,
criminally, or under control by extortion. Quietly manipulating
King would be a political objective of the Kennedy brothers. A
bonus, Hoover held career-ending information on the Kennedys.
RFK risked a backlash if he did not authorise the wiretaps. So,
the Kennedys helped set up the equally sexually adventurous
Martin Luther King as a bullseye target for J. Edgar Hoover.
Documents released in 2019 of the RFK approved tapes, show
a startling parallel between JFK and Martin Luther King. They
detail King's wild sexual activities with dozens of women as he
crossed America campaigning against racial inequality. William
Sullivan, Assistant Director of the FBI, wrote in a 1964 memo
that King joked to his friends in his bugged Washington hotel
room *he had started the International Association for the Advancement of
Pussy-Eaters*. Another FBI recording claims King *looked on, laughed
and offered advice* while a friend, a Baptist minister, raped one of
his *parishioners*. The tapes said to show the assault were being held
in 2019 in a vault under court seal at the US National Archives.
The revelations on the tapes, in FBI summaries, were found by
historian David Garrow who won a Pulitzer prize in 1987 for
Bearing the Cross (William Morrow, 1986) his life of Rev. King.
His biography also won the *Robert F. Kennedy Book Award* – ironic
as he approved the wiretap on King.

Garrow gave details of his findings in the British monthly
magazine *Standpoint* in June 2019. He revealed the FBI planted
miniature transmitters in two lamps in rooms booked by King in
January 1964, at the Willard Hotel which is near the White House.
FBI agents in nearby rooms listened in electronically with radio
receivers, the conversations silently transferred to tape recorders.
King was accompanied by a friend, Logan Kearse, the pastor of
Baltimore's Cornerstone Baptist Church, who had arrived in
Washington with what an FBI summary describes as 'several

women *parishioners* of his church'. Kearse invited King to meet the women in his room, where they 'discussed which women among the *parishioners* would be suitable for natural and unnatural sex acts'. The FBI document adds: 'When one of the women protested that she did not approve, the Baptist minister immediately and forcibly raped her' as King watched. At the same hotel the following evening, King and a dozen other individuals 'participated in a sex orgy' including what one FBI official described as 'acts of degeneracy and depravity … When one of the women shied away from engaging in an unnatural act, King and several of the men discussed how she was to be taught and initiated in this respect. King told her that to perform such an act would "help your soul".'

At one point J. Edgar Hoover sent an incriminating tape and an anonymous letter to King, calling him an 'evil abnormal beast' and warning him that your adulterous acts, your sexual orgies were 'on the record for all time'. The letter ended with a veiled suggestion that King should commit suicide 'before your filthy, abnormal, fraudulent self is bared to the nation'. When King learnt of the tape's contents, he is said to have told one aide over a wiretapped phone line that the FBI was 'out to get me, harass me, break my spirit'.

The tension with the Civil Rights surveillance and the animosity involved in its undertaking was put to one side with what – in off-office comments Hoover reckoned 'the Limeys up to their old tricks' – a prominent UK politician was caught with his trousers down in California. Ominous decades ago, no more than the lift of an eyebrow in the twenty-first century, the incident allowed the FBI director to improve his relationship with RFK and, in turn, allow him to endear himself to the British government. Secrets were valued currency in those days of mistrust and potential Armageddon but continually it was personal indiscretion which afforded ammunition for leverage and favours.

The UK Liberal MP and future leader of his party, Jeremy Thorpe, was known by MI5 and the FBI and the CIA and other security agencies for his homosexuality, which was illegal in the UK. In a quid pro quo, Hoover gave RFK a 'passionate' letter written and sent by Thorpe to an American man known as *Bruno* he'd met during a 1961 visit to San Francisco: 'If I'm ever driven out of public life in Britain for a gay scandal then I shall settle in San Francisco.' An FBI memo reads: 'The letter makes reference to a possible homosexual relationship between [redacted] and Jeremy Thorpe. The letter was written by Thorpe and bore a return address of the House of Commons, London. The Attorney General stated that he wanted to inform [redacted] of this matter on a personal basis "as the British can't afford another disclosure of this kind".'

The letter, dated April 1961, was discovered in 1963 when Bruno was arrested in New York for breaking probation following a theft conviction. Thorpe writes in the letter: 'It was an unkind stroke of fate that we should only have met at the very end of my stay in San Francisco... I don't know how you feel, but although we only met so briefly, I miss you desperately. How I adored San Francisco... the one city where a gay person can let down his defences and feel free and unhunted. Somehow, we must meet again, either I must get on to San Francisco on some mission, which the British or American taxpayer will pay for! Or one summer we must get you to Europe for a really good holiday.'

Thorpe offered to help Bruno find work. He asked him to write to him at his home or at the House of Commons but warned that 'the letter should be marked personal!' Thorpe also requested a photograph and enclosed one of himself, explaining: 'I have a spare passport one which I send along. I'm afraid it's a bit smudged at the back. But it will remind you of my front!' He signed off by saying: 'I can't tell you how happy I am to have met you. Yours most affectionately, Jeremy.' RFK knew too well the importance of keeping personal secrets personal. Which helped, even fourteen years later, during Thorpe's trial for conspiracy to murder his lover Norman Scott, a young riding instructor with whom he'd had a long affair. A gunman had lured Scott to the moors and in a madcap comedy of error shot dead his Great Dane, Rinka, in October 1975. The Old Bailey heard that Thorpe, concerned that the relationship would be made public, told a fellow Liberal MP: 'We've got to get rid of him... it is no worse than shooting a sick dog.'

Thorpe refused to give evidence. He was said to be fearful of the witness box. Only with the new FBI documents did the reason become clear. The prosecution had his letter to Bruno and he did not want to be quizzed about his sexual adventures. Which appeared rather incidental given the 'evidence' being accumulated on Dr King.

David Garrow said that the FBI material on King includes hours of surveillance recordings that were sealed by court order for fifty years in January 1977. Yet, significant documents have been made available following judicial appeals. Garrow said in UK interviews that he had spent several months digging through a King-related document dump on the National Archives website, among them electronic copies of documents that were five hundred pages long. In *Bearing the Cross*, Garrow discussed what he then knew of King's extramarital adventuring but admitted he had no idea of the scale or the extent until he saw the FBI files. 'I always thought there were ten to twelve other women, not forty to forty-five.' He said he believed that in the evidence of King's indifference to rape 'poses so fundamental a challenge to his historical stature as to require the most complete and extensive historical review possible.'

Something, arguably, Martin Luther King is not alone in requiring.

RFK wanted intelligence services at home and abroad on side as he did not want his brother asked about his connections with Mariella Novotny and her friends, especially with the talk in Washington of Bobby Baker's off-the-books 'hospitality' network. Out in the open, that alone would devastate the Kennedy government. There was great fear in the echo of an echo, as 1963 raced toward the primary elections of 1964 with the ever-darkening cloud of Vietnam threateningly on the horizon. History is packed with unlikely truths and happenings and sometimes the absurdity is what makes them impossible to hide for ever.

Chapter Seventeen

Reality

'The time may come, we've gotta just have to try to do something about [Vietnamese leader Ngô Đình] *Diệm.'*

JFK in conversation with Henry Cabot Lodge Jr on his appointment as ambassador to Vietnam, 15 August 1963. The tape was discovered in 2020 and had been previously denied.

As testament to the almighty, and lifetimes, of efforts to protect the JFK image – still a sainted figure to many millions – it took six decades for the discovery of evidence of his involvement in foreign assassinations which, arguably, provoked the greater follies and tragedies of the Vietnam War.

It brings the JFK story full circle circle, back again to conversations with his one-time Boston political rival Henry Cabot Lodge Jr, one of the most versatile and graceful American politicians of the twentieth century.

The 'lost' talk between Lodge and the President in the Oval Office on 15 August 1963 – it went from 11 a.m. to 11.35 a.m. – is remarkable. In 1991, the US State Department said 'no record has been found' of that so vital conversation. Then, there was supposedly no knowledge of JFK's White House tapes, made years before Richard Nixon's more infamous ones, until the 1980s when JFK's secretary Evelyn Lincoln revealed they existed. It was the diligence of a Texas historian, Professor Luke Nichter, which alerted us to the taped conversations. In his book *The Last Brahmin: Henry Cabot Lodge Jr and the Making of the Cold War* (Yale University Press, 2020) he questions the conventional history of America's 1960s' involvement in the Vietnam War. We sourced the full taped conversation from the National Security Archive at the George Washington University in Washington DC and in comments JFK points toward *executive action* capability for killing foreign leaders.

When Lodge was appointed US ambassador to Vietnam in the summer of 1963 the Kennedy Administration was feeling abused by the American media reporting from Saigon – JFK told *The New York Times* to take its correspondent David Halberstam out of Vietnam, because he didn't like his reports on America's failures in the war – and was suspicious of South Vietnam President Ngô Đình Diệm. And wondering if they'd be better off without him.

Diệm, and his younger brother and adviser, Ngô Đình Nhu, who was married to the troublesome Trần Lệ Xuân, known internationally as Madame Nhu and, with Diệm unmarried, as the besieged nation's First Lady, kept court together at the Independence Palace in Saigon. It was not all happy families. Bickering replaced table talk. Outside the palace, there was intrigue as the despotic government employed torture and persecution to keep control, cruelly oppressing Buddhists which allowed world outrage.

At that 15 August White House meeting, the transcript report reads 'the President very much concerned by what was going on in Vietnam. He referred particularly to the famous Associated Press picture of the Buddhist monk, Quang Duc, burning himself alive. I suppose that no news picture in recent history had generated as much emotion around the world as that one had. President Kennedy referred to that picture, to the overall importance of Vietnam, and to what was going on in Saigon – to the fact that apparently the Diệm government was entering a terminal phase. He also mentioned the extremely bad relations that the [American] Embassy had with the Press. He said: "I suppose that these are the worst Press relations to be found in the world today, and I wish you, personally, would take charge of Press relations."'

Lodge briefs JFK on his meeting the previous evening with Thân Thị Nam Trân, wife of Vietnamese Ambassador to the US Trần Văn Chu'o'ng and, vitally, the mother of Madame Nhu. JFK and his new ambassador Lodge discussed Lodge's challenges and the President bluntly tells him: 'The time may come, though, we've gotta just have to try to do something about Diệm, and I think that's going to be an awfully critical period. I don't know how well prepared you are for that out there, or who we would sort of support, or who we would and I think that's going to be the key – your key problem this year. This woman's right. You don't see other situations that go on without disintegrating [unclear] information. It may be that they ought to go, but it's just a question of how quickly that's done, and if you get the right fellow who...'

There's no direct talk of 'a coup' from JFK but he makes clear he'd be willing to accept regime change under certain circumstances. Lodge cautions on the difficulties of controlling a coup, warning that Madame Nhu's mother believed that she, along with Diệm, Ngô Đình, were all going to be assassinated. The transcript offers:

Lodge: 'They're all going to be assassinated: her daughter [Madame Nhu], son-in-law Nhu and the President, Diệm. And she said, "[unclear] They're all going to be assassinated. I don't think there's any question about it." The only hope they have is to get out. And she said, "I hope you," Lodge, "will advise them to get out."'

Kennedy: 'She doesn't think it can be saved – is that it?'

Lodge: 'No. It cannot be saved. And she said, "If you've advised them to go out and they refuse to take your advice let me know and I will come out and try to talk with my daughter." Now this daughter, Madame Nhu, has always been violent and impossible and – not crazy, not stupid, but…'

Kennedy: 'Yeah.'

Lodge: '…but crazy. Right. And violent, and wilful…'

Kennedy: 'Yeah.'

Lodge: '…and angry. When she was here in Washington a couple of years ago, she took an overdose of sleeping pills and they had to pump out her stomach. She's just been a terrible trial to both of them, always. She says that she talks like this and a lot of them talk like this – because Diệm, and Nhu, this is what they really think, and they like to hear her talking like this…'

Kennedy: 'Yeah.'

Lodge: '…which is quite revealing.'

Kennedy: 'Is she a Buddhist – this woman [Thân Thị Nam Trân]?'

Lodge: 'Oh, yes. She's a Buddhist and she's a very devout one. And Madame Nhu was born a Buddhist and then…'

Kennedy: 'Became Catholic.'

Lodge: '…a convert. I don't know how good of a Catholic she is anyway.'

Kennedy: 'She's political. She'd put a lot of the church [unclear] [laughs].'

Kennedy: '…everybody always – everybody gets attacked – you remember all that stuff about Greece at the end of the war? You know, when the communists really almost took over Greece, you know?'

Lodge: 'Yeah.'

Kennedy: 'And all that was written in the American Press was the fascist nature of the Greek government. So I don't think there's any doubt that the Press are instinctively – a lot of them are liberal and some very – and they harry against any authoritarian regime they [unclear]. Then there's the – so I don't know – I've never – I assume that probably this fellow's [Diệm] in an impossible situation to save, but I just want to be sure we're not getting our policy made for us by a couple of smart, young reporters.'

Lodge: 'Of course, their viewpoint at the time – they're looking at a story – they're looking at something sensational. And they're not – they don't realise that an authoritarian government is what the people have always had in most parts of the world.'

Kennedy: 'That they have to have, it's just that there really isn't anybody else to run it – just this bitch [Madame Nhu], of course. She's made it – she's made it – well, as I say, I think we have to leave it almost completely in your hands and your judgment. I don't know whether we'd be better off – whether the alternative would be better.'

Pause.

Kennedy: '… Two years ago, everybody was saying we're all through out there in six months. And you know, then we're [unclear] coming out that we'd have to put American troops in there… I just figure that we don't want to get carried away until you've had a good chance to look at it.'

On 2 November 1963, with deniable White House approval, the CIA supported South Vietnam's military when they launched a successful coup d'état led by General Du'o'ng Văn Minh and arrested Ngô Đình Diệm and Ngô Đình, after the generals called the palace offering Diệm exile if he surrendered. Fearful for their safety, Diệm and his entourage escaped and found refuge in a Catholic church, only to be recaptured. They were stabbed by bayonet and shot, assassinated on the direct orders of Văn Minh.

JFK was 'shocked' by the killings but his surprise was credited to 'good acting'. Henry Cabot Lodge, aware of the circumstances, had warned the Vietnamese leaders to go into exile. After the coup, Richard Nixon wrote: 'The heavy-handed participation of the United States in the coup which led inevitably to the charge that we were either partially responsible for, or at the very least condoned the murder of Diệm and his brother, has left a bad taste in the mouths of many Americans. This may not seem important now, but I don't need to tell you that the villains of today may become the martyrs of tomorrow.'

A diary entry by JFK reads, 'We must bear a great deal of responsibility for it.'

The regime change, and the replacements puppets toppled on like falling dominoes, just as inevitably brought the deployment of the first US Marines to the beaches of Da Nang in March 1965. It was the start of the full American military involvement in Vietnam which was a challenge for America's new President, Lyndon B. Johnson, another mess left for someone else. President Johnson took his oath of office aboard Air Force One on 22 November 1963. More than sixty years on, those six seconds of photographic images from Dallas, on the day a President died and an industry was born, remain freeze-framed in memory, those tragic ticks of time still the most studied and debated in American history: JFK, hubris again, risking himself in an open-top limousine, standing tall, held as an erect target by his back brace; Jackie Kennedy in her pink suit and matching pillbox hat; JFK grinning and waving, the crowds cheering and the gunshots shattering the world, ending a thousand days of the Camelot carousel.

Joe Kennedy, whose influence was insidious and malign, the template for the sexual adventures Kennedy pursued during his Presidency, could not take in the happenings of Dallas. Two years earlier, on 19 December 1961, a thunderous stroke left him without speech and almost totally immobile; trapped in a wheelchair and within himself with the antecedents of organised crime in America, his involvement compelling as a factor for what happened in Dallas. JFK never escaped his father.

There is one JFK story which still catches the breath.

Marlene Dietrich, who had that intense affair with Joe Kennedy in the south of France in the 1930s – and on the dancefloor stuck her hand down young JFK's trousers – visited him at the White House on 11 September 1963. In her diary she writes that in the afternoon she wrote a letter to the ailing Joe Kennedy and then notes, 'White House drinks Jack.'

Until her death, aged ninety in 2006, Dietrich enjoyed the gossip around her 'quickie' at the White House that evening which began with JFK's all but instant approach. She was twenty years older.

'You know, Mr President, I am not very young.'

Moments later: 'Don't mess my hair, I'm performing.'

Three minutes later, JFK is asleep. Dietrich, running late for an award presentation, gets herself together and wakes the President. He calls his valet ('clearly used to this sort of thing') and with a towel around his waist, he takes her to the small elevator across the hall from the bedroom and 'shook my hand as if I were the Mayor of San Antonio'. But something is bothering him: 'Did you ever go to bed with my old man?'

The supreme diplomat: 'He tried but I never did.'

As if involved in a competition with his father, a triumphant JFK: 'I always knew he was lying.'

Nearly thirty years later, Dietrich's daughter Maria Riva, who'd danced with the twenty-one-year-old JFK at Elsa Maxwell's Riviera summer ball, recounted the immediate follow on to that White House encounter in a biography of her mother (*Marlene Dietrich: By Her Daughter*, Knopf, 1992). 'My husband when in America on business, stayed at my mother's apartment. He was there the day she returned from Washington. She came through the door, saw him, opened her large, black crocodile handbag, extracted a pair of pink panties and held them under his nose, saying: "Smell! It is him! The President of the United States! He was wonderful!"

'My husband moved to a hotel.'

Such remembrances darken the shadow across the life and times of John F. Kennedy, promoted by sentimental and careless myth manufacture as purity, only interested in a moral approach to leading the nation, crushing the Mafia, and the CIA, and promoting Civil Rights and protecting America and the world from communism. That was and is the legend. His death was such a sudden and world event that the blindingly bright memory of the assassination continues to erase – to inexplicably redact – much of what went before which, when recalled, is almost always evaluated through the prism of the Dallas denouement. It's been his get-out-of-jail card for living memory. His relationship with Judith Exner directly connected him to the senior echelons of the American Mafia; he repeatedly misled or lied to the American people about his health; he began the politics of style over substance, becoming an entertainer and making television pervasive in public life, of sound bites over policy, a good haircut trumping ideas, where those who seek political office should behave like a movie star in the fantasy factory of Hollywood where you must suspend belief. Finding a life so unbelievable, no screenwriter would dare crush the story of JFK into such a short lifetime. Reality, reckless and shameful as it is, imposes no such limits.

POSTSCRIPT

Denouements

'Three can keep a secret, if two are dead.'
Carlos Marcello, Mafia godfather, 1962

Bobby Kennedy made his bid for Presidency in 1968 and was at the heels of Eugene McCarthy until he beat the frontrunner in the Californian Democratic primary on 5 June. It was a time to celebrate, and the party location was the Ambassador Hotel on Wilshire Boulevard, Los Angeles. The Secret Service did not provide security for candidates, only nominees, and the LAPD, as they had always done for the Kennedys, planned to look after Bobby Kennedy.

On 4 April that year, Martin Luther King, aged thirty-nine, had been assassinated in Memphis, Tennessee, but Bobby Kennedy's advisers thought having uniformed police around the Ambassador was 'too provocative'. The LAPD's Daryl Gates recalled of the evening: 'Kennedy's people were adamant, if not abusive, in their demands that the police not even come close to the senator while he was in Los Angeles.'

Normally, that wouldn't have mattered. The LAPD never wanted VIP trouble in their kingdom. If high-profile targets were in town they would, unknown to most, have an undercover cop as their driver and a plain-clothes police presence.

But Bobby Kennedy and his staff were aware of this tactic and refused it. Officially, there were no uniformed or known plain-clothes LAPD officers protecting Bobby Kennedy. After delivering his victory speech, he made his way out of the hotel through the ground-floor kitchen. There he was hit by three bullets from a .22 calibre pistol. He was pronounced dead at 1.44 a.m. on 6 June 1968 at the Good Samaritan hospital. OCID, as always, ignored authority and did what *they* thought was correct. Unknown until the publication of this book is that several members of OCID were secretly inside the Ambassador Hotel when Bobby Kennedy was assassinated; and much of the evidence obtained by the intelligence squad detectives remains secret, conveniently *lost* among all the others in the history of the Los Angeles Police Department.

All but the Kennedy family *consigliere*, Johnny Rosselli got a Mafia farewell in the hot July of 1975, when he was still in charge of the Chicago Mob's gambling interests in Las Vegas. He was living quietly with his sister, Mrs Joseph Daigle, in Plantation, Florida, a little to the west of Fort Lauderdale. He was, his neighbours said, a nice, silver-haired gentleman who liked to walk his poodle and talk about such local environmental concerns as the caterpillars munching the foliage. Although he had arthritis of the spine, he played golf regularly. Another local *wiseguy* had been assassinated on the golf course earlier in the year and Rosselli never played the same course twice in a row. Still, he rejected his lawyer's advice to hire a bodyguard. He was choked to death, his legs sawn off and his body sealed in a fifty-five-gallon oil drum. Heavy chains were coiled around this casket and holes punched in the sides to make it stay underwater when it was dumped in the ocean off the Florida Golden Coast. But Rosselli rose from the depths: the gases from his decomposing body floated the oil drum to the surface. Three fishermen found it in Dumfoundling Bay near North Miami Beach. Police ran the victim's fingerprints with the FBI and up came the ID: John

Rosselli, seventy-one, emphysema sufferer and a Mafia executive who'd been involved in landmark capers and made the error of telling about them. In June 1975, Rosselli testified before the Senate Intelligence Committee (SIC) investigating the excesses of the CIA. This is where he should have counted up to five and pleaded the Fifth Amendment. Rosselli not only talked, he provided the details of how he and Sam Giancana had been recruited by the CIA to assassinate Fidel Castro.

Five days before Rosselli sang, his Chicago boss and close Sinatra associate Sam Giancana was murdered in the kitchen of his heavily protected home in Oak Park, Illinois. He was shot in the back of the head as he was frying spicy Italian sausage and peppers and, after he collapsed to the floor, the killer, Tony Spilotro, flipped the body over. He blasted the man who shared a lover with Sinatra and JFK six more times with a .22 calibre pistol – once in the mouth, five bullets under the chin. He was silenced the old-fashioned way. Giancana, who knew more secrets than most, was scheduled to testify, like Rosselli, for the Church Committee, before the SIC, about CIA collusion with the Mafia to kill President Kennedy. Giancana was buried beside his wife in his family mausoleum at Mount Carmel Cemetery in Hillside, Illinois; a cigar is often wedged in the door of the tomb.

When Giancana was called before a Grand Jury on 1 June 1965, he wouldn't talk and was jailed for a year, the duration of the judicial hearings. He hated his time inside and, on his release, he abdicated his Chicago empire and moved to Cuernavaca, Mexico, and began plundering the southern Americas. He also, usually with singer Phyllis McGuire, enjoyed trips to London and Paris and kept his Mexican hosts 'sweet' with profitable shares in his illegal enterprises. He enjoyed nearly a decade before the Mexican government gave in to US diplomatic pressure and extradited him to give evidence in Washington. Back in America, his social life was curtailed by heavy police protection. The authorities knew Giancana's life was at high risk.

And he went, the Chicago way, on 19 June 1975, eleven months after his return to America and days before he was to give evidence before the Church Committee. Anthony 'Tony the Ant' Spilotro (played by Joe Pesci in *Casino*, 1995) was, according to files, responsible for twenty-four Mafia murders. He took over duties in Las Vegas from Johnny Rosselli and worked with Frank Rosenthal (Robert DeNiro in *Casino*) managing the skim – the illegal profits – from a quartet of Vegas Strip casinos. Spilotro himself ran out of luck on 14 June 1986 when he upset the boys in Chicago. He and his brother Michael were discovered eight days later, buried in an Indiana cornfield: they had been hit on the head and strangled to death by 'friends'. Which seems appropriate recompense, as Sam Giancana had watched over Spilotro's career, arranged his move to Las Vegas and, according to testimony from Salvatore Bastone, one-time capo of the Chicago outfit, 'was fucking crazy about him'. He told the story without telling the story: 'Sam sure loved that little guy Tony Spilotro. It was Sam who wanted Tony Spilotro out in Vegas. Even with all the problems with the skim and all, Sam always stood behind the guy. Tony was over to Sam's house all the time. He lived right by there. Did you know Tony even figured out a way where he could get in through the back of Sam's place without anybody seeing him? He'd go through other people's yards, go over fences, all sorts of shit.'

Salvatore Bastone was clear that murder-by-friends was a convenient way of doing business. Was Sam Giancana killed because of what he could and would say about the Kennedy assassination? 'There's never just one reason for shit like what happened to Sam. There's a million of 'em.'

Joseph Kennedy outlived three of his sons. He died at home at Hyannis Port on 18 November 1969.

PART FOUR

Death of a President

'The CIA clearly did lie about the case. There were many cases where they seem to have tried to cover their tracks.'

G. Robert Blakey, Chief Counsel, House Select
Committee on Assassinations, 19 November 2013

Mike Rothmiller writes:

Since Dallas, countless conspiracy theories have flourished. Some are imaginative and impossible to believe. In contrast, others are grounded in factual information, with the blanks filled in to complete the circle. However, none can substantiate their theories with solid evidence, which is not surprising. The US government has refused to release many records surrounding the assassination. Not releasing some documents may have been valid at the time, but many decades later, it is not. The people of America and the descendants of President Kennedy have a right to know the entire story, no matter where blame, criminal liability or embarrassment may fall.

As a former detective, I have many unanswered questions. However, I will remain sceptical of any future assassination information the government provides. I'm presenting this information through the eyes of an intelligence detective.

As with my official investigations into the Mafia, I tried to eliminate as much background noise as possible and summarise factual, meaningful data to assist you in understanding the various components possibly leading to the assassination and the conspiracy to influence the official Warren Report investigation. I've included verbatim transcripts of various official documents and significant portions of others. As in a trial, readers are the jurors and must decide the documents' relevance and significance to this case.

Dallas, Texas
22 November 1963
Around 12.30 a.m.
Lee Harvey Oswald and his wife, Marina, were not living together. Lee rented a room in Gladys Johnson's Oak Cliff boarding house at 1026 N. Beckley Avenue, Dallas, Texas, for eight dollars a week. At the same time, Marina was living with Ruth Paine in the Dallas suburb of Irving, Texas. With a mysterious break of habit, Lee arrived at the Paine home Thursday night instead of the usual Friday night. Marina noticed Lee was uneasy and having difficulty sleeping.

6.30 a.m.
Marina said Lee was tense while dressing for his job at the Texas School Book Depository. After a cup of coffee, Lee strangely removed his wedding ring and placed it in a cup atop Marina's dresser. Next, he put $170 from his wallet and into the cup with his ring. Marina noted Lee was anxious, but she didn't know why. Marina asked if he was OK but didn't receive an answer.

Lee's co-worker, Buell Wesley Fraizer, picked Lee up for the drive to the Texas School Book Depository. Buell noticed Lee was carrying a long item wrapped in paper and asked what it was. Lee claimed they were curtain rods for his room at the boarding house.

Fort Worth, Texas
22 November 1963
Approximately 7.00 a.m.

On the last day of his life, President Kennedy and Mrs Kennedy awoke in their suite at the Texas Hotel and began readying themselves for the day.

Approximately 8.45 a.m.

A large crowd waited patiently in the rain for the President and Mrs Kennedy to exit the hotel. A small platform was erected near the hotel's front entrance, allowing the President to address the throngs of enthusiastic supporters.

'There are no faint hearts in Fort Worth,' President Kennedy began, *'and I appreciate your being here this morning. Mrs Kennedy is organising herself. It takes longer, but, of course, she looks better than we do when she does it.'*

After the laughter stopped, he mentioned the nation's need to be 'second to none' in military defence and space exploration. He hoped for continued economic growth and *'the willingness of citizens of the United States to assume the burdens of leadership'*. After his brief comments, he shook hands with admiring onlookers before re-entering the hotel.

9.00 a.m.

Back inside, Kennedy addressed a breakfast meeting of the Fort Worth Chamber of Commerce, with the theme of his speech being military preparedness. *'We are still the keystone in the arch of freedom,'* he said. *'We will continue to do our duty and the people of Texas will be in the lead.'* He ended his speech, smiled and acknowledged the thunderous applause.

10.30 a.m.

The President and Mrs Kennedy returned to their hotel suite and prepared to travel to Dallas. Perhaps due to a deep-seated fear or premonition, the President said to his wife, '*You know, last night would have been a hell of a night to assassinate a President.*' It's believed his uneasy comment referenced their late-night motorcade through Fort Worth.

The Presidential Party departed the Texas Hotel and the motorcade travelled directly to Carswell Air Force Base. The President's flight aboard Air Force One would take less than fifteen minutes and mark the last stop of his life.

Arriving at Love Field Dallas, the President and Mrs Kennedy quickly de-planed and immediately walked to a fence line to greet a waiting crowd of supporters. They walked the fence line for several minutes, shaking hands.

The President wore a grey business suit, a long-sleeve, white shirt with thin vertical blue stripes and a dark blue tie with lighter designs. Interestingly, just before Kennedy entered the waiting limousine that carried him to his death, he changed neckties and placed the one he had worn earlier into his coat pocket. Later, Mrs Kennedy gave that tie to Preston Bruce, the White House doorman, saying, '*The President would have wanted you to have this.*'

Elegantly dressed and radiant, Mrs Kennedy wore a pink Chanel, double-breasted raspberry pink coat and skirt. Her coat's lapel was navy blue and she wore a pink pillbox hat and white gloves. She received a fresh bouquet of red, long-stem roses, which she carried to the waiting Presidential limousine.

With the weather clearing, Secret Service Agent Win Lawson removed the plastic bubble top from the President's limousine. Kennedy made it clear that he wanted to be accessible to the public and as much as possible, when circumstances and weather permitted. He also didn't want Secret Service Agents riding on the back of the limousine.

Texas Governor John Connally and his wife Nellie were already waiting in the second row of seats of the black, highly polished, six-seat, open convertible, Presidential Lincoln Continental limousine. A small American flag was mounted on a short staff above the right front fender (bumper). In the same position on the left fender was a flag bearing the Seal of the President. Without question, the image of that long, sleek limousine projected immense power.

11.50 a.m.

Several of Lee Harvey Oswald's co-workers saw him eating lunch on the first floor of the Texas School Book Depository. At that moment, the President's motorcade departed Love Field to begin its ill-fated journey.

Two hundred thousand enthusiastic Texans lined the streets of Dallas and the President's limousine presented a tempting target as it moved closer to his death. Within the Texas School Book Depository Lee Harvey Oswald had prepared a makeshift sniper's nest at a corner window on the sixth floor. His position would provide a clear view of the Presidential motorcade when it passed below.

Two armed Secret Service Agents occupied the front seats of Kennedy's limousine. Agent William Greer was driving and Assistant Special Agent in Charge Roy Kellerman sat beside the driver. President Kennedy and Mrs Kennedy were seated in the rear; slightly higher than the Connallys. The President sat directly behind the Governor and Mrs Kennedy was behind Nellie Connally. Vice President Lyndon Johnson and Mrs Johnson followed two cars behind.

22 November 1963
Approximately 12.00 p.m. (central time),
Cambridge, UK

A reporter from the *Cambridge News* received an anonymous call. The caller told the reporter he should call the US embassy in London for some big news and hung up.

After the reporter learned of Kennedy's assassination, he informed the Cambridge police of the strange call. The police immediately notified British Intelligence MI5, who notified the CIA station in London. MI5 calculated that the call was made to the newspaper twenty-five minutes before Kennedy was shot. In all likelihood, this was a crank call, but that has never been confirmed.

22 November 1963
12.30 p.m., Dallas, USA

Thousands of enthusiastic people waved and shouted to the President and Mrs Kennedy as they passed. The President and his wife smiled and waved to the joyous crowds. Slowly, the motorcade turned from Main Street at Dealey Plaza. Rapid rifle shots echoed across the plaza as the limousine slowly passed the Texas School Book Depository. Some witnesses claimed they heard two shots, while others heard as many as six.

The 2024 Presidential Candidate Robert F. Kennedy Jr, son of Senator Bobby Kennedy and nephew of President John F. Kennedy, reached out to Mike Rothmiller to discuss the assassinations of President John F. Kennedy and Robert F. Kennedy's 1968 assassination in Los Angeles. Both Kennedy Jr and Rothmiller possessed insider knowledge and knew the Warren Commission Investigation was a facade at best. They also knew the LAPD's official investigation into Bobby Kennedy's murder lacked credibility on numerous fronts.

While many of RFK Jr's findings are well thought-out and correspond with provable facts and findings of other investigators, it doesn't imply that we, as authors, agree with all his positions on issues not related to the assassinations.

Robert F. Kennedy Jr is an attorney and serious investigator. During our discussion it was clear he based his opinions and conclusions on solid evidence and strong circumstantial evidence. An investigator may not have all the answers; however, through experience and thoughtful deliberation of the known facts, it is possible to understand a puzzle without all the pieces. For example, if you studied a jigsaw of a tiger with only the eye pieces missing, a reasonable person can accurately conclude the image is that of a tiger.

RFK Jr has spent decades reviewing every detail of the assassinations and interviewed scores of people with insider knowledge. When your uncle and father are both murdered and scores of questions remain unanswered, it is only natural for a person to seek the truth, no matter how long it takes. And that is precisely what Robert has done and his investigations continue. His findings must be seriously considered.

Regarding President Kennedy's assassination, RFK Jr told Detective Rothmiller that there were eighty-eight witnesses in Dealey Plaza; twenty-one were police officers. Those cops said they heard shots from the grassy knoll to the front and right of the President's limousine. We must pay special attention to the police officers' belief that shots came from the grassy knoll because they are trained observers who fire their sidearms regularly to meet a certain proficiency level. Also, several officers were Second World War combat veterans and knew the sound of rifle fire and how to determine its origin. The police officers certainly understood how the sound of a gunshot echoes from surrounding tall buildings and can present a false impression of the point of origin.

There were buildings to the rear and the Texas School Book Depository was to the right of the President's limousine. However, there were no buildings behind the grassy knoll located to the right and in front of the President, no buildings to the front and no buildings to the left to cause an echo. However, depending on where a witness stood, they may have heard some echo. Therefore, I must assume the officers' belief that they heard shots from the grassy knoll is probably correct.

RFK Jr related the stories of two critical witnesses; he said two of President Kennedy's special assistants, Dave Powers and Kenny O'Donnell, were riding in a limousine directly behind the President. Both men were combat veterans and knew the sound of rifle fire. Both instantly thought the President was caught in a military-style sniper's crossfire when the shots rang out. Meaning two snipers were firing simultaneously from different positions. Kennedy had entered the snipers' kill zone. They witnessed the President slump in his seat after the first shot hit him. They also saw the President's head explode with the fatal shot.

Both heard shots coming from in front of the President. Later, the FBI tried to pressure the men into changing their story 'for the good of the country'. Shots coming from in front of the limousine did not fit the official story secretly ordered by President Johnson.

Eventually, Kenny O'Donnell did bow to the pressure and changed his statement, claiming the rifle shots came from behind the President. Interestingly, Dave Powers refused to change his statement and was not called to testify before the Warren Commission.

RFK Jr also mentioned that sixty witnesses later said the FBI altered what they said. Authors Anthony Summers and Carol Goetz uncovered evidence that the FBI rewrote the testimony of key witnesses to conform their observations of the single-shooter theory.

I've discussed President Kennedy's assassination several times with a highly decorated Marine Corps sniper who served in Vietnam and later as a senior police officer. First, he studied the famous Zapruder home movie and had many troubling questions. He followed up with a visit to the Texas School Book Depository. He used his sniper training and experiences in Vietnam to calculate the kill zone from the window from which Lee Harvey Oswald allegedly fired all the shots. He also walked and, with a sniper's eye, studied the surrounding area of Dealy Plaza and the grassy knoll and the white picket fence. After considering all the necessary calculations of a sniper, he walked away with many troubling questions and ominous concerns. Although not impossible, he believes it would have been extremely challenging for Oswald, or a trained sniper, to have fired all the shots within 2.5 seconds with a used Italian bolt action 6.5 x 52mm Carcano Model 38 infantry carbine and hit a moving target. The Warren Commission listed it as a 'Mannlicher-Carcano' rifle.

As a trained sniper, I asked how he would have planned the assassination. He said he would place one sniper in a tall building, such as in Oswald's window position and another on the grassy knoll or the railway bridge overpass in front of the President's motorcade. In those positions, a sniper would fire down on the President as he passed and the sniper on the bridge or grassy knoll would fire into the approaching limousine. Interestingly, his overall concerns and hypothetical sniper placement match those of other military and police snipers who have examined the location.

Based on scientific analysis of the Zapruder film, the Warren Commission determined the time between the President's and the Governor's observable reactions was too short to have allowed, according to the Commission's test firings, two shots being fired from the same rifle. FBI sharp-shooters who test fired the gun for the Commission employed a telescopic sight on the rifle. The minimum firing time between shots was approximately 2.25 to 2.30 seconds. The time between the observable reactions of the President and the Governor, according to the Commission, was less than two seconds.

RFK Jr said that Robert Tanenbaum, who served from 1975 to 1977 as Deputy Chief Counsel to the House Select Committee on Assassinations, told him, 'Oswald was working for the CIA since at least 1957. This is a fact we know from manifold sources.'

The above represents solid circumstantial evidence that a competent investigator understands and would then seriously consider the very real possibility of a conspiracy.

The various investigations weakly concluded the first shot missed Kennedy, striking the street. The second shot entered Kennedy's upper back and exited at the base of his throat and that bullet (the 'magic bullet') also stuck Governor Connally in front of Kennedy. Another shot was quickly fired and a pink cloud of bloody mist exploded from Kennedy's head, filling the nearby air with brain matter and pieces of his skull. The wound would prove fatal. He was rushed to Parkland Memorial Hospital and arrived unconscious with a weak and failing heartbeat. Once the doctors saw the head wound, they knew he would not survive.

Years later, I spoke with Dr Larry Klein who was in residency at Parkland. He was in Trauma Room One when Kennedy arrived and stood beside Mrs Kennedy. He said all the attending physicians he spoke with believed the wound in the front area of Kennedy's throat was an entrance wound. Later, it was alleged to be an exit wound from the bullet that hit Kennedy in his lower shoulder. That bullet supposedly exited his body and then hit Governor Connally.

In September 2023, *People* magazine published an interview with former Secret Service Agent Paul Landis, who was standing on the side bar (running board) of the car immediately behind Kennedy's limousine. He discussed his actions when Kennedy was shot, and his body was removed from the limousine at Parkland Hospital. Just after President Kennedy was lifted from the rear seat, placed on a hospital gurney and rushed into Trauma Room One, Landis said he noticed a fully intact bullet 'sitting on the back seat ledge, where the cushion meets the metal on the car.' He saw it was a critical piece of evidence, so he grabbed the nearly pristine bullet and placed it in his pocket. He said he was concerned someone would take it as a souvenir. After the President was declared dead, Landis said, 'I took it out and I set it by the President's left foot and it was like a white cotton blanket on the table and the bullet started to roll off the table and I reached out and grabbed it and there was a little wrinkle in the blanket. So I put the bullet so that it wouldn't roll off. It stopped in that blanket.'

I understand his stated motive for retrieving the bullet. The limousine's rear seat and floorboard were covered with Kennedy's blood, pieces of his brain and skull. That gruesome scene would attract countless curious cops, Secret Service Agents, news media and ER workers seeking a glimpse. Anyone could have taken the bullet or it may have been lost when the limousine was transported back to Washington, DC. Weeks later, the limo was stored in a secured location in Washington, since it was considered part of a crime scene. Soon, Secret Service Agents and others with access to the limo complained of the dreadful odour emanating from the decomposing pieces of Kennedy's scalp, skull fragments, and brain matter. They requested to have the limo cleaned and reconditioned. If the bullet remained in the limousine, it may or may not have been found during cleaning.

As a detective, I'm at a loss to understand Landis's actions of not safeguarding a vital piece of evidence, failing to book it as evidence and failing to mention it to his supervisor or anyone else. His action was an incredible disservice to everyone involved in the investigation and has fuelled decades of misinformation. However, I respect him for finally disclosing this valuable information. It adds to the theory that two snipers fired at President Kennedy and casts doubt on the 'magic' bullet theory proposed by the Warren Commission.

Landis and Secret Service Agent Hill stayed with Jacqueline Kennedy at Parkland Memorial Hospital while the medical staff treated the President. After returning to Washington, DC aboard Air Force One, Landis and Hill accompanied Mrs Kennedy to Bethesda Naval Hospital, where President Kennedy's autopsy would be performed.

FBI agent Francis X. O'Neill Jr's report of 26 November 1963, stated that, during the autopsy, the doctors noticed the bullet wound in Kennedy's back. Dr Humes probed the wound with his finger and believed it wasn't deep. Examining X-rays, 'the individuals performing the autopsy were at a loss to explain why they could not find no bullets' in the President's body. During the autopsy, Dr Humes learned that Secret Service Agent Richard Johnson had recovered a bullet from a stretcher at Parkland Hospital and had already given it to the FBI. It was then that Dr Humes speculated that the bullet must have dislodged from

President Kennedy's back during an aggressive cardiac massage at Parkland. They assumed the back wound was also fired from behind the President.

After completing the autopsy, Mr Hagen, Edwin Stroble, John Van Haesen and Thomas Robinson from Gawler's Funeral Home embalmed the body and prepared it for burial.

Unaware of Landis's actions, the Warren Commission hypothesised that a single bullet entered Kennedy's back, exited at the lower front of his throat and struck Governor Connally. That conclusion was dismissed by many.

If Landis was truthful about his actions, his secrecy caused immense damage to the investigation and caused additional confusion for decades. It may have allowed a second sniper to escape arrest and prolonged a major conspiracy. Considering the numerous lies, intentional obstructions of the assassination investigation and the alleged altering of photographs depicting Kennedy's injuries, the following can be postulated as one possibility supporting Landis's statement. We cannot say if this is correct since there isn't enough independent hard evidence. It is provided for consideration.

The Landis statement, if accurate, points to an explosive possibility when combined. The idea is with the observations of some doctors who treated Kennedy at Parkland Memorial Hospital and eyewitnesses to the shooting. Let us recap: Dr Charles A. Crenshaw, who battled to save Kennedy's life in Trauma Room One, said the wound on the front of Kennedy's throat was an entrance wound, meaning that the shot was fired from the front, not from the Texas School Book Depository. Some witnesses in Dealy Plaza said they heard shots from the grassy knoll or the railway overpass directly in front of the limousine. It is implausible a shot was fired from the railway bridge overpass since police and railroad workers were observing the motorcade from the bridge. Landis said he found the bullet 'sitting on the back seat ledge, where the cushion meets the metal on the car'.

The diagram drawn by the pathologists performing the autopsy depicts a wound just below Kennedy's right shoulder, near the shoulder blade. In the limousine, Kennedy's back was at the approximate height and just inches from where Landis claims he found the bullet. Why does this matter? If accurate, it provides additional evidence that Kennedy was shot from two directions, proving there were two gunmen.

If his back wound was indeed an entrance wound fired by Oswald from the sixth floor, the bullet's trajectory was at a severe downward angle. One would logically expect the bullet's exit wound to be lower than the entrance wound. It would not exit Kennedy's lower throat since, once it entered his body, the bullet would need to make a drastic upward turn to exit at the base of his throat. It is highly doubtful that this occurred. The bullet was nearly pristine and bore no significant deformities, indicating that it did not 'ricochet' off a bone inside Kennedy's body. If it were a through-and-through wound entering from the back, it would likely maintain its initial downward trajectory and exit below Kennedy's throat, probably near his chest or abdomen. But that is not the case.

One can, in theory, consider that a shot fired at a downward angle from the grassy knoll or another elevated location in front of Kennedy struck him in the front lower portion of his throat, causing an entrance wound. The bullet then passed through his upper body, continuing slightly downward and exited from the wound in his back. That would be the logical bullet trajectory. If accurate, it would explain how the bullet ended up in the position Landis says he found it and disrupts the Warren Commission's 'magic' bullet theory.

Suppose a new bullet trajectory study was conducted by measuring the angle of fire with the limousine's position, including the roadway's three-degree downward slope. In that case, it may prove that the witnesses were correct and a second gunman was firing from the grassy knoll or another location.

The illustration in the plate section is part of the official House Select Committee on Assassinations (HSCA) report. Note the arrow in the first image depicts the bullet's path when fired from above and behind – meaning the Texas School Book Depository. It shows the President – incorrectly – leaning forward. The President was sitting upright, his back brace not allowing him to slump forward.

The same image has been adjusted to depict the President seated upright. The dark line indicates a bullet's trajectory if fired from a slightly elevated position in front of Kennedy. This trajectory would have the bullet exit Kennedy's back at the approximate autopsy-indicated location.

The Bethesda autopsy report presented to the Warren Commission described the back wound as 'oval-shaped', six by four millimeters and located above the upper border of the shoulder blade. The shape is a significant finding for the following reasons: first, it indicates that the bullet was not travelling in a straight trajectory. It would have made a nearly perfect circle entrance wound if it was. The proposed 'exit' wound at the front of Kennedy's throat would have been oval-shaped or demonstrated a more considerable deformity. It did not.

However, a bullet fired from the front would cause a round entrance wound to Kennedy's lower throat (as observed by some Parkland doctors). As the bullet travelled through his body, it started a slight tumble and it could cause an oval-shaped exit wound in Kennedy's back. More importantly, if the bullet exited his back, it could have come to rest in the area where Landis states he found it. Some ballistic experts say that the rifle used by Oswald is accurate and the standard round-nose Italian military bullet he used (see plate section) was somewhat unstable and could tumble after hitting soft tissue. This tendency adds credence to the oval-shaped wound on Kennedy's back being an exit wound.

The bullet hole in the back of Kennedy's shirt appears slightly elongated – or oval-shaped. It is improbable that an entrance would cause such a shape, but a bullet mildly tumbling as it exited the body could. As a detective, I saw scores of bullet entry and exit wounds close up or via homicide close-up photographs. A bullet (not a shotgun) entry wound was always round, matching the bullet's shape. Exit wounds were larger and nearly always misshaped due to the bullet expanding, deforming or tumbling as it passed through the body. This is reflected in the image of Kennedy's throat wound (see plate section).

At times, if a bullet only passes through flesh without striking a bone and doesn't change trajectory, the exit wound may resemble the entrance wound. On close examination, the edge of the wound will demonstrate a slight outward tearing of the skin. However, it is doubtful this occurred with Kennedy.

Shots from the railway bridge

At the time of the assassination, railway worker and eyewitness Sam Holland was standing on the railway bridge overpass and testified to the following: he was in the company of two uniformed police officers, a plain-clothes officer from an unknown agency and an estimated fourteen to eighteen other railway workers and onlookers. He heard four shots and when asked about the location of the shots, Mr Holland said, referring to the picket fence atop the grassy knoll, 'I have no doubt about it. I have no doubt about seeing that puff of smoke come out from under those trees, either.'

To indicate a possible second gunman's location, Mr Holland further testified that the rifle shots differed in sound: 'No, it was different sounds, different reports.' Regarding the shot from behind the picket fence atop the grassy knoll, he said, 'It wasn't as loud as the previous report.'

This is a significant observation. Rifle shots fired nearly simultaneously from two locations will present a different sound pattern. As a military veteran and detective, I have extensive experience in hearing gunfire and noticing such changes.

Other factors play into sound assessments, such as the separation in the distance between the two shooters, the angles of their fire, the direction of the rifle's muzzle when fired, weather, wind, etc. All of this adds to the noticeable change in sound.

Supposing Landis's and Holland's statements are correct. In that case, we must seriously consider the possibility of a second sniper firing from behind the picket fence atop the grassy knoll. However, it does not provide conclusive proof. Logically, we can consider that the shot striking Kennedy in the throat came from the grassy knoll or another slightly elevated position to Kennedy's front. The shot hitting Governor Connally and the fatal shot to Kennedy's head was fired by Oswald from the sixth floor of the Texas School Book Depository. Landis's statement will and should be investigated, dissected, and analysed. End of thesis.

Unfortunately, Landis's 2023 testimony comes at such a late date it will prove extremely difficult, if not impossible, to uncover new evidence of a conspiracy and those involved. With that said, as a detective, I find what he did with the bullet is questionable.

22 November 1963, Parkland Memorial Hospital, Dallas

Seconds after President Kennedy and Governor Connally arrived at the hospital, Kennedy was rushed into Trauma Room One while Connally was being treated for a gunshot wound in another room. A team of surgeons hovered over the President's body, knowing their medical skills could not save him.

1.00 p.m., Dallas. Inside Parkland's Trauma Room One

President Kennedy had flatlined. Dr Kemp Clark, Chief of Neurosurgery, looked up from the President's body and, in a low and trembling voice, said, 'Gentlemen, President Kennedy has died.'

Most of the observers in the emergency room quietly exited. Dr Salyer was standing at the head of the operating table as a priest and

Mrs Kennedy approached the President. The priest administered the last rights of the Catholic Church to President Kennedy.

Years later, Dr Salyer recalled that horrible moment, 'As I stood at the table, Mrs Kennedy approached it and I remember her looking at me as if that was OK. I nodded and watched as she moved close to the President's body. She leaned across him to reach for his left hand, removed his wedding ring and placed it on one of her fingers and then she simply held her husband's hand in a final goodbye. 'I was still standing beside the table, numb and disbelieving, when a few men entered the room with a wooden casket, placed the President's body inside it, then carried him away.'

Another attending physician, Dr Robert McClelland, remembers it slightly differently. He said Jackie took his ring and placed her ring on the President's hand. He described her as self-contained and not crying or hysterical: 'She stood there very dignified, very quiet and walked slowly down to the end of the gurney where the President's bare right foot was protruding out from the sheet that he was covered with. She stood there for a moment, leaned over and kissed his foot, then walked out of the room. That was the last we saw of her.'

On 12 November 2015, before a live audience in Texas, Dr McClelland discussed his observations and opinion after examining President Kennedy's massive head wound and after viewing the Zapruder film of the assassination. We must respect his opinion because he had extensive experience as a surgeon examining and treating gunshot wounds. He said, 'There's a massive hole in the back of his head that's at least five inches in diameter. And at that time, we couldn't really tell whether the shot had been fired from the front or the back. And not until many years later, when I first saw the Zapruder film of the assassination, did I then come to the realisation that the bullet had apparently been fired not from the back, but from the front behind the picket fence on the grassy knoll.'

Another attending physician was Dr M. T. Pepper Jenkins, Chief of Anesthesiology. He led the resuscitation team. In 1993, he recalled this horrible moment in the emergency room when Jackie Kennedy approached him. 'She would come circling through and a member of the Secret Service would come in and get her by the arm and take her out. She looked at a fifty-yard stare, she didn't see anything that appeared. I think you could have done this [he waved his hand in front of his face] and I don't think she would have blinked. She was white, drawn and base. Looking very remote, quite shocked, I would say. And she was carrying her hands [one hand cupped over the other, cradling something] like this for the first two or three times she came through the room. Her left hand over her right hand and then one time, she came in and nudged me with her elbow and as I looked around, she handed me what was in her right hand. Which was a big chunk of the President's brain. That was a bad moment, I can tell you.'

1.00 p.m., Parkland Memorial Hospital.
President Kennedy is officially declared dead.

Washington, D.C.
RFK Jr told Detective Rothmiller of his father's actions and thoughts immediately after President Kennedy's assassination: it was the afternoon in Washington when Attorney General Robert F. Kennedy learned his brother was shot. His first thought and rightfully so, was that the CIA was responsible. He immediately called a high-ranking CIA officer and asked, 'Did your outfit have anything to do with this horror?' Of course, the CIA officer denied any involvement or knowledge.

CIA Director John McCone immediately went to Kennedy's home. The two men were talking in the den when FBI Director J. Edgar Hoover called to tell Bobby that his brother was dead. Kennedy motioned McCone to follow him outside, where he posed a chilling question. He was angry and did not hold back, asking McCone if the CIA killed his brother. At the time, McCone said no. Several months later, McCone confided in Kennedy that he believed there was a conspiracy in Dallas to kill the President.

Later that day, Kennedy called Harry Ruiz, an anti-Castro leader, to determine if they were involved in the assassination. By then, he believed the CIA was likely responsible. Without question, that thought tormented him until he was assassinated in 1968.

Now, decades later, we realise Kennedy's assumptions were most likely correct. The CIA was not forthcoming with the truth.

RFK Jr mentioned he believed the CIA and possibly the Mafia were involved in President Kennedy's assassination and his own father's murder. Over the decades, RFK Jr has uncovered significant information that would cause any detective to take notice and seriously consider his conclusions, based on both solid and circumstantial evidence.

Detective Rothmiller believes RFK Jr was completely truthful in his assertions. Over the years, he has done an outstanding job uncovering significant details that paint a questionable, if not incriminating, picture of the CIA.

Additionally, RFK Jr said that had his father been elected President, he would have launched a new investigation into his brother's murder. His first actions as President would be to fire the FBI director and the CIA boss and replace them with competent, loyal investigators. Many knew he would pursue his brother's murder and that terrified the CIA and deep state. Unfortunately, I believe any chance of learning the truth behind Kennedy's murder died with RFK's own assassination.

If Robert F. Kennedy Jr finds himself in a position to launch a new investigation into the assassinations, as a former organised crime detective, I'd gladly serve as one of his investigators.

1.25 p.m., Parkland Memorial Hospital

With President Kennedy's death, the US Presidential line of succession elevated Lyndon Johnson to the Presidency. Within minutes, under heavy guard, Johnson was whisked from Parkland Memorial Hospital to Love Field, where he and his wife boarded Air Force One.

The coffin containing President Kennedy's body arrived later and was loaded into the aircraft. Inside the passenger compartment of Air Force One, Johnson took the oath of office and became the thirty-sixth President of the United States. By his side, Jackie Kennedy stoically stood, still wearing her blood-soaked, pink outfit.

Approximately 1.14 p.m.

Dallas police officer J. D. Tippit was on patrol and noticed a man resembling the description of President Kennedy's assassin walking in a residential area. Tippet stopped his patrol car and called the man over; it was Lee Harvey Oswald. Oswald approached and briefly spoke with Tippit from the passenger side. It is unknown what was said, but something piqued Tippit's suspicions. He exited the patrol car and, while walking around to the front, Oswald pulled out a .38 calibre pistol and shot Tippit twice at point-blank range. As Tippit lay on the ground, severely wounded, Oswald stepped up and fired a third shot into his head, instantly killing him.

Between 1.20 p.m. and 1.30 p.m.

Witnesses said they saw Lee Harvey Oswald enter the Texas movie theatre, 231 Jefferson Blvd, without purchasing a ticket. The features playing that day were *Cry of Battle* and *War is Hell*. The police were notified, and a large contingent of officers and detectives surrounded the theatre within minutes. Inside, officers located Oswald seated in the balcony area. A brief fight ensued between Oswald and the officers before he was taken into custody and transported to police headquarters.

8 p.m., Bethesda Naval Hospital

The autopsy findings are discussed later in this book.

Washington

Six military pallbearers carried President Kennedy's flag-draped coffin into the East Room of the White House, where it lay in repose for twenty-four hours. From the White House, the body was placed on a horse-drawn caisson and escorted to the Capitol Building Rotunda to lie in state for eighteen hours. Over 250,000 mourners passed through the Rotunda to view the flag-draped casket.

23 November 1963, during the evening

The Dallas FBI office received a telephone call from a man speaking in a calm voice and saying he was a member of a committee organised to kill Lee Harvey Oswald.

The FBI immediately notified the Dallas Chief of Police of the threat. The Chief reassured the FBI that Oswald was provided with sufficient police protection.

24 November, Sunday, early morning

The FBI again called the Dallas Chief of Police, warning of a possible plot against Oswald. Again, the Chief assured the FBI that adequate protection was being provided.

11.21 a.m.

As detectives escorted the handcuffed Oswald through the police department's basement, past a large crowd of reporters and police, Jacob Leon Rubenstein, a.k.a. Jack Ruby, quickly stepped from the crowd, pushed a .38 calibre revolver against Oswald's left torso and fired one shot. As the bullet tore through Oswald's body, he grimaced in pain and fell to the floor. Within minutes, Oswald was unconscious, placed in an ambulance and rushed to Parkland Hospital, where he died shortly after arriving. In a strange twist, President John Kennedy had died in the same emergency department two days earlier.

The unanswered question of that day is how Jack Ruby entered the highly secured basement of the Dallas Police Department while Oswald was being transferred. While working as a detective in LAPD's OCID, I reviewed an *extremely sensitive* document providing a possible and plausible answer. Jack Ruby was connected to the Mafia, owned a local, cop-friendly bar with B-girls and oversaw a stable of prostitutes not far from the Dallas police headquarters. Over time, many Dallas cops drank free at his bar and some used the services of his prostitutes – the report said that several police officers and a few high-ranking Dallas PD officials were provided with free sex services by Ruby's prostitutes. As a result, Ruby could blackmail officers and receive favours.

The intelligence report said several unnamed officers allowed Ruby to enter the basement, some knowing he planned to shoot Oswald, while others did not. Some believed Ruby was highly emotional and sought revenge on Oswald for killing the President. Others believe he was ordered to kill Oswald as the final step in a joint CIA and organised crime operation to assassinate Kennedy. However, no one knows Ruby's true motives.

25 November 1963, a day of funerals.
The nation mourns.

In Washington, DC, world leaders assembled to pay their last respects to a murdered President. Over a million mourners lined the streets as millions more watched live on television. President John F. Kennedy's flag-draped coffin departed the Capitol Rotunda en route to the cathedral of St Matthew the Apostle for services.

The coffin was carried on a black caisson pulled by white horses, followed by a riderless, coal-black, morgan quarter horse named Black Jack. The saddle held highly polished, black boots reversed in the stirrups, a poignant symbol of the fallen leader's last ride. The caisson was preceded and followed by thousands of uniformed military personnel.

At the cathedral, Cardinal Richard Cushing led the requiem mass. Over 1,200 guests attended the solemn service with leaders and representatives from over ninety countries.

After the service, Kennedy's body was transported to Arlington National Cemetery by the black caisson for burial. Today, an eternal flame lit by Mrs Kennedy still burns over the President's grave.

Other Kennedy family members buried near the President include the President's two brothers, Robert F. Kennedy and Edward M. Kennedy. There is a marker for the President's eldest brother, Joseph P. Kennedy, who was killed in the Second World War. Next to President Kennedy lies his wife, Jacqueline Bouvier Kennedy.

Dallas, Texas
Police Officer J. D. Tippit was thirty-nine years old. He was married and had three young children. Hundreds of Dallas police officers attended his funeral and served as an honour guard. Burial was at Laurel Land Memorial Park.

Pastor C. D. Tipps Jr of the Beckley Hills Baptist Church administered the funeral service and quoted from First Thessalonians, the same Bible quoted by Cardinal Richard Cushing at the funeral mass of President Kennedy.

The pastor said, 'He was doing his duty when he was taken by the lethal bullet of a poor, confused, misguided, ungodly assassin.' The pastor added, 'Human words are futile.' After the service, three dozen roses spread on top of the casket were removed and the coffin opened, allowing more than a thousand of Tippit's fellow officers to file past and say a final goodbye.

Fort Worth, Texas
Around 4:00 p.m. at Rose Hill Cemetery in Fort Worth, Texas, a small group gathered at an unadorned open grave. Nearby, Lee Harvey Oswald's body waited in a parked hearse for pallbearers to carry it to the grave. The only family members attending were Oswald's wife Marina, with their daughter, June, his brother Robert and their mother, Marguerite, who

held Oswald's infant daughter Rachel. The family sat alone on metal folding chairs next to the grave.

There was a problem. There were not enough family or friends in attendance to serve as pallbearers. With FBI agents, reporters and curious onlookers, the funeral director eventually convinced several reporters to serve as Oswald's pallbearers. They carried his casket to the grave and stepped back. Some had mixed feelings about their task.

Reverend Louis Saunders, the executive secretary of the local council of churches, stood nearby and Marguerite asked if he would say a few words. He had left his Bible in the car and, from memory, recited the twenty-third psalm, 'The Lord is my Shepherd', and a passage from John 14, 'In my father's house are many mansions'. Saunders delivered one of the shortest eulogies known. He closed with, 'Mrs Oswald tells me that her son, Lee Harvey, was a good boy and that she loved him,' he said. 'And today, Lord, we commit his spirit to your divine care.'

The Warren Commission investigation, the US Senate Committee Investigations on Assassinations and the House Committee on Assassinations concluded that, *in all likelihood, a conspiracy did exist to assassinate the President and acoustic evidence indicates two snipers fired at Kennedy.*

From a detective's point of view, there were alarming aspects of the investigation. Within hours of the assassination, rumours of a conspiracy spread like wildfire across America. Did the Mafia murder Kennedy? Did the Cubans or Soviets have him murdered? Did multiple assassins fire in unison from the Texas School Book Depository and the 'grassy knoll'? Was it a conspiracy of major corporations generating fortunes from the Vietnam War? Did the CIA orchestrate the killing? Was it a conspiracy between the CIA and the Mafia? Or was it a political coup to replace President Kennedy with Lyndon Johnson? Some were far-fetched, while others emerge as plausible.

As decades passed and more classified documents have been released and dissected by investigators, most evidence still pointed to Lee Harvey Oswald as the lone assassin. That assumption was understandable, considering the lies and misinformation the CIA and FBI expressed early on.

The live television broadcast of Oswald being shot inside the basement of the Dallas Police Department by Jack Ruby raised many new questions. Was he also part of the conspiracy? Was Oswald's murder the final step in the plot? No one can answer those questions with certainty. Thousands of documents relating to the assassination remain classified and thousands of others have probably already been secretly destroyed. Every person who could have possessed vital information regarding any conspiracy is dead: it is doubtful we will ever know.

Nonetheless, we can say that President Lyndon Johnson and others would go on to shatter the basic rules of criminal investigations and, by doing so, opened the conspiratorial door and cast a permanent, nefarious shadow of suspicion over the entire government investigation, the CIA and FBI. These items provide sufficient fuel and substance for conspiracy theorists and true detectives. We cannot dismiss every conspiracy theory, thanks to the government's highly questionable and unethical conduct during the official investigation. Many individuals do not accept the government's findings and present a valid counterargument.

As a former intelligence detective, I've seen hard evidence that all levels of the government have engaged in conspiracies to commit crimes, falsify documents and overthrow or assassinate foreign heads of state. Why? Because that is the action of governments and people in power. In contemporary times, America has witnessed the CIA, FBI, and Department of Justice falsify documents, invent evidence and ignore objective, factual evidence of crimes. They did this because senior executives inside those agencies despised a politician and sought to protect other politicians who were their friends.

Evidence shows those associated with the Warren Commission investigation did the same. The CIA and FBI twisted facts and ignored and lied to the commission regarding prior contacts or knowledge of Lee Harvey Oswald. The Commission lied in its final report by following President Lyndon Johnson's directions to say who was and wasn't involved in the assassination of President Kennedy. These facts prove that nearly every agency involved in the investigation lied and conspired to fulfill President Johnson's secret mandate. As a result, the Commission's findings cannot be accepted as totally accurate or the absolute truth. The Warren Commission was a propaganda tool.

It didn't work.

AFTERWORD

Bad Memories

'I have always depended on the kindness of strangers,'
Blanche Dubois, *A Streetcar Named Desire*,
Tennessee Williams, 1947

Peter Lawford is a tragic figure and plays a little-known cameo in a suitable parable for the Kennedy family priorities, for celebrity politics in Washington and Hollywood, perhaps simply for pragmatism, and for fame.

It involves the mortal remains of the author Truman Capote, the one-time toast of America's literary and society world. His ashes were in the possession of Joanna Carson, the former wife of the man who for decades was America's favourite television talk show host. Fearful for their safety, in 1988 she took them to Westwood Village Memorial Park in west Los Angeles where much of the cast of Hollywood past is interred. Devastatingly, there was no crypt available among the stars resting there like Marilyn Monroe and her longtime friend and Kennedy brother-in-law, Peter Lawford who, like Capote, died in 1984. Overwhelmed by celebrity, Truman Capote (ashes), and Johnny Carson (ex-wife), and being unable to help, the mortician was mortified. As Laurence Leamer tells it in *Capote's Women*, G. P. Putnam, 2021, the circumstances made him suitably obsequious. 'I'm sorry about your accident,' he said to Mrs Carson while pointing at a sticking plaster on her forehead. Pause. She looks curiously at him and then a dismissive, 'That's to prevent wrinkles.'

Caught on the back foot, he ponders while Joanna Carson strolls down the Walk of Memory Lane which skirts through the cemetery. She's gazing at the marble wall of crypts, desperate for her obsessively adored friend Truman to be placed within. Suddenly, the burial businessman grasps the moment like a falling trapeze artist: Peter Lawford! He chases after Mrs Carson:

'The Kennedys haven't paid and we would be willing to cut a special deal with you and remove Mr Lawford.'

As Leamer tells it in his book, Joanna Carson couldn't face life without some of Capote and split his ashes in two. She added her dog's ashes to fill the urn which was duly sealed in a Westwood crypt. She kept the rest in a carved Japanese box on her mantelpiece until her death in 2015, when the Capote ashes were auctioned, selling for $45,000. Peter Lawford's mortal remains were fluttered out over the Pacific without ostentatious ceremony.

Possibly forgetful, the Kennedys never did pay for his four years on Memory Lane.

BIBLIOGRAPHY

Allgood, Jill, *Bebe and Ben: Bebe Daniels and Ben Lyon* (Robert Hale, 1975)

Adams, Cindy Heller, *Lee Strasberg: The Imperfect Genius of the Actors Studio* (Doubleday, 1980)

Allen, Maury, *Where Have You Gone, Joe DiMaggio?* (Dutton, 1975)

Aldrich, Richard J., *The Hidden Hand* (The Overlook Press, 2002)

Anderson, Janice, *Marilyn Monroe* (Paragon, 1994)

Arnold, Eve, *Marilyn Monroe – An Appreciation* (Knopf, 1987)

Axelrod, George, *Will Success Spoil Rock Hunter?* (Samuel French, 1957)

Bacall, Lauren, *By Myself* (Knopf, 1979)

Baker, Carlos, *Ernest Hemingway* (Scribner, 1969)

Bartlett, Donald; Steele, James B., *Empire: The Life, Legend and Madness of Howard Hughes* (Norton, 1979)

Basinger, Jeanine, *The Star Machine* (New York: Vintage, 2009)

Beauchamp, Cari, *Joseph P. Kennedy Presents: His Hollywood Years* (Knopf, 2009)

Beauchamp, Cari, *Joseph P. Kennedy's Hollywood Years* (Faber and Faber, 2009)

Belafonte, Harry; Shnayerson, Michael, *My Song: A Memoir of Art, Race, and Defiance* (Canongate, 2012)

Berg, A. Scott, *Goldwyn: A Biography* (New York: Riverhead, 1998)

Blair, Joan and Clay, *The Search for JFK* (Putnam's, 1969)

Block, Alan A., *Masters of Paradise, Organised Crime and the Internal Revenue Service in The Bahamas* (Transaction, 1991)

Bogdanovich, Peter, *Who the Devil Made It: Conversations with Legendary Film Directors* (Arrow Books, 1998)

Bogdanovich, Peter, *Who the Hell's In It: Conversations with Hollywood's Legendary Actors* (Faber & Faber, 2005)

Bosworth, Patricia, *Marlon Brando* (New York: Viking, 1999)

Bosworth, Patricia, *Montgomery Clift* (Harcourt, Brace Jovanovich, 1978)

Breslin, Jimmy, *Damon Runyon* (Ticknor and Fields, 1991)

Brinkley, Alan, *John F. Kennedy: The American Presidents Series: The 35th President, 1961–1963* (Times Books, 2012)

Brownstein, Ronald, *The Power and the Glitter: The Hollywood–Washington Connection* (New York: Vintage, 1992)

Brown, Peter; Barham, Patte, *Marilyn: The Last Take* (Dutton,1992)

Brown, Peter Harry; Broeske, Pat, *Howard Hughes: The Untold Story* (Viking, 1996)

Buntin, John, *L.A. Noir* (Orion, 2014)

Cahn, Sammy, *I Should Care: The Sammy Cahn Story* (New York: Arbor House, 1974)

Cannon, Doris Rollins, *Grabtown Girl: Ava Gardner's North Carolina Childhood and Her Enduring Ties to Home* (Asheboro, NC: Down Home Press, 2001)

Capra, Frank, *The Name Above the Title: An Autobiography* (Boston: Da Capo, 1997)

Capua, Michelangelo, *Janet Leigh: A Biography* (Jefferson, NC: McFarland, 2012)

Clarke, Gerald, *Get Happy: The Life of Judy Garland* (Sphere, 2001)

Clooney, Rosemary; Barthel, Joan, *Girl Singer: An Autobiography* (New York: Doubleday, 1999)

Caro, Robert A., *Lyndon Johnson: The Passage of Power, Volume 4* (Bodley Head, 2014)

Carter, Graydon, *Vanity Fair's Tales of Hollywood* (Penguin, 2009)

Cirules, Enrique, *The Mafia in Havana* (Ocean Press, 2004)

Cockburn, Alexander; St Clair, Jeffrey, *Whiteout: The CIA, Drugs and the Press* (Verso, 1999)

Collier, Peter; Horowitz, David, *The Kennedys* (Summit Books, 1984)

Dale Scott, Peter, *Deep Politics and the Death of JFK* (University of California Press, 1996)

Dale Scott, Peter, *Crime and Cover-Up: The CIA, The Mafia and The Dallas–Watergate Connection* (Westworks, 1977)

Damone, Vic; Chanoff, David, *Singing Was The Easy Part* (New York: St Martin's, 2009)

Davis Jr, Sammy; Boyar, Jane; Boyar, Burt, *Why Me? The Sammy Davis Jr Story* (New York: Farrar, Straus & Giroux, 1989)

Davis Jr, Sammy; Boyar, Jane; Boyar, Burt, *Sammy: An Autobiography* (New York: Farrar, Straus & Giroux, 2001)

Denker, Henry, *The Kingmaker* (HarperCollins, 1974)

Dobbs, Michael, *One Minute to Midnight*, (Hutchinson, 2008)

Drosnin, Michael, *Citizen Hughes* (Holt, Rinehart, Winston, 1985)

Eisenberg, Dennis; Uri, Dan; Landau, Eli, *Meyer Lansky: Mogul Of The Mob* (Paddington Press, 1979)

English, T. J., *Paddy Whacked* (William Morrow, 2006)

English, T. J., *The Havana Mob* (Mainstream, 2007)

Evans, Peter, *Nemesis: Aristotle Onassis, Jackie O. and the Love Triangle That Brought Down the Kennedys* (Harper Collins, 2004)

Evans, Peter; Gardner, Ava, *Ava Gardner: The Secret Conversations* (New York: Simon & Schuster, 2014)

Evans, Robert, *The Kid Stays in the Picture* (Hachette Books, 1994)

Exner, Judith Campbell; Demaris, Ovid, *My Story* (Grove, 1977)

Farrow, Mia, *What Falls Away: A Memoir* (Bantam Press, 1997)

Field, Shirley Anne, *A Time for Love* (Bantam Press, 1991)

Fraser-Cavassoni, Natasha, *Sam Spiegel: The Biography of a Hollywood Legend* (Little, Brown, 2003)

Friedrich, Otto, *City of Nets* (Harper Perennial, 2014)

Gabler, Neil, *Walter Winchell* (Picador, 1995)

Gardner, Ava, *Ava: My Story* (Bantam Books, 1990)

Gentry, Curt, *J. Edgar Hoover: The Man and his Secrets* (W. W. Norton and Company, 2001)

Ghaemi, Nassir, *A First-Rate Madness: Uncovering the Links Between Leadership and Mental Illness* (The Penguin Press, 2012)

Giancana, Antoinette; C. Renner, Thomas, *Mafia Princess: Growing Up in Sam Giancana's Family* (New York: William Morrow, 1984)

Giancana, Sam; Giancana, Chuck; Giancana, Bettine, *Double Cross: The Explosive Inside Story of the Mobster Who Controlled America* (Skyhorse, 2016)

Goode, James, *The Story of The Misfits* (Bobbs-Merrill, 1963)

Goodwin, Doris Kearns, *The Fitzgeralds and the Kennedys: An American Saga* (Simon & Schuster, 1987)

Gosch, Martin A.; Hammer, Richard, *The Last Testament of Lucky Luciano* (New York: Little, Brown & Company, 1975)

Graham, Sheila, *Hollywood Revisited* (St Martin's Press, 1985)

Grobel, Lawrence, *The Hustons* (Skyhorse, 2014)

Harris, Marlys J., *The Zanucks of Hollywood: The Dark Legacy of An American Dynasty* (Crown, 1989)

Hersh, Seymour, *The Price of Power* (Summit Books, 1983)

Hersh, Seymour, *The Dark Side of Camelot* (HarperCollins, 1998)

Hersh, Seymour, *Reporter: A Memoir* (Allen Lane, 2018)

Heymann, C. David, *Joe and Marilyn* (Emily Bestler Books, 2014)

Heymann, C. David, *RFK: A Candid Biography of Robert F. Kennedy* (E P Dutton, 1998)

Hilty, James W., *Robert Kennedy: Brother Protector* (Temple University Press, 2000)

Hotchner, A. E., *Doris Day: Her Own Story* (Star, 1977)

Huston, John, *An Open Book* (Da Capo Press, 1994)

Israel, Lee, *Dorothy Kilgallen* (Delacorte Press, 1979)

Jacobs, George; William Stadiem, *Mr S: My Life with Frank Sinatra* (It Books, 2004)

Kaplan, James, *Frank: The Making of a Legend* (Sphere, 2012)

Kaplan, James, *Sinatra: The Chairman* (Sphere, 2015)

Kelley, Kitty, *His Way: The Unauthorised Biography of Frank Sinatra* (Bantam Books, 1986)

LaGuardia, Robert, *Monty: A Biography of Montgomery Clift* (Arbor House, 1977)

Lawford, Patricia Seaton; Schwarz, Ted, *The Peter Lawford Story* (Carroll & Graf, 1988)

Lev, Peter, *Twentieth Century Fox: The Zanuck–Skouras Years, 1935–1965* (Austin: University of Texas Press, 2013)

Levy, Shawn, *Rat Pack Confidential: Frank, Dean, Sammy, Peter, Joey and the Last Great Showbiz Party* (Crown, 1999)

Lewis, Jerry; Kaplan, James, *Dean and Me: A Love Story* (Crown, 2007)

Lawford, Patricia Seaton; Schwarz, Ted, *The Peter Lawford Story* (Skyhorse, 2015)

Logevall, Fredrik, *JFK: Volume One: 1917–1956* (Viking, 2020)

Mailer, Norman, *Oswald's Tale: An American Mystery* (Random House, 2007)

Mailer, Norman, *Marilyn* (Hodder & Staughton, 1981)

Manchester, William, *The Death of a President* (Pan Books, 1968)

McClintick, David, *Indecent Exposure: A True Story of Hollywood and Wall Street* (William Morrow, 1982)

McDougal, Dennis, *The Last Mogul: Lew Wasserman, MCA and the Hidden History of Hollywood* (Crown, 1998)

Messick, Hank: *Lansky* (Putnam's, 1971)

Moldea, Dan E., *The Hoffa Wars: Teamsters, Rebels, Politicians and the Mob* (Paddington Press, 1978)

Moldea, Dan E., *Dark Victory: Ronald Reagan, MCA and the Mob* (Viking, 1986)

Monroe, Marilyn; Hecht, Ben, *My Story* (Stein and Day, 1974)

Monroe, Marilyn; eds. Buchthal, Stanley; Comment, Bernard, *Fragments* (Harper Collins, 2010)

Muir, Florabel, *Headline Happy* (Holt, 1950)

Nasaw, David, *The Patriarch: The Remarkable Life and Turbulent Times of Joseph P. Kennedy* (New York: Penguin, 2013)

Nichter, Luke A., *The Last Brahmin: Henry Cabot Lodge Jr and the Making of the Cold War* (Yale University Press, 2020)

Noguchi, Thomas, *Coroner* (Simon & Schuster, 1983)

Otash, Fred, *Investigations Hollywood* (Henry Regnery Co, 1976)

Plokhy, Serhii, *Nuclear Folly: A New History of the Cuban Missile Crisis* (Allen Lane, 2021)

Powers, Thomas, *The Man Who Kept the Secrets: Richard Helms and the CIA* (Knopf, 1979)

Raab, Selwyn, *Five Families: America's Most Powerful Mafia Empires* (Griffin, 2006)

Ragano, Frank; Raab, Selwyn, *Mob Lawyer* (Charles Scribner's Sons, 1994)

Reid, Ed; Demaris, Ovid, *The Green Felt Jungle* (Ishi Press, 2010)

Riva, Maria, *Marlene Dietrich: By Her Daughter* (Bloomsbury, 1992)

Rose, Frank, *The Agency: William Morris and the Hidden History of Show Business* (New York: HarperBusiness, 1996)

Rothmiller, Mike; Goldman, Ivan G., *LA Secret Police* (Pocket Books, 1992)

Rothmiller, Mike; Thompson, Douglas, *Bombshell: The Night Bobby Kennedy Killed Marilyn Monroe* (Ad Lib, 2021)

Rothmiller, Mike; Thompson, Douglas, *Frank Sinatra and the Mafia Murders* (Ad Lib, 2022)

Schlesinger Jr, Arthur, *Robert Kennedy and His Times* (Houghton Mifflin,1978)

Schulberg, Budd, *Moving Pictures: Memories of a Hollywood Prince* (Ivan R. Dee, 2003)

Schulberg, Budd, *The Harder They Fall* (Random House, 1947)

Schulberg, Budd, *The Disenchanted,* (Allison & Busby Classics, 2013)

Server, Lee, *Robert Mitchum: Baby, I Don't Care* (Griffin, 2002)

Server, Lee, *Ava Gardner: Love Is Nothing* (New York: St Martin's Press, 2006)

Server, Lee, *Handsome Johnny: The Mob's Man in Hollywood* (Virgin Books, 2018)

Shearer, Stephen Michael, *Gloria Swanson: The Ultimate Star* (Thomas Dunne Books, 2013)

Sinatra, Tina, *My Father's Daughter* (Simon & Schuster, 2000)

Spada, James, *Peter Lawford: The Man Who Kept the Secrets* (Bantam Press, 1991)

Spada, James; George Zeno, *Monroe: Her Life in Pictures* (Doubleday, 1976)

Stack, Robert; Evans, Mark, *Straight Shooting* (Macmillan, 1980)

Starr, Kevin, *Golden Dreams: California in an Age of Abundance 1950–1963* (OUP, 2011)

Sugerman, Myron, *Chronicles of the Last Jewish Gangster: from Meyer to Myron* (Myron Sugerman, 2017)

Summers, Anthony, *Goddess: The Secret Lives of Marilyn Monroe* (Macmillan, 1985)

Summers, Anthony, The Kennedy Conspiracy (Sphere, 1998)

Summers, Anthony; Swan, Robyn, *Sinatra: The Life* (Corgi, 2006)

Swanson, Gloria: *Swanson on Swanson* (Random House, 1980)

Tierney, Gene, *Self Portrait* (Wyden, 1977)

Thompson, Douglas, *The Dark Heart of Hollywood* (Mainstream/Random House, 2012)

Thompson, Douglas, *Shadowland* (Mainstream/Random House, 2011)

Tosches, Nick, *The Devil and Sonny Liston* (Little, Brown, 2000)

Tosches, Nick, *Dino: Living High in the Dirty Business of Dreams* (Doubleday, 1992)

Turkus, Burton B.; Feder, Sid, *Murder Inc.* (Da Capo Press, 1992; reproduction of 1951 edition)

United States Treasury Department, *Mafia: The Government's Secret File on Organised Crime* (HarperCollins, 2007)

Tye, Larry, *Bobby Kennedy: The Making of a Liberal Icon* (Random House, Reprint Edition, 2017)

Von Tunzelmann, Alex, *Red Heat: Conspiracy, Murder and the Cold War in the Caribbean* (Simon & Schuster, 2011)

Wagner, Robert J.; Eyman, Scott, *Pieces of My Heart: A Life* (Hutchinson, 2009)

Waldron, Lamar; Hartmann, Thom, *Legacy and Secrecy: The Long Shadow of the JFK Assassination* (Counterpoint, 2008)

Waldron, Lamar; Hartmann, Thom, *Ultimate Sacrifice: John and Robert Kennedy, The Plan for a Coup in Cuba and the Murder of JFK* (Counterpoint, 2008)

Weiner, Tim, *Legacy of Ashes: The History of the CIA* (Penguin, 2012)

Wilkerson, Tichi; Borie, Marcia, *The Hollywood Reporter, The Golden Years* (Coward-McCann, 1984)

Wilson, Earl, *Sinatra* (W.H. Allen, 1976)

Wilson, Edward, *The Midnight Swimmer* (Arcadia Books, 2011)

Winters, Shelley, *Shelley: Also Known as Shirley* (Granada, 1980)

Wolfe, Donald H., *The Assassination of Marilyn Monroe* (Little, Brown, 1998)

Yablonsky, Lewis, *George Raft* (Mercury House/W. H. Allen, 1975)

Zolotow, Maurice, *Billy Wilder in Hollywood* (W. H. Allen, 1977)